Bunty's New World

Bunty's New World

(Sequel to *Bunty's War.*)

A young woman's diary records hilarity, despair
and success in her new world, America, after
surviving World War Two's onslaught in England.

Ida Greene

ISBN: 1544122845
ISBN 13: 9781544122847

Contents

Dedication

To my husband, Al Greene,
without whom
this book
could not have been written

Preface

A CAR'S HORN tooted outside. "I'm off, Bunty, see you at supper time." My husband's voice floated toward me from the front door, calling me by my nickname.

Who is Bunty? Well, I was born in Uganda, Central East Africa, when it was still a British protectorate, and where Jack Amiss, my father, had been sent by the British Board of Trade as captain of a merchant ship on Lake Victoria, second largest lake in the world after Lake Superior. I was named Ida after my mother. When I was two years old my parents brought me home to settle in Sunderland, on the northeast coast of England, where they had both been born and raised. Dad's shipboard engineering career moved on to one in water filtration and purification.

The family began to call us "Big Ida" and "Little Ida". Mom didn't like that idea! So the family nicknamed me "Bunty", and the name stuck. After several years we moved to a pretty southern suburb of London, where I grew from girl to woman in a life turned upside down by World War Two.

"O.K., dear, have a good time--see you later." I watched from the window as Al Greene walked out to the car and his waiting golf buddies, golf bag slung over his shoulder. He bent and stowed the bag in the car, then they were off for a day on their favorite golf course.

My life's journey had by now brought me to Connecticut and retirement, and I still hadn't finished unpacking. Challenged by unopened packing boxes, now that I was alone for the day I could mutter to myself out loud without anyone thinking: "Poor dear, she's finally lost it!"

So, I muttered to myself: "And I thought we had *downsized!* Just look at all these boxes full of 'stuff'. Wherever will we put it all? Oh, well, I'll just have to start going through it, see what we haven't used for a few years, and 'downsize' again!"

I sat down on the porch floor and pulled the nearest packing carton toward me. Inside was a battered white cardboard box, tied with string. That box had traveled with us throughout Al's company transfers over the years, filled with reminders of memories too precious to discard: special letters, the kids' kindergarten pictures, our wedding photos, a silver and white wedding invitation. At the bottom of the box was a small pile of diaries. I knew mine were there, but here were more! To my amazement, I recognized Al's handwriting. He had kept a diary, and I didn't know! I began to read his daily jottings, telling what he was doing on the same day as mine. I compared mine with his, written as we began our journey together into a new life in a postwar world, and smiled as I remembered my addiction to American movies, which was when I decided to call my mother "Mom" instead of the English "Mum."

Time ceased to exist as I re-lived those days of experiences that were so unusual that I thought: "Bunty, there's enough adventure here for a whole book! I could call it *Bunty's New World.*"

So here's the book. The names of some people and places have been changed; American spelling and expressions are mixed with British ones, and I have reconstructed conversations as I remembered they could have been. I hope you will enjoy reading it as much as I enjoyed writing it.

Introduction

THE END OF World War Two was still not in sight. On V-E Day (Victory in Europe Day), Tuesday May 8, 1945, a nation rejoiced as Britain, in her seventh year of war with Germany, was at last released from attack from the skies. In our tree-lined suburb, Upper Woodside, south of the city of London, for years we had suffered through vicious air raids, including those in the Battle of Britain and the London Blitz. Our house was so severely bomb-damaged that we were forced to leave it and become refugees in North Wales for two years, after which we returned to our patched-up home in London.

When the Allies were advancing toward Holland after D-Day, 1944, Hitler, in a last-ditch effort with which he thought he could still win the war against Britain, unleashed his Vengeance Weapons: the V-1s, deadly remote-controlled flying bombs nicknamed "doodlebugs", followed and eclipsed by the terrifying V-2's, intercontinental ballistic missile rockets. The city of London, including the southern suburbs where we lived, bore the brunt of these attacks, as they had done throughout the Battle of Britain and the London Blitz earlier, but miraculously, my family and I had survived!

At eighteen, I was called out of college to National Service. I went to work as a secretary at the London office headquarters of British Overseas Airways Corporation (now British Airways), which was government-controlled in wartime by the British Air Ministry.

At this point in time, my social life was sadly lacking; the local boys I knew were all away in service, and I was bored and lonely. An office friend suggested that I join her periodically after hours as a volunteer at

"Rainbow Corner", London's large American Red Cross Club, to serve coffee and doughnuts to the G.I.s (abbreviation for "Government Issue", the nickname commonly given to American Army enlisted men). We were also eligible to attend the dances held in the ballroom, and it was at one of these that I had been introduced to Al Greene, a tall, shy, attractive G.I., stationed in London with a U. S. Army Signal Corps radio communications group. His manner and deliberate speech reminded me of film star James Stewart. I knew he was the man for me, but would he propose?

"Of course not," I told myself: "he hasn't known me long enough for that, and anyway I'm not sure I want to be a married woman--yet!"

The war in the Pacific was still raging, and American servicemen were being shipped there from the European Theater. Al might have to go. Would I lose him?

Engaged!

AL AND I knew that we were falling in love almost as soon as we were introduced by Elsie Celli, director of Rainbow Corner. Handsome and unassuming (reminding me of James Stewart,) Al had by now come home with me to Upper Woodside to meet my parents--standard procedure for me with all my new friends--and he had stayed overnight several times before returning to duty at the U.S. Army radio room in London. Rumors were flying that his unit might be shipped to Germany soon. His diary entries and mine tell the story:

Al: "MONDAY, JUNE 18: DAY OFF. STAYED LAST NIGHT AT BUNTY'S HOME. TODAY SHE HAS TO WORK. WILL SEE HER AT RAINBOW CORNER DANCE TONIGHT. GOT UP AT 10 A.M. TALKED TO MOM AMISS. DID DISHES (BROWNIE POINTS!) LEFT FOR CITY ABOUT 3 P.M. WENT TO BILLET, THEN TO RAINBOW CORNER FOR MY LAST HOUSE COMMITTEE MEETING. FAREWELLS. DANCE. SAW BUNTY LEAVE. FOLLOWED. CAUGHT UP AND POPPED QUESTION. 'YES?' (I THINK--I HOPE!). WENT HOME WITH HER. TALKED TO HER FOLKS. STAYED OVERNIGHT."

Bunty: "TODAY I'M JUST SWEPT OFF MY FEET! THIS EVENING AT RAINBOW CORNER, AL GREENE ASKED ME TO BECOME HIS WIFE!"
I had said "goodnight" to Al and left the Rainbow Corner dance to catch the last train at 10 p.m. back to Upper Woodside. I felt totally wretched: "I may never see him again," I fretted, "and he didn't even say 'goodnight' to me. What's wrong with him?"

As I hurried from the ballroom to catch the last train home, I heard running feet behind me. Looking back, I saw Al hurtling down the hallway. I stopped. He ran up to me, breathless, and took hold of my hand. I waited. He caught his breath. "Bunty, it's taken me this long to come to my senses. I can't let you go! I want to ask you something that will mean the world to me. Bunty, I'm asking you if you will become my wife?"

I couldn't believe my ears! Al Greene had just proposed to me! I was astonished, and (for once) speechless. At this early stage in a new relationship it was incredible to me that a quiet, thoughtful man like Al would suddenly propose marriage. But Al Greene meant business! He took both my hands; his handsome face was serious and his blue eyes looked deep into mine. "I know this is sudden, Bunty, but I couldn't be more sure of what I am saying. I just heard today that my unit is leaving for Germany on Thursday, to join the rest of the guys in my Signal Corps battalion. Plans are that we'll be shipped as an entire group from there to the Pacific for active duty. I can't stand the thought of losing you. I may never get back this way, and I *do* know I want to marry you. Please say 'Yes'"

I closed my eyes; all I could think of was that I was in a movie with James Stewart! Time stood still as I tried to digest what Al had just said. Chaotic thoughts raced through my brain: "Am I on my head or my feet?...I need more time to think...what should I say to him?" I didn't know. But he was the only man I'd ever felt this way about. I wondered what Mom and Dad would think.

What should I do? What should I say?

I tried to speak, but my voice had disappeared altogether. My thoughts suddenly crystallized. I looked at Al, and managed to croak: "Oh, we'll have to go home and talk this over with Mom and Dad. If we hurry, we can catch the last train." I never did remember saying "Yes!"

We walked home from the commuter station hand in hand, and sat down with the cups of hot cocoa Mom had brought into the dining room. Dad, Mom and I sipped the comforting drink, content to exchange simple chatter about our days' activities.

Al didn't attempt to drink his cocoa. He cleared his throat, looked Dad squarely in the eye, and said firmly: "Mr. Amiss, I am going to be shipped to Germany on Thursday with my communications unit, and before I go I would like to ask you for your daughter's hand in marriage."

The shocked silence that descended upon the room was almost palpable. Dad was looking pained as he groped for words; Mom looked as if she had swallowed a mouthful of sour grapes.

Dad reverted to his north country accent, which usually happened when he was under stress: "Well, me lad, this *is* a surprise! But it's plain as the nose on me face that you're just homesick! I'll grant you Bunty's a fine lass, but she's too young to be thinking of marriage yet. Go home, lad, and think it over."

Al sat up in his chair, straight as a ramrod and unsmiling, looking much older than his twenty-one years. "I *have* thought it over, Mr. Amiss," he said, slowly and deliberately. "I love your daughter, and I believe I can make her happy and give her a good life with me in the U.S.A."

Dad began to realize that this was no sudden impulse on Al's part, but he still had reservations, the greatest of which he now put into words: "You know, lad, Bunty has a good life here. We've given her a good education. She's all we have. We can and do give her the best of everything, and she is used to that. I must ask you: what are your financial prospects, Al?"

Al looked as though he had fully expected this question. His face took on a new look of confidence. "Well, before I enlisted in the Army I had begun to work for the American Telephone and Telegraph Company, one of the largest, most respected and wealthiest companies in the U.S.A. When I enlisted, they guaranteed to keep my job open for me whenever I would return to civilian life. I've already earned a more-than-adequate living wage with the Company, and I have prospects of good advancement with them. A.T.& T. is called a 'cradle to grave employer', because of the security and benefits it provides for its employees."

As all of this sank in, both my parents were struggling to come to grips with the full implications of Al's request. They obviously liked Al, whom they had only met on several brief occasions before, but this was totally unexpected.

The silence lengthened. Al gripped my hand so hard I thought it would fall off.

Dad finally said: "Well, then, it's up to Bunty, isn't it?"

The ball was squarely in my court. Engagements in England traditionally gave time for long-range planning for an unhurried wedding. Knowing there was no chance that I could be married before Thursday, I said, tentatively: "Well, I think we *could* be engaged!"

Al: "WEDNESDAY, JUNE 20: UP EARLY. BUNTY AND I TOOK TRAIN TO LONDON. WENT TO MY BILLET. PICKED UP ALL MY ACCUMULATED RATIONS TO BRING HOME TO MOM AMISS. WROTE LETTER TO MY MOM TELLING HER ABOUT OUR PLANS. BOUGHT BUNTY AN ENGAGEMENT RING. BEAUTIFUL THING. THREE DIAMONDS, OUT-OF-THE ORDINARY SETTING. RUMORS NOW ARE THAT WE WILL SHIP OUT ON FRIDAY. STOPPED IN AT RAINBOW CORNER TO TELL ELSIE CELLI OUR NEWS AND TO ANNOUNCE IT AT DANCE. BACK TO UPPER WOODSIDE OVERNIGHT."

Bunty: "AL GOT A DAY'S EXTENSION. HE NEED NOT REPORT UNTIL FRIDAY. CALLED THE OFFICE. TOOK THE DAY OFF. AL BOUGHT ME AN ADORABLE DIAMOND ENGAGEMENT RING. I BOUGHT HIM A GOLD SIGNET RING. WENT TO RAINBOW CORNER DANCE AND ANNOUNCED OUR ENGAGEMENT."

In those days it was unusual in England for a man to wear a wedding ring, but often engagement rings were exchanged: a gold ring with diamonds or other precious stones for a woman, a gold signet ring for a man. Our rings were "Utility" nine carat gold, the balance being an alloy: silver or copper. This small percentage of gold was the maximum allowed by the government for use in jewelry in wartime Britain, due to conservation of gold reserves, but even if our rings had been pure twenty-four carat gold, they couldn't have meant more to us both.

Al had taken the little diamond ring in his hand and said: "You know, my love, what these three little diamonds say? 'I-LOVE-YOU.'" He slid the tiny ring onto my ring finger and asked me again: "Bunty Amiss, will you be my wife?"

This time I replied: "Yes, Al, I will. And will you, Al Greene, be my husband?" I slid the signet ring on his finger.

"Yes, Bunty, I love you, and I will--**AND HOW!"**

Al bent and kissed me on the mouth, right there in the jewelry store in front of the elderly store clerk who had helped us find a ring for me that Al could afford. Out of the corner of my eye, I thought I saw him wipe away a tear. Nothing had ever affected me like this kiss! I tingled all over. Upon occasion I'd had had butterflies in my stomach, but this time the butterflies went wild! My diary said it all: "SO NOW I KNOW--HE REALLY *IS* THE ONE!"

That evening at Rainbow Corner we stopped in to see Elsie Celli. Petite and pert in her American Red Cross uniform, Elsie looked up from her desk, a smile crinkling around her warm brown eyes as she greeted us. I held out my hand with its new little ring. She exclaimed with joy: "Well, how about that? When I introduced two of my favorite people I didn't expect I would be playing Cupid! Congratulations!" She enfolded us in a bear hug. "Be sure to tell the kids at the dance tonight. I'll bet there have been rumors!"

Al: "FRIDAY, JUNE 22: GOT UP EARLY. SAID GOODBYES TO BUNTY AND HER PARENTS. WENT UP TO LONDON TO MY BILLET. PACKED AND AWAITED EVENTS WITH MY UNIT. WAITED ALL DAY! LEFT VICTORIA STATION AT 10 P.M. ARRIVED NEWHAVEN AT 11:15 P.M. BOARDED BOAT MIDNIGHT. ROAMED AROUND ON DECK IN DARK. LOST MY UNIT, BUT LITERALLY BUMPED INTO THEM AGAIN. DISCOVERED WE HAD TO SLEEP OUTSIDE ON DECK IN DECK CHAIRS. PROCURED BLANKET. ROLLED MYSELF UP IN IT. TRIED TO GET COMFORTABLE. FELL OFF DECK CHAIR. RATS! SLEPT FITFULLY OVERNIGHT ON DECK CHAIR. CROSSED CHANNEL 9 A.M."

Bunty: "AL WAS SHIPPED TO GERMANY AT 10 P.M. BOO, HOO! AT HOME, WE'RE VERY TIRED AND BEWILDERED AFTER ALL THE RUSH." Mom, Dad and I were all still stunned. Dad had given me an especially long hug as he left for his latest government water purification job. Mom seemed more quiet and thoughtful than usual. For a few days I had the feeling she wasn't far from tears, but she showed no resentment or self-pity in front of me for the loneliness she must have been fearing when I would leave to go to America, after we had been so close all these years.

I wasn't quite sure how I felt. I looked down at the three little diamonds in my new ring, the tacit reminder of Al's three little words: "I love you," as he slipped it on my finger. I said to myself: "Bunty, what have you been rushed into? Here's a new and completely unheralded chapter in your future. Already you are wondering whether or not you can handle the changes looming ahead: marriage, then leaving your parents and your country for a new land and a totally new way of life."

Most of that night I lay awake: "Think positively, you idiot! Don't worry so much; with Al in Germany you'll have time to get your mind around it all. You know you have a pretty wonderful man there." Since the beginning of the war in 1939, I'd had to accept and deal with the many events that had changed my life so dramatically, but they were not of my own choosing. Here was something entirely different: my own actions now could change my whole future!

After more tossing and turning I gave a mental shrug. "Oh well, in the meantime it's fun to be engaged! There will be loads of time for me to get used to the idea of this marriage business. Yes, Al wants to marry me, and I told Al I would marry him, but we're not married yet, and after all--worst case scenario--broken engagements are quite common!"

Having found some comfort, I turned over and went to sleep.

Al: "SUNDAY, JUNE 24: WE'RE IN PAREE! CHANNEL CROSSING WAS CALM. TRAIN FROM DIEPPE TO PARIS. BILLETED AT HOTEL PALAIS DE NOUVEAUTE. THERE'S A RAINBOW CORNER AMERICAN RED CROSS

CLUB HERE! TOOK A TOUR OF PARIS ARRANGED BY A.R.C. WROTE BUNTY."

Bunty: "WROTE LETTERS TO GRAM, PAUL AND AUNTIE BELLE, ANNOUNCNG MY ENGAGEMENT. WAITING FOR ADDRESS FOR AL. WONDER WHERE HE IS?"

I carefully composed the words to write to my grandmother and the two people in whom I had confided since childhood: Paul Bates, now a seminarian preparing for Roman Catholic priesthood, and Auntie Belle. Gram could be counted on to tell all Mom's Ditchfield family the news that I would be leaving England to live in an unknown place called Little Cedar River, New Jersey, U.S.A. Auntie Belle, wife of Dad's youngest brother, Arthur Amiss, was my favorite aunt to whom I felt closest; I hoped she would understand. I didn't know what my childhood friend Paul would think or say.

Three replies to my engagement announcement rapidly arrived. Paul wished me a long and happy marriage. Auntie Belle's reply was encouraging: she trusted my judgment "because you were always a sensible child, Bunty." My grandmother addressed her reply to Mom. It began: "Ida, have you gone stark, raving mad, allowing Bunty to do such a silly thing?"

Al: "WEDNESDAY, JUNE 27: LEFT PARIS ON TROOP TRAIN LAST NIGHT AT 2000 HRS. HARD WOODEN SEATS. STOPPED AT REIMS TO EAT AT MIDNIGHT. LONG, UNCOMFORTABLE TRIP. ARRIVED LUXEMBOURG AT 1030. LOOKED OVER TOWN. HIT HAY. NO BLANKETS. USED RAINCOAT AND FIELD JACKET. SLEPT LIKE LOG. GOT BLANKETS FOR TONIGHT."

Bunty: "FORMULATED LETTER TO BILL ABOUT MY ENGAGEMENT. ALSO WROTE TO MAGGIE AND BESSIE IN WREXHAM. BERLIN HAS BEEN PARTITIONED INTO FOUR SECTORS BY RUSSIA, U.S., BRITAIN AND FRANCE."

I dreaded writing the letter to Bill. He was one of the two American aerial gunners Dad had brought home for a weekend last year, when he was supervising the installation of water purification equipment for use on their air base. Bill and his married buddy Frank Kopeck had found respite from their bombing missions at our home in Bishop's Hill, spending their 48-hour passes with us throughout the months they had been stationed in England. Bill had a crush on me, but I thought of him only as a dear friend. Now back in the States, his letters were asking if he could send me an engagement ring. I drafted my letter to him in pencil, going over and over the wording to make it as kind and gentle as possible before it was finally copied in ink. I thought: "Whatever I write, I know how hurt he will be, but it has to be done. I wonder how he will take it?" For the next few days guilt made me miserable, although in my heart was a sense of relief, too. I needn't have worried; I never heard from Bill again.

Reminders of the war were still making headlines in our newspapers. History was happening in Germany on this same day in the new postwar Europe. American, British and French forces entered Berlin, joining the Russians by prior agreement in partitioning the city into four sectors, like lions in the jungle sharing a kill.

Engaged!

Al Greene's Bombshell

Al: "FRIDAY, JUNE 29: AROSE 1615. CHOW. ASSEMBLED LUGGAGE. CARBINES PACKED. PULLED OUT LUXEMBOURG CITY 0930 BY TRUCK TO GERMANY. VERY PRETTY COUNTRYSIDE. MOST FIELDS WELL-TENDED. ALL TOWNS REALLY WRECKED. ARRIVED WIESBADEN, GERMANY 1430. WAS GIVEN ROOM, MINI TOP FLOOR OF BUILDING--ALL TO MYSELF! MET OTHER GUYS IN UNIT. BED."

Bunty: "TWO LETTERS AND POSTCARD FROM AL, WRITTEN IN PARIS! ONLY TOOK TWO WEEKS TO GET HERE! OH, WHAT A WONDERFUL GUY! WROTE FOURTEEN PAGE LETTER BACK TO HIM."

Al and I wrote to each other every day, and before I realized what was happening, I was falling deeper in love. We wrote about our daily adventures, also our thoughts, beliefs, hopes and dreams; I knew this man through his letters better than I had known any of the boys who had passed through my life over the years. He was all I could ever have hoped for: gentle, kind, sincere and loving, and I knew I could look forward to a full and happy life, sharing it with him.

Al had been a member of the House Committee at Rainbow Corner, which "ran" the club activities, planning outings and special events and recruiting help for them. Its membership consisted of an equal number of Red Cross club volunteers and American G.I.s stationed in London, presided over by the club's American Red Cross staff. Today I had been invited to their meeting as a guest.

A.R.C. Staff member Blossom Brown joked: "Boy, Bunty, Al sure threw us a curve ball when he came out and asked you to marry him! Just shows you, you gotta watch out for these quiet ones!"

"Oh, I'm giving myself plenty of time, Blossom. We probably won't be married until after the war; Al could be shipped to the Pacific from Germany." I filled them in on news they were waiting to hear about Al's whereabouts after he left London. Home again, I exulted to Mom: "Gosh, Mom, I didn't realize Al's prestige with this group! It makes me so proud of him to know he was so well-liked, and how much they miss him and his contributions to the committee. Oh, yes, and they congratulated me and I had a great time flashing my ring around to be admired. I'm really enjoying being engaged!"

Little did I know what was just around the corner.

Al: "WEDNESDAY, JULY 4: TALKED WITH BUNTY ON TELEPRINTER. ASKED HER TO MARRY ME NOW INSTEAD OF WAITING UNTIL AFTER THE WAR."

Bunty: "'TALKED' WITH AL TODAY BY TELEPRINTER FROM GERMANY, ARRANGED BY HIM WITH THE RADIO ROOM BOYS IN LONDON. HE WANTS TO MARRY ME NOW, NOT WAIT UNTIL AFTER THE WAR!"

A "skeleton crew" had been left behind where Al had worked at the Ministry of Information building in London. When we became engaged, Al took me to meet his buddies at the U.S. Army Publicity Service Battalion radio room. Located in the basement of the building, buried deep under the city of London, it was considered bomb-proof and had been made almost invisible as well as being inaccessible to the public. After D-Day, news bulletins from the European front were sent here by radio, scrambled, then transmitted by the Army Signal Corps across the Atlantic, to be unscrambled, censored, then released to the U.S. news media. Today was Independence Day in the U.S.A., but it was not a holiday in England or for the radio room, which was in operation twenty-four hours a day, seven days a week.

On the morning of this July 4, the phone rang on my desk. An American drawl said: "Say, Bunty, this is Chuck from the radio room; remember me? Your fella Al says he'll be on the teleprinter at four o'clock this afternoon in Germany and he wants you to come over here and talk with him. That O.K. with you, kid?"

"Yes, of course." I was breathless with surprise and excitement. I could hardly wait to leave the office and take the Tube (underground railway) across the city to arrive at the radio room at the appointed time.

Minutes after they let me in through the locked door, the radio room boys welcomed me, congratulated me, admired my ring, and sat me down in front of the teleprinter. Al "signed on" and I saw his printed words on the paper as it rolled out of the machine in front of my eyes. Happily typing away in Germany, he probably didn't guess the effect these words were having on me at the other end. I felt as if he had dropped another bombshell.

"Hi, honey. Say, there are rumors over here that my battalion will be leaving Germany soon for the Pacific. I think we should begin making plans so we can be married as soon as possible before I leave the E.T.O." (European Theater of Operations.) "If you agree, as soon as I get permission to marry I'll apply for a special furlough to come to England for the wedding. It will probably take some time, but I think we should get things started. Please say 'yes', darling."

I realized with a jolt that the fun of being engaged, which I was enjoying to the hilt, would soon be over. If I said "yes", I would soon be a married woman with all the duties and responsibilities that would bring. What a sobering thought! But my loving best friend in Germany was waiting for my answer. How could I say anything but "yes?" I typed back: "O.K., darling, go ahead."

"There's one more thing, Bunty," Al typed. "You'll need to write a letter to Headquarters telling my Commanding Officer that you want to marry me. You'll need to state your full name, address, nationality and date of birth. Here's the address."

Chuck rolled up the teleprinter paper into a neat scroll and handed it to me. When I got home I unrolled it and read it to Mom and Dad, who seemed to reel all over again with the shock of the imminence of Al's and my intended marriage.

After a few moments of silence, Dad said: "Well, Bunty, he seems determined that you'll marry him before he leaves the E.T.O., and you've agreed with him. He's getting things going at his end, so I suppose we'll have to do the same here. There will be plenty of red tape for him to go through, what with the Americans' regulations about their men marrying foreign girls."

Ending with what I thought sounded like a lingering hint of hopefulness, Dad added: "I wonder if he'll have time to pull it off before he's sent to the Pacific?"

Panic-stricken, I confided to my diary: "I NEED MORE TIME TO GET USED TO THIS!" But the machinery was already in gear. I mailed my letter to the C.O. the following day.

Bunty: "THURSDAY, JULY 5:   CHURCHILL DEFEATED IN GENERAL ELECTION. ALL OF PHILIPPINES AND BURMA NOW LIBERATED FROM JAPANESE BY ALLIES."

"I can't believe it! How could they be so ungrateful to Winnie after he carried us through those awful war years?" Mom echoed the feelings of many, upon hearing the news of Winston Churchill's defeat in the election. "Winnie", as we affectionately called him during the war, had been the right man in the right place at the right time. He had successfully completed the superhuman task he undertook as Prime Minister in 1940, rallying a flagging country perilously near defeat. He had devoted every waking moment and all of his energy to the war effort. But now the war in Europe was over. Forward-looking voters saw Churchill as an aging man of the "old guard", who might not succeed in the difficult task of bringing Britain back to peacetime solidarity and progress.

Politically, Britain's great wartime leader represented the Conservative elite. "Working middle-class" Brits were ready for social reform and new broad initiatives now that peace had returned to their homeland, so they had voted to bring the Labour Party back.

Dad was incensed at the idea of a Socialist government takeover. A dyed-in-the-wool Conservative, he ranted: "Silly fools, don't they know that the country will go to pieces with those idiots in charge?"

Mom and I rolled our eyes and said nothing.

The war dragged on in the Pacific. The Philippines and Burma, each suffering through the bloodbath that preceded victory, had finally been reclaimed by the Allies, despite the unfamiliarity of Japanese guerilla warfare with its snipers, which rendered Allied tanks and fire-power useless against the punishing attacks of an ever-vanishing enemy. By June and July, U.S forces had experienced an incredibly high cost in bloodshed and carnage in order to take back territory from the Japanese.

Al: "MONDAY, JULY 9: I'VE BEEN SENT ON A RADIO TEAM TO BAD NAUHEIM. PACKED, ARRIVED BAD NAUHEIM 1630. STOWED GEAR AT BILLET. RED CROSS CLUB IS IN POSH SPA HOTEL. SWIMMING POOL, LAKE WITH PADDLEBOATS, TENNIS COURTS, BATHS. WENT SWIMMING. HOT DIGGETY DOG! I COULD GET USED TO THIS! WROTE TO BUNTY TO TELL HER ALL ABOUT IT."

Bunty: "NANTIE IS STAYING FOR A WEEK FROM SUNDERLAND. PAT PRINGLE CAME OUT TO BISHOP'S HILL FOR TEA. WENT TO SEE BETTY WHITE WHO HAS OFFERED TO LEND ME HER WEDDING DRESS. TRIED ON SHOES AND VEIL, TOO. THEY ALL FIT ME--GREAT LUCK!"

One by one, Mom's sisters were coming to visit. It was beginning to feel like peacetime again! My Aunt Eleanor, or "Nantie" as the grandchildren called her, was a great favorite at Gram's house. I can still picture her sitting on the floor with my young cousins and me, keeping us enthralled as she taught us simple card games to play.

Pat Pringle arrived at Bishop's Hill shortly after Nantie. Pat knew Al before I did; I fancied she had had a crush on him. Her office at the Ministry of Information building was near Al's radio room, and when he first took me there he had introduced us. We became friends on the spot. Pat was a sweet soul, attractive but not pretty due to a few unnecessary pounds that made her face and figure a little too pudgy, hiding the good bone structure underneath. I had invited her to Bishop's Hill so my parents could know her awhile before I asked her to be maid of honor at my wedding. Pat left after tea time, and I headed over to see Betty White.

The thought of my not being married in a church had never entered the minds of Mom, Dad or myself. But Mom and I had a typically feminine reaction: we looked at each other and wailed: "Whatever will we *wear?*" Providence had provided the answer for me.

Mrs. White and her live-at-home daughter Betty were still frequent visitors at our house. They had stayed many nights with us, in anguish, while they waited for news of their only son and brother, Roger, who was missing in his R.A.F. bomber over Germany in the war, and also when the dreaded telegram had come: "Killed in action." They were both excited when I told them about my engagement. Betty burst out: "Oh, Bunty, if you'd like to borrow my wedding dress, you can come and try it on to see if it fits."

Now divorced from her unfaithful husband, Betty had been married just prior to the war when white satin brocade was still to be had. By 1945, even if I could have found such extravagant fabric to buy, new wedding regalia might take a whole year's clothing coupons. If I borrowed from Betty, the coupons could be spent on other clothing I would need for my honeymoon! With today's discovery that Betty's lovely white brocade dress, wispy silk net veil and silver shoes were almost as new as the day she wore them and that they actually fit me, my feet barely touched the ground as I ran home to tell Mom. Now I could almost believe I was going to be a bride!

Al: "SUNDAY, JULY 15: LETTER FROM BUNTY, ONE FROM SISTER AMY. SPENT ALL EVENING READING THEM. GOTTA LOOK FOR WEDDING RING. THOUGHT OF PLANS FOR FUTURE FOR BUNTY AND ME, PLEASANT THOUGHTS. WENT TO CHURCH 1100. GOOD SPEAKER, MESSAGE: 'HE WHO SHALL BE GREATEST AMONG YOU WILL BE YOUR SERVANT. A GOOD MAN IS A GREAT MAN: COURAGE, HONESTY, USEFULNESS.' **WOW!** HE MUST HAVE BEEN THINKING OF 'G. I. JOE'! WENT TO ORGAN RECITAL 1630, EXCELLENT. CHOW. U.S.O. SHOW FROM 1930 TO 2100. GOOD. FRATERNIZATION BAN HAS BEEN LIFTED. STAYED IN WHILE THE GUYS WENT OUT TO FRATERNIZE!"

Bunty: "MOM SHOWED ME HOW TO MAKE APPLE PIE. PREPARED ALL VEGETABLES FOR DINNER. I'VE GOT TO START GETTING DOMESTICATED! WENT TO CHURCH IN EVENING, THEN VISITED WITH MRS. WHITE AND BETTY."

"I'd better get a few new skills if I'm going to be a housewife," I declared to Mom.

"Oh, anyone can run a 'Hoover', dust and polish, but it's time you learned how to cook, dear. We'll start with pies, now that apples are in season; in fact, you can go and pick a few of the ripe ones off our trees in the back garden, if you like. Cooking is easy; I've always said: 'anyone who can read can cook.'"

I soon discovered it wasn't that simple!

Wedding Banns and Bob

Al: "TUESDAY, JULY 17: BAD NAUHEIM. PLAYED TENNIS. RECEIVED LETTER FROM MY MOM AND AMY CONGRATULATING ME ON MY ENGAGEMENT. EVERYTHING LOOKING ROSY. WROTE TO BROTHER BILL. TOOK MINERAL BATH. WENT TO SEE STAGE SHOW STARRING FAMOUS BRITISH ACTRESS BEATRICE LILLIE. GREAT SHOW. BOY, THIS IS THE LIFE! TOO BAD IT'S A TEMPORARY ASSIGNMENT. WISH IT WOULD GO ON FOR EVER!"

Bunty: "POTSDAM CONFERENCE BEGAN. LETTER FROM BESSIE IN WALES ENCLOSING PHOTOS TAKEN LAST EASTER ON MY VISIT. FEEL AS IF I'VE LIVED A LIFETIME SINCE THEN! HAD A VISIT FROM PAUL."

The Potsdam Conference, held in Potsdam, Germany, was a follow-up to the Yalta Conference among the "Big Three", Churchill, Roosevelt and Stalin, earlier in the war; this time to negotiate terms for the end of World War Two. The conference lasted from July 17 through August 2. President Roosevelt had died since the last conference; President Truman now represented the United States. After July 26, Britain was now represented by the Labour Party leader, Prime Minister Clement Attlee.

Long after the war, declassified commentaries on the conference revealed that Truman had hinted to Stalin that the U.S. had a nuclear weapon.

Paul Bates stepped into our house as he had done so many times over the years. Still tall, blond and handsome as ever with his dancing blue eyes and the dimple in his cheek, he had stayed in touch with frequent letters while he was at the Roman Catholic seminary in the next county to ours, but this was the first time he had appeared on our doorstep since I wrote to him to announce my engagement. He quickly settled into a soft dining room chair and relaxed with a cup of tea, and behind the black shirtfront and white clerical collar I could still see the childhood friend I had always known. He smiled at me, and the dimple appeared. I interrupted: "Oh, Paul, you've still got that dimple!"

"Well, Bunty," he retorted, "I offered it to you years ago, remember, but you never did take it; I still think dimples are for girls!"

We chuckled together, remembering some of the outlandish things we did as children and young teenagers before the war. Then Paul sobered. "Just think, here's another milestone for both of us. I'll be starting to prepare for ordination, and you'll be starting on an exciting new chapter of your life, too. I'm glad for you *and* for me."

Paul's words were vastly different from those in the last letter I would ever have from Bruce, the boy I'd had a terrific crush on when I was fourteen. He was now a Royal Navy second lieutenant, resplendent and handsome in his newly-acquired officer's uniform, and before I met Al he had been a steady date at St. John's church Fellowship Dances, and also a regular visitor to my office to pick me up for dinner and a London show when he was home on leave. Now, we thought, he was either in the Mediterranean or the Pacific with his ship, an L.S.T. (Landing Ship, Tank). An avid correspondent, he had begun to sign his letters: "With all my love". This time, he had concluded his reply to my letter announcing my engagement with: "Bunty, I hope you know what you are doing!"

And then there was "Little Arnie," who had been my reliable friend at Rainbow Corner before I met Al. Stationed in London at the big American A.P.O. (Army Post Office), he was the typical American movie "boy next door", with his farm-fresh, open face, uncomplicated temperament, and

Midwestern drawl. He was what the Rainbow Corner volunteers called a "non-wolf", refreshingly different from some of the brash, worldly G.I.s who frequented the dances. His only known vices were his passion for Coca-Cola and ice cream; in short, I found him safe!

Like many of the London-based G.I.s, Arnie had a bicycle, and it wasn't long before he was stowing it in the luggage compartment on a commuter train to Upper Woodside, then riding it to Bishop's Hill from the train station. Lately, I was getting weary of the fact that he sometimes turned up unannounced on weekends at our front door; he seemed to be beginning to think he lived at Bishop's Hill. But even the neighbors liked him!

Arnie must have noticed the electricity between Al and myself when we had met, but he still persisted. I'm sure the situation was obvious to him the day he came unannounced to Bishop's Hill when I had invited Al to lunch! I didn't know how to make it plain without hurting his feelings; he would just have to learn the hard way!

Arnie wasn't at the dance when Al and I announced our engagement. I believe someone must have told him the news. I truly felt sorry for him, but my conscience was clear in that we had never shared confidences and I had never let him think he was anything more than a good friend.

Al: "THURSDAY, JULY 19: STILL AT BAD NAUHEIM. LAP OF LUXURY! TENNIS, BADMINTON, PADDLEBOATS, SWIMMING, FRENCH VARIETY SHOW. WOW! TODAY, GOOD NEWS: WAS TOLD THAT I'LL BE STATIONED HERE WORKING IN THE RADIO DEPT. YIPPEE! REPORT FOR DUTY SATURDAY. HAD A MINERAL BATH AND MASSAGE BEFORE DINNER. WROTE TO MOM AND BUNTY."

Bunty: "SENT AL GERMAN-ENGLISH DICTIONARY AND PHRASE BOOK PER HIS REQUEST. ALSO SENT HIM A COPY OF CHURCH OF ENGLAND MARRIAGE SERVICE. HE'S WAITING FOR REASSIGNMENT, BUT HOPES TO STAY AT BAD NAUHEIM. NEWS IS THAT S.H.A.E.F. HAS BEEN DISBANDED."

It was just as well that I hadn't been able to see Al's diary, especially when I wrote in mine: "WORKED LIKE A DOG TODAY AT OFFICE--CAME HOME DEAD TIRED!" I heard about Al's reassignment to Bad Nauheim today when Chuck called me from the radio room and said: "Hey, Bunty, yer feller Al asked me to call to tell ya he will be stationed at Bad Nauheim for at least another month*!"*

Great news! This would delay Al's departure for the Pacific, but he was by now already bogged down in the red tape of the G.I. marriage application process. Was a month's delay going to be enough? The American authorities made no secret of the fact that they discouraged marriages between their servicemen and girls living in the countries where they were stationed. It was rumored that Commanding Officers helped to make this as lengthy a process as possible, no doubt hoping to discourage their men from pursuing the mountain of paperwork involved. But the G.I.s weren't giving up, least of all Al!

In order to obtain permission to marry me, Al was required to fill out an Affidavit of Support detailing his salary, allowances, insurances and other financial assets, also whether he had other dependents. This information had to be confirmed from a maze of Army records. In the days before computers, everything was sent by "snail mail", which was aptly named! Once completed and witnessed, the affidavit required a written statement from Al's Commanding Officer verifying the information to be correct. Neglect sometimes killed these applications, as they meandered from one Army in-box to the next. The possibility of our marriage before Al left Europe was looking very dim. Even Al's letters sounded despondent.

Another sign that the American military liberation operations in Europe were complete was a notation in Al's diary that S.H.A.E.F. (Supreme Headquarters of the American Expeditionary Forces) had disbanded. I remember the patch that had appeared before D-Day on the sleeve of so many of the G.I.s at Rainbow Corner, with the S.H.A.E.F. emblem--a flaming sword, and above it the rainbow of deliverance.

Al: "SUNDAY, JULY 22: WENT TO CHURCH. SERMON DEALT WITH PRAYER. EXCELLENT SPEAKER. CHOW. TENNIS. ON DUTY 1530. NO RADIO TRAFFIC. WROTE LETTER TO BUNTY."

Bunty: "MOM AND I STAYED AFTER CHURCH TO SEE VICAR OF ST JOHN'S ABOUT HAVING WEDDING BANNS POSTED."

Posting the wedding banns, the intention of a couple to marry, is an ancient custom in the Church of England. It is thought to date back to the 1600s; its purpose has always been to ask the congregation to disclose anything they know that might render a marriage unlawful. The banns are read on three consecutive Sundays, along with the names of the prospective bride and bridegroom, and the question is asked.

Mom had rallied amazingly to the realization that her only child was serious about this marriage. Outwardly, she seemed to be what Dad called "hot and bothered", but I believe she actually began to enjoy the planning. Notes appeared on lined writing pads and the backs of envelopes all over the house, as she jotted down reminders to herself of the preparations she would need to make. Not the least of these was arranging for the wedding banns. "Well, Bunty," she said, "it looks as if we have a wedding on our hands, so we'll have to make sure that all the preliminaries that the Church of England requires are done in plenty of time."

Our jolly Vicar, Reverend Throckmorton, took us into his study after church that Sunday. "So you're getting married, Bunty?" He chuckled, and his plump little midriff jiggled up and down as he spoke: "I remember you from the time you were in Sunday School."

I prayed that he didn't remember the time I brought a small frog to my Sunday School class in my pocket, and it escaped with disastrous results! Mom began to look distinctly "hot and bothered," but he went on cheerfully: "Now don't worry, Mrs. Amiss, we'll soon get things started. The first reading of the banns will be next Sunday, and I'll be glad to perform the ceremony as soon as we have a firm date."

"A firm date," I thought, "will we ever have one?"

Al: "TUESDAY, JULY 24: SECOND DAY ON DUTY AT RADIO STATION. TOUGH. BEGAN PRACTISING MORSE CODE TO GET MY SPEED UP. REALLY TIRED!"

Bunty: "RECEIVED SURPRISE PACKAGE FROM AL, MAILED WHEN HE WAS IN PARIS: LIPSTICK, POWDER, NAIL POLISH, AND WOW, 'CHANEL NO.5' PERFUME! GAVE MY NINTH AIR FORCE BROOCH TO BUZZ."
It was like Christmas in July, literally--such scarce luxuries in a package. And wafting around smelling of Chanel Number Five was the ultimate status symbol among the girls I knew, both during and after World War Two. The package had taken a whole month to get here! When Al was in Paris en route to Germany he must have shopped and sent the package as a surprise, as he hadn't mentioned it in any of his letters. I thought to myself exultantly: "What a great husband he's going to be!"

At the office, I looked at the little silver brooch in my hand--a replica of the wings of the U.S. Ninth Air Force given to me by Bill, which I had proudly worn in 1944 until he and Frank had completed their quota of missions after D-Day and were now back in the U.S. Memories of the months we enjoyed the company of Frank and Bill came flooding back. They were good days, and my friendship with Bill had, according to him, seen him through some rough spots during his bombing missions; something to cling to. But it was time to break with the past and its reminders, now that I had made a commitment to the man whom I knew to be the right one for me.

"Here, Buzz, I have something special to give you."

Our office boy peeked around my office door and came in, curiosity written on his face. "Oh, Bunty, are you sure you want to part with it? It's really smashing of you to think of giving it to me."

"Buzz, I'm giving it to you for safe keeping, and I know you're the right person to do just that for me."

Buzz dashed off to show Bill's wings to co-workers Syd and Brad.

Al: "SATURDAY, JULY 28: DAY OFF. PLAYED TENNIS FOR COUPLE HOURS. GETTING NICE TAN. WENT TO SEE G.I. SHOW 'OFF LIMITS'

GIVEN BY ANOTHER DIVISION. GOOD IN SPOTS, ESPECIALLY MEN'S CHORUS. SHOW TOO LONG. SOME LOUSY SKITS. AM LEARNING A FEW GERMAN PHRASES EVERY DAY. MUST NOT BE TOO BAD, THEY SEEM TO UNDERSTAND ME!"

Bunty: "ALLIES HAVE CRIPPLED JAPANESE FLEET AT KURE. NICE LETTER FROM AL'S SISTER AMY WITH PHOTO. SHE'S LOVELY. BOB KOPECK ARRIVED UNEXPECTEDLY FROM GERMANY ON FURLOUGH!" Retribution for Pearl Harbor came with the Allied raid on Kure, where the assembled Japanese fleet was decimated, leaving only one warship serviceable.

It has been estimated that over one thousand B-29 bombers had participated in an unrelenting succession of air raids on the Japanese mainland. But Japan's Prime Minister announced that the Japanese would fight to the last man; they would never surrender. It was clear that the only road to a final Japanese defeat would be an Allied invasion of her home islands, possibly extending the war for another year or beyond; a bloodbath with continuing loss of life on both sides.

In today's mail was a long, pleasant letter from Al's sister Amy. We had not received any correspondence from his mother since her one brief sentence in Amy's letter congratulating me on my engagement to Al. I worried aloud to Mom: "She sounds like Bill's mother, *chilly!*"

Amy's new letter was warm and welcoming. The enclosed photo showed a slender, pretty girl in a long, white formal dress. It was taken, she explained, on her initiation into the Order of the Eastern Star. This made Brownie points with Dad--he had been a Master Mason for years. I had sent Al's mother a letter the week before, giving her some of our family background and enclosing a photo of myself, along with one of Mom and Dad. In my letter, I made sure to tell her how surprised we all were at Al's sudden proposal, adding that I could quite understand what a shock the news of our engagement must have been for her. I asked myself: "Is she just another American mother who thinks her son has been seduced by a foreign girl? I really had hoped she would write--or has everything I have written displeased her?" I would just have to wait and see.

On this quiet Sunday morning, Dad was home between jobs for a week, and we were all having a cup of tea together. The doorbell rang, and Dad heaved himself out of his chair to open the front door. We heard the distant rumble of a man's voice, followed by Dad's, booming: "Well, well, well, what have we here? Come in, Bob, come in."

Mom and I looked at each other and said simultaneously: "Who's Bob?"

An American Army staff sergeant was ushered into the dining room. There was no mistaking him as Frank Kopeck's older brother: the same short, compact body, rugged facial features and infectious smile. "Hi, I'm Bob Kopeck. Great to see you all! Sorry I couldn't give you any warning; just came on ahead and found my way here with my kid brother Frank's directions. I've got a week's furlough--hope that's O.K. with you!"

Barely recovered from our astonishment, Mom and I found ourselves enveloped in Bob's bear hugs. "You've been so swell to Frank, and with the letters we've written back and forth I feel I know you already." He reached into his duffle bag. "I brought some items I thought you could use." Out came a canned ham, some bacon, sugar, and a large German smoked sausage. Mom was beside herself with delight. Bob had made a friend for life! Mom recovered her composure and, true to form, offered Bob a cup of tea.

Dad said: "Well, Bob, we're glad to see you, after enjoying your letters and wondering when old 'Blood and Guts' Patton would let you come on leave to England. Mom will show you where to take your things upstairs, and when you're settled we'll chat awhile."

Over Bob's shoulder, as he followed Mom, came the reply: "O.K., Pop Amiss, I'll be down in a jiffy!"

Looking fresh as a daisy, Bob was anxious to explore London, so I offered to take him for his first taste of that wonderful city. He ate a quick couple of slices of the beige National Loaf, spread with our butter and jam ration, and more tea, then we set off on the bus. He bubbled with enthusiasm when he recognized famous landmarks in the city, making it a joy for me to show off my favorite spots. When we arrived back at Bishop's Hill, Bob was looking a little wilted from all the walking, but after dinner he rallied when Dad said: "Come on, lad, let's go up to the 'Pig and Whistle' for a pint or two."

Our local pub was "The Conquering Hero," which Dad inevitably called "The Pig and Whistle." He said he thought that sounded more down to earth.

Keeping up Appearances

Al: "SUNDAY, JULY 29: LONG DAY. CHURCH. WORK. CHOW. FIGURED MY TWO CANS OF AMERICAN BEER WEREN'T DOING ANY GOOD ON THE SHELF. DRANK THEM. FINISHED LETTER TO BUNTY IN RECORD TIME!"

Bunty: "TOOK BOB UP TO LONDON. HAD MY FIRST CHINESE LUNCH AT RESTAURANT IN THE WEST END. SHOWED HIM SOME OF THE THEATRE DISTRICT, THEN WENT TO RAINBOW CORNER FOR MY AFTERNOON VOLUNTEER MEETING AND STAYED FOR THE DANCE." What would the neighbors think? They had met Al and knew about our engagement. He had no sooner gone away than a new man in a U.S. uniform appeared and left the house this morning arm in arm with Bunty Amiss shortly after he arrived! I could imagine them gossiping: "Another American? Thought she was engaged to Al Greene! Whatever kind of a girl is she turning into? And what's happened to her father? Last night he and this fellow went off together to the 'Conquering Hero'--he seems to like this new one as much as he liked Al!"

Bob was more sophisticated than his younger brother Frank. He had a bachelor's degree and a good job as a chemist in Ohio before he enlisted. He knew just what to order at the Chinese restaurant. For some unknown reason, Dad was suspicious not only of the Chinese, but also of their food, so we never "ate Chinese." Today, I sampled egg drop soup, chow mein, egg foo yung--as mysterious as they were tasty. I thought: "Better not tell Dad; Bob needn't hear his lurid tales of those Chinese ports he visited when he was in the Merchant Navy!"

From the theatre district with its famous theatres and eateries, we walked down Shaftesbury Avenue toward Piccadilly Circus. Bob said: "Say, Bunty, what's that thing all boarded up in the middle of the traffic circle down the street? And what are all those girls doing hanging around it?"

I looked ahead to the middle of the road where several tiers of stone steps in concentric circles were topped with a shroud of plywood. Sitting and standing on the steps were young girls with very short skirts, showing lots of leg. "Oh," I replied, "that's Piccadilly Circus (the Roman word for 'circle'). Under the plywood is a nineteenth century commemorative fountain with a statue of Anteros standing above it on one leg, poised with his bow and arrow. In Greek mythology he was actually the *brother* of Eros, the Greek god of love ('Cupid' to the Romans), but now everyone calls the statue 'Eros'. He was boarded up in wartime for safety during the air raids. I've heard that prostitutes hang out there because they think that the god of love will bring them good business! Those girls are often nicknamed 'Piccadilly Commandos.' You should ask Frank to tell you about the time he and Bill were standing with me on those steps, waiting to cross the road, and we heard one of them shout at me: 'Oo do you think yoo are, girly? This 'ere's my spot. Git orf it!'"

Bob gave an appreciative chuckle. We had arrived at the front entrance of Rainbow Corner, and I ushered Bob inside. He went off to the "Dunker's Den" for a cup of coffee, while I went to my monthly volunteer meeting.

When my meeting was over we had dinner, then climbed the ornate staircase to the ballroom. One of my fellow volunteers came over. She said, reproachfully, "You know, Bunty, Arnie hasn't been here since you announced your engagement to Al. We think you've broken his heart." She gave Bob a disapproving look and waited. By now we had been joined by several more in the group that Al and I knew. I introduced Bob in an effort to make things clear: "This is Bob Kopeck. My family knew his brother when he came to England in the Ninth Air Force. We've corresponded with his folks in Ohio for almost a year now. Bob is visiting us on furlough from Germany."

Feeling vindicated, I decided to enjoy myself. Bob led me expertly through foxtrots, waltzes, jitterbugs and tangos. He was such a good dancer that I was enjoying every minute, but I could almost feel the waves of sympathy for poor Al and little Arnie wafting in my direction. Bob was having a wonderful time, but I was glad when we had to leave to catch the last train for Upper Woodside. I was determined not to take Bob back to Rainbow Corner!

In reality, although they had never met, Al knew all about Bob, having heard the story of Bill and Frank, and how Bob had arrived in the E.T.O. just in time to fight enemy tanks in the Battle of the Bulge. Al had no other preference for a best man at our wedding, so he suggested we ask Bob to serve, if he could get leave from Germany.

Al: "WEDNESDAY, AUGUST 1: TWELFTH ARMY GROUP DISBANDED YESTERDAY. WHEN WILL IT BE OUR TURN? WENT TO BAD HOMBERG TO VISIT GUYS FROM LONDON-- ANOTHER SPA--NEAR FRANKFURT, FAMOUS FOR ITS CASINO. LUXURY HOTELS LIKE ONES AT BAD NAUHEIM. LEARNED SOME GERMAN PHRASES. WENT SWIMMING IN HOTEL POOL WITH GUYS. GREAT! BACK TO BAD NAUHEIM. WROTE LONG LETTER TO BUNTY. SURE DO LOVE THAT GAL."

Bunty: "LEFT WITH BOB BY TRAIN TO VISIT OLD FRIEND OF BOB'S DAD, WILLIAM HIGHGROVE, IN HERTFORDSHIRE. NICE DAY."
While Al was swimming in a posh hotel pool, Bob and I were visiting an elderly widower at Hitchin, north of London. Dr. Kopeck and he had met in England in World War One, and had stayed in touch all these years. When he was in England, Frank had gone to visit Mr. Highgrove, and now Bob had also arranged a visit. He asked me to go with him.

A little over an hour on the train brought us to our destination. Bob hailed a taxi and gave the driver the address. The cab stopped at a beautiful old house of weathered brick with leaded glass bay windows and a meticulously kept flower garden. Mr. Highgrove was expecting us. He came to the door, both hands outstretched in welcome. He showed signs of aging, but still held himself erect with shoulders squared. His hazel eyes twinkled in a handsome sun-bronzed face. A thinning crop of gray hair and a little military moustache completed his appearance. He had recently lost his wife to cancer; Bob offered his condolences.

"Thank you, Bob. I shall mourn Edna's passing for the rest of my life, but we just have to pull ourselves together and go on, don't we? Now let's have some lunch." He rang a little bell. A motherly, middle-aged woman appeared. "Molly, these are special visitors: this is Bob Kopeck, the son of my dear friend, Dr. Kopeck, in the U.S.A., and this is his friend, Bunty Amiss. I wonder if we could have some tea, and how about some of your lovely sandwiches and plum cake?"

Molly smiled and nodded to us, and disappeared as silently as she had arrived.

"Molly is my housekeeper," explained Mr. Highgrove, "We've had her with us since she was a young girl. Good as gold itself."

Many cups of tea, sandwiches and slices of plum cake later, we were given a tour of Mr. Highgrove's flower garden full of multicolored annuals and perennials, surrounding a sundial. A small fishpond was in his back lawn, a favorite feature of suburban gardens in England. "Of course, I bring them in to spend the winter in my aquarium," he said, waving a hand at the six beautiful golden carp swimming lazily around in the water, "they are so relaxing to watch, indoors or out."

It was hard to say goodbye to this gentle, lonely man, but Bob promised to visit him again before he left the E.T.O.

Al: "SATURDAY, AUGUST 4: WENT WITH COURIER TO WIESBADEN. I'VE BEEN GRANTED PERMISSION TO MARRY AFTER SEPTEMBER 9, BUT I'M NOT DUE FOR A FURLOUGH UNTIL OCTOBER 6. SO LONG TO WAIT! TALKED TO BUNTY ON PRINTER TO LET HER KNOW AND MAKE ARRANGEMENTS."

Bunty: "WENT TO LONDON RADIO ROOM AND TALKED TO AL ON THE TELEPRINTER AT WIESBADEN. GREAT NEWS! PERMISSION

GRANTED FOR HIM TO MARRY ME! HAD MY PHOTO TAKEN, THEN WENT FOR FITTING FOR MY NEW SUIT. BOB TALKED TO ME ABOUT MARRIAGE LIKE A DUTCH UNCLE!"

Al's army group was headquartered at Wiesbaden, south of Bad Nauheim. He hitched a ride there frequently with the daily courier run when he needed to go to the P.X.(Post Exchange), visit his old buddies from London, collect his rations and pay, connect with the "brass" about his furlough, and to use the teleprinter to contact me.

The teleprinted message came clattering in front of my eyes, as I sat in the radio room in London.

"Honey," Al typed, "good news! I've been given permission for us to marry any time after September ninth. Bad news: I'm not due for a furlough before October sixth. I think I might be able to do something about that, but just keep your fingers crossed that I won't be shipped out before I do! I think you should go ahead and buy the wedding ring you want; when my furlough comes through there may not be enough time to get one."

I typed back: "O.K., I'll shop for a ring, dear, and while I'm up here in the city I plan on having a formal photo made to send to your folks. I haven't had one taken since I was getting ready to be evacuated to Canada, back in 1940--I don't want them to think I still look like that!"

Several poses later, I hurried from the photographer's back to Upper Woodside to see our local tailor, Mr. Anderson, for my first fitting for a new suit.

"Hello, Mr. Anderson. It's going to feel so good to have a nice custom-made suit to wear after all the shortages, especially in my size! My old prewar one really looks pathetic, and it's rather tight across the bosom--definitely not eligible for a honeymoon!"

The elderly man who had had a lifetime's career as a custom tailor was well-known in the neighborhood for the perfection of his work. He wagged his finger at me: "Now look, young lady, your Mum found this suit-length of fine woolen material on her last visit to the northeast, and I'm going to make sure it looks absolutely perfect on you. But you're go-ing to have to be patient during your fittings. My fingers aren't as nimble as they used to be, so it might take longer than you want to stand still for me. I like the pattern you and your Mum chose--thank goodness it won't look like those skimpy Utility suits in the stores! You couldn't get one with pleats, nowadays, but your skirt will have some nice ones."

Hoping to sound reassuring, I smiled and said: "Oh, by the way, I heard you had made Betty White's wedding dress before the war. Guess what? She has offered to let me borrow it from her. I'm so thrilled--and it's so beautiful! And I promise to stand ever so still for you, Mr. Anderson, only I hope you'll let me change feet once in awhile!"

When I arrived home, I found Bob relaxing in a lawn chair. As we chatted, he lectured me, like the brother I never had, on what to expect from marriage and how to handle it. Mom had never brought up the subject, but had instead given me a book to read called *Sane Sex Life and Sane Sex Living*, which had been a shock to my naïve, untutored mind. Bob gave me a lot of new pointers, but even so, the more I thought about it the more nervous I became!

Next day, Bob reluctantly departed for Germany, promising to apply for a furlough once we knew the wedding date.

Al: "MONDAY, AUGUST 6: WASHED SOME UNDERSHIRTS BY HAND. UGH! MUST FIND A LAUNDRY. WENT ON DUTY AT RADIO STATION FROM 1200 TO 1815. PLAYED SOME TENNIS. CHOW. BED."

Bunty: "LETTER FROM AL. MM-MM-MM! ALSO LOVELY LETTER FROM HIS MOTHER. WHAT A RELIEF, SHE DOESN'T HATE ME, AFTER ALL! AUNTIE BELLE, AUDREY AND DOROTHY ARRIVED FOR A WEEK."

Reading our diaries many decades later, I wondered: "Why did neither of us write about the dropping of the atomic bomb on Hiroshima today? It hastened the end of World War Two, but why wasn't it mentioned by either one of us in our diaries?" Then I remembered that at that time it was commonplace to hear about multiple air raids being carried out on Japan involving more than a thousand aircraft, but we had no inkling of the American government's well-kept secret of having created an atomic bomb.

Later, in the newspaper I read the text of President Truman's radio message to the American people. He announced the attack on Hiroshima, mentioning one aircraft and one bomb; not enough to impress the casual listener, but his prepared speech went on to say that the bomb that had been dropped carried the equivalent of more than twenty thousand tons of T.N.T. He then revealed the investment of two billion dollars in the secret development of the bomb to have been "an expensive gamble, but one that we have won." He added that even more powerful weapons were in the developmental stage. Truman's speech said nothing about the effect the bomb would have on its target. Now I realized that, at the time it was dropped, it would be some time before reports could reveal its enormity. That would surely have made it into Al's and my diaries!

Meantime, at Bishop's Hill, it was looking like peacetime, with the visit of more family members from Sunderland. Mom had hardly recovered from Bob's visit when Auntie Belle and my two cousins arrived to spend a week with us. Our house really must have looked as if it had a revolving door--I'm sure the neighbors thought so!

My fears of Al's mother's coolness were dispelled by her letter, which was warm and touching, welcoming me into the family.

Al: "THURSDAY, AUGUST 9: GOT ALL MY LAUNDRY TOGETHER AND WASHED MY UNDERWEAR IN AN OLD GERMAN WASHING MACHINE. CONTEST AROSE BETWEEN MACHINE AND ME, BUT AT LEAST MY UNDERWEAR DOES LOOK A TRIFLE CLEANER--OR MAYBE THE DIRT IS JUST SPREAD AROUND MORE EVENLY! WENT ON DUTY 1230 TO 1830. RAINING FOR PAST FEW DAYS."

Bunty: "I'M TAKING TIME OFF FROM THE OFFICE. SINCE AUNTIE BELLE ARRIVED, WE HAVE NOW TAKEN THE KIDS TO HAMPTON COURT AND ST. PAUL'S CATHEDRAL. TOOK A DAY FOR MYSELF TODAY. SPENT THE DAY WITH PAT PRINGLE."

Al and I were both involved in domestic affairs and again our diaries didn't mention the dropping of the second atomic bomb, on Nagasaki.

The horrific result of the vast damage and human carnage caused by this second atomic bomb and its lethal predecessor had not yet begun to be disseminated or comprehended.

The use of these two atomic weapons is still debated and highly controversial. Theodore Van Kirk, the last living member of the crew of the B-29 *Enola Gay*, which dropped the first bomb, said: "It's hard to talk of morality and war in the same sentence. Where was the morality in the bombing of Coventry, or Dresden, or the Bataan Death March, the Rape of Nanking, or the bombing of Pearl Harbor?"

In my own mind, I could only rationalize it by thinking of the alternative: the loss of millions more Allied and Japanese lives in a war that could have dragged on for another year or longer.

On the home front, today I was getting to know Pat Pringle better. Al had suggested her as maid of honor at our wedding. She lived with her ailing mother in an apartment on the other side of London; devotion to her Mom kept Pat from enjoying much of a social life.

We did what girls do best: went shopping, then relaxed over a slushy romantic movie to rest our feet! I asked her to be my maid of honor, and she was thrilled. She gurgled: "Oh, and I have a pink bridesmaid's dress I can wear. Will it do?"

I could hardly believe my good luck: "Will it do, Pat? You bet it will!" Another problem solved! Pat was my kind of gal.

Rescued by a Holocaust

Al: "FRIDAY, AUGUST 10: RAINING HARD. BEGINNING TO INSTALL MORE COMMUNICATIONS EQUIPMENT. DUTY ALL MORNING. SPENT ALL AFTERNOON INSTALLING POWER LINES. GOODBYE, GERMAN WASHING MACHINE--NOW WE HAVE A LAUNDRY. MARKED ALL MY UNDERWEAR READY. WOW, WHAT A BREAK!"

Bunty: "WENT TO BUY MY WEDDING RING. NINE CARAT GOLD, UTILITY, WITH A LITTLE FLORAL DESIGN. RECEIVED SURPRISE PACKAGE FROM KATE AND FRANK IN THE U.S.--LACE UNDERWEAR AND NAIL POLISH."

I thought: "Well, I never dreamed I'd have to buy my own wedding ring! But it's still wartime, so I guess I'm not the only one!"

The sales clerk remembered selling us my engagement ring. I enthused: "Oh, I just love wearing it, and it's been admired by lots of people. Thanks for helping us find such a beautiful one that we could afford."

"And how is your fiance, Miss?"

"Oh, he's fine, thank you. He's stationed in Germany. He'll be coming back to England for our wedding, but we may not have enough time to shop for a wedding ring, so I'm doing it today."

He sounded apologetic. "Well, as you know, Miss, we only have Utility rings, but I have two I can show you." He showed me two nine-carat gold rings and I chose the one with tiny flowers etched around it.

I grumbled to myself: "Here I was, just getting used to the idea of a wedding, but now I have no idea <u>when,</u> or even <u>if!</u>"

I had corresponded with Frank Kopeck's young wife, Kate, while he and Bill were our surrogate family in 1944. Now that Frank was back in the U.S.A., we still kept in touch. Obviously, Kate and Frank had faith in the "<u>if!</u>" They had sent me a surprise wedding gift: delicate pink and white lacy underwear and three different shades of nail polish--all impossible to find in England--to be cherished and made to last as long as possible.

Al: "MONDAY, AUGUST 13: WENT WITH COURIER TO WIESBADEN AND HAD MY NAME PUT ON LIST FOR FURLOUGH IN SEPTEMBER. LETTERS TODAY FROM MY MOM, AMY AND BUNTY. THEY ARE ALL NOW IN CONTACT."

Bunty: "BACK TO WORK. HAD A CALL FROM CHUCK AT LONDON RADIO ROOM. AL HAS LEFT A MESSAGE FROM GERMANY TO SAY HE'S ON THE LIST FOR A FURLOUGH IN SEPTEMBER! WHOOPEE!"

Chuck's nasal accent came through my phone at the office. "Hey, Bunty, gotta message for ya. Al sez to tell ya he's on the list for a priority furlough in September. Ah thought you should know right away. Geez, that fella gets all the luck!"

"You sound quite envious, Chuck! Thanks for relaying the message. Now, at last, I'll be able to get to work organizing a wedding!" I sat for a moment, digesting the full meaning of Al's message in the phone call. I thought: "Wow! This guy *is* full of surprises! Now, with a little bit of luck, the wedding could be in September instead of October. We have a month, but without a date how am I supposed to plan?"

Mom rose to the occasion. "Bunty, even if we don't have a date, we've got to be prepared." She consulted her notes on her pad of lined paper and a few backs of envelopes, and began to make a priority list.

Al: "WEDNESDAY, AUGUST 15: HAD A TYPHUS SHOT. OUCH! WAR WITH JAPAN IS OVER TODAY! CAN'T QUITE BELIEVE IT YET. HAVE A COLD. TOOK HOT BATH, WROTE TO BUNTY. BED."

Bunty: "JAPAN AGREED TO UNCONDITIONAL SURRENDER! IT'S THE END OF WORLD WAR TWO! ALL THOSE YEARS OF WORRY AND HORROR HAVE ENDED AT LAST. TOOK DAY OFF FROM WORK. JOLLIFICATIONS IN BRITAIN, BUT NOTHING LIKE THE SCALE OF V-E DAY."
It seemed like a lifetime since September 3, 1939 when Britain had been plunged into World War Two. Now, miraculously, came the surrender of the remaining Axis power. In its seventh year for us in Britain, at last the scourge of world war was over.

I said to myself: "I can hardly believe it! Al won't have the threat of being in harm's way any longer. Now at last we can realize the promise of a life together." I said a prayer of heartfelt thanks, but as yet had no idea of the terrible, tragic cost of peace as a result of the atom-bombing. I couldn't have guessed that Al and I were rescued by a holocaust.

Brits again filled the streets of London with celebration, but this was not as unrestrained as on V-E Day, and there was no dancing in the street at Bishop's Hill. Our family still had cause to worry. My two second cousins, both newspaper reporters, had been captured and interned in a Japanese concentration camp during the British retreat in Malaya. We still didn't know if they were alive. But the war in the Pacific had been remote in our minds; thank God we had never been on its receiving end.

Al: "SATURDAY, AUGUST 18: THEY ARE BEGINNING TO SHIP THE GUYS HOME TO U.S. ONE OF OUR FELLOWS GOING WEDNESDAY. ON RADIO DUTY 1120 TO 1800. STUDIED AND PRACTISED MORSE CODE."

Bunty: "DAD, MOM AND I TOOK THE TRAIN TO GODSTONE IN SURREY TO CHECK OUT ROMANTIC OLD INN FOR A HONEYMOON HOTEL. FOUND A BEAUTY--IT'S SOOPERDOOPER!"

A wedding should be followed by a honeymoon, and my well-organized mother had canvassed her friends to find us the perfect place to stay: an old English country inn. Their unanimous vote had been for the White Hart Inn, nestled in a Surrey village, and I fell in love with it. "This is the place," I bubbled. "Now we've a honeymoon destination, but how can we make a reservation without a wedding date? Why is life so darn' complicated?"

At the reception desk the clerk was sympathetic. "I can quite appreciate your problem, Miss," she said, "we've run into this quite often, with things so uncertain. But don't you worry, I'll put you down for late September."

Yes, the inn was "super-duper!" I giggled as I re-read my diary, years later, noticing the Americanisms creeping into it. I was so fascinated with American English that I began a translation list in the back of my diary. I never could have guessed that what my glossary offered would represent just a drop in the bucket of trouble I would have later!

Bunty: "SUNDAY, AUGUST 19: MADE A QUICK TRIP TO LONDON TO VISIT ELSIE CELLI AND THE RED CROSS GIRLS AT RAINBOW CORNER. THE CLUB IS LIKE A FUNERAL PARLOR! TODAY IS A NATIONAL DAY OF PRAYER. WENT WITH MOM AND DAD THIS EVENING TO ST. JOHN'S VICTORY THANKSGIVING SERVICE."

Amid all the rejoicing over the ending of the war, Rainbow Corner had changed. The lively place I remembered was now just another spot for G.I.s to grab a quick meal as they passed through London on the way to their reassignment to Europe, or to board a ship taking them back to the U.S.A. The American Red Cross girls were going home. Elsie Celli was bursting with excitement. "Bunty, I'm so thrilled about the news of your wedding. Now listen to my news: I expect to be married myself, shortly after I go home to Boston."

We hugged each other. I felt a pang of sadness to think I would be losing such a loyal friend, but Elsie's shared joy dispelled the sadness. "Another ship had passed in the night," as Dad would have said.

Throughout Britain, people flocked to their churches for a National Day of Prayer--one of many which had been called by King George V1 throughout the perilous days of World War Two--this time to celebrate the end of the war with a service of thanksgiving. At St. John's Evensong service, Mom, Dad and I gave thanks that in this seventh year since it began, we were now free of the bondage of war and also of the tyranny it had represented.

Al: "THURSDAY, AUGUST 23: BEGAN TAKING TENNIS LESSONS FROM THE HOTEL'S TENNIS PROFESSIONAL. HE CAN'T SPEAK A WORD OF ENGLISH, BUT GOOD AT HAND SIGNALS. DUTY FROM 1800 TO 2100. BED."

Bunty: "COLLECTED MY PHOTO PROOFS. CHOSE BEST ONE TO BE MADE INTO PRINT TO SEND TO ALL AND SUNDRY. LAST PHOTO AS A SINGLE WOMAN! WILL SEND A PROOF TO AL. PAUL CAME TO VISIT."
I had written to Paul telling him I would be collecting the proofs today, and he had made a special trip from the seminary with some equipment so he could laminate them and make them permanent. My favorite proof was on its way to Al the following day.

Al: "SUNDAY, AUGUST 26: TENNIS LESSON, MY GAME IMPROVING. PACKED UP MY DRESS UNIFORM TO SEND TO BUNTY FOR ME TO

WEAR AT THE WEDDING, THEN PACKED BARRACKS BAG TO GO TO NEW ASSIGNMENT AT RADIO STUTTGART."

Bunty: "ATTENDED CHURCH SERVICE AT ST. JOHN'S THIS MORNING TO HEAR WEDDING BANNS READ. PETER DONOVAN BROUGHT HIS FIANCEE TO MEET US!"

Although superstition declared that it was unlucky for a bride to hear her own wedding banns, I thought I'd better check out the last reading at the morning service today, to make sure they had the right names! The Vicar intoned: "I publish the banns of marriage between Ida Heywood Amiss and Albert Samuel Greene. If any of you know just cause or impediment why these persons should not be joined together in Holy Matrimony, you are to declare it. This is the third time of asking."

There was a nice warm silence from the congregation. After the service I walked back home and reported: "Well, nobody seems to object if Al and I get married, so I guess we've overcome one more hurdle! This marriage business is a lot more complicated than I ever dreamed it would be!" Little did I know that this would be only the tip of the iceberg!

My childhood friend, Peter Donovan, hadn't popped up in my diary since 1944. His family had moved away from Upper Woodside. We had lost track of each other after his leg had been badly crushed in an accident when he was a dispatch rider in the R.A.F., followed by his many subsequent surgeries and long hospitalization in south Wales. Always somewhat proprietary where Mom, Dad and me were concerned, he had appeared to be miffed as we played host to a stream of homesick Americans. Now "invalided out" of the R.A.F. because of his shattered leg, he wanted us to meet Rhonda, his attractive new fiancée, with whom he had fallen in love, as Mom had suspected, when his visits with us suddenly tapered off before his accident. I liked Rhonda immediately, and Mom and I were both so glad that Peter had come "home" to show her off. They were planning a September wedding, too.

Al: "MONDAY, AUGUST 27: RODE WITH COURIER TO WIESBADEN. LEFT PACKAGE WITH MY DRESS SHOES AND UNIFORM AT A.P.O. TO BE SENT

TO BUNTY FOR WEDDING. PICKED UP RATION CARD AND SIGNED COPY OF PERMISSION TO MARRY. MADE ARRANGEMENTS TO GO WITH COURIER TOMORROW TO HEIDELBERG AND ON WITH ANOTHER TO STUTTGART. SPENT THE NIGHT IN WIESBADEN ON JOE AND HOWIE'S SPARE COUCH. I FELL OFF IT TWICE, BUT IT'S GREAT TO HAVE FRIENDS WHEN YOU NEED 'EM!"

Bunty: "WORKED MYSELF TO A STANDSTILL AT THE OFFICE. EVERY-ONE SEEMS TO BE TAKING A FEW DAYS OFF. TELEPHONE WENT CRAZY. SOMETIMES WE HAVE SOME INTERESTING FREIGHT. TWO ARISTOCRATIC DOGS PASSED THROUGH THE CARGO DEPARTMENT IN CRATES TO HAVE THEIR DOCUMENTATION CHECKED BEFORE GO-ING ON TO LISBON AND STOCKHOLM RESPECTIVELY! IT'S BEGIN-NING TO LOOK LIKE PEACETIME!"

In the absence of my boss, Freddy and the rest of the staff, who all appeared to have taken off to celebrate the surrender of Japan, Brad and I were holding down the office. It had become frantic with nonstop activity that had seemed to pick up like magic the minute the war was over. The following day was a repeat. I wrote: "I'M EXHAUSTED AND BRAD IS NEARING A NERVOUS BREAKDOWN--WHERE IS EVERYBODY?"

Al: "WEDNESDAY, AUGUST 29: GOOD BILLET AT STUTTGART. BEST CHOW I'VE TASTED SINCE LEAVING ENGLAND. NICE TENNIS COURT AND SWIMMING POOL. SPENT MORNING SIGHTSEEING. BOMB DAMAGE TERRIBLE IN CITY. SENT BUNTY COPY OF PERMISSION TO MARRY."

Bunty: "WROTE TO BOB'S C.O. TO ASK PERMISSION FOR HIM TO SERVE AS AL'S BEST MAN. ORDERED WEDDING INVITATIONS. AL IS NOW STATIONED IN STUTTGART."

I doubted that Bob would be granted another furlough so soon after his recent one, but it was worth a try. I carefully composed the letter to his C.O., explaining how much we would appreciate it, then crossed my fingers.

There was still no sign of a wedding date. The invitations had to be ready for me to send out, so I simply ordered them to be printed without one!

Al: "FRIDAY, AUGUST 31: RECEIVED PHOTO PROOF FROM BUNTY. WONDERFUL. COULD HARDLY KEEP IT IN MY POCKET. KEPT TAKING IT OUT AND LOOKING AT IT. RECEIVED PACKAGE WITH MY DRESS SHOES AND UNIFORM BACK FROM THE A.P.O. I FORGOT TO PAY THE POSTAGE! GUESS I MUST BE IN LOVE, OR SUMPIN'!"

Bunty: "SURPRISE PACKAGE FROM BOB! WHAT A HONEYMOON HE WANTS ME TO HAVE! SHEER NIGHTGOWN, BLACK LACE UNDERWEAR, NYLONS, FROTHY SLIPS! WOW!"
I opened Bob's package, spread out each lacy garment, and just sat and looked at them. After seeing only ugly Utility underwear during the war, I couldn't believe my eyes. I thought: "I'll try everything on tomorrow, but for now I just want to enjoy looking at it all."

Al's move to Stuttgart could possibly mean that he would soon be shipped back to America with his group. My heart sank. Would we ever be married? What about all the wedding preparations?"

The Elusive Bridegroom

Al: "SUNDAY, SEPTEMBER 2: MAILED PACKAGE YESTERDAY WITH DRESS SHOES AND UNIFORM ONCE AGAIN! IS MY FACE RED! HOPE IT ARRIVES IN TIME! FOUND AMERICAN RED CROSS CLUB. GOOD CHOW THERE. WROTE LETTERS HOME. BED."

Bunty: "THE WAR IS OVER! JAPAN SIGNED OFFICIAL DOCUMENT OF UNCONDITIONAL SURRENDER. TRIED ON MY NEW LINGERIE. SMASHING!"

IT STILL ISN'T clear when World War Two officially ended. V-J Day (Victory over Japan Day) is now celebrated in the U.S. on August 14, the date when news of Japan's impending surrender broke. It was celebrated in Britain on August 15, when Japan had announced its unconditional surrender. Some authorities say it should be celebrated on September 2, when Japan signed the surrender document. Whatever the correct date, I celebrated by prancing around my bedroom, scantily clad in see-through underwear, trying on each beautiful, delicate garment. I couldn't believe they were mine, as I luxuriated in the feeling of each slinky item like the ones I had seen during the war only in Hollywood movies. Mom chuckled as I appeared in front of her to model each ensemble. Overcome with the sight of my new intimate wardrobe, she gasped: "Aha, so this is what Bob meant in his letter when he said he was sending you some 'honeymoon delight.' I thought he meant candy!"

Enter Laurie

Al: "TUESDAY, SEPTEMBER 11: WENT TO SEE TRANSMITTER AT STUTTGART YESTERDAY. SITUATED HIGH ON HILL. LOVELY VIEW.

VISITED RED CROSS CLUB FOR COFFEE AND DOUGHNUTS. WENT TO PARK TO READ. DUTY. CHOW. BED."

Bunty: "WENT TO G.I. WIVES CLUB MEETING AT RAINBOW CORNER. MET A GIRL WHO IS GOING TO LITTLE CEDAR RIVER, NEW JERSEY!!! MOM HAS FINISHED MINOR ALTERATIONS ON WEDDING DRESS."
"Mom, I didn't know that as an official fiancée I'm eligible to attend the monthly G.I. Wives Club meetings at Rainbow Corner," I had declared, "I think I'll give it a try after work today."

There were now so many marriages between G.I.s and English girls that Elsie Celli had created these monthly meetings, to acquaint the "G.I. Brides" who lived in the London area with each other and to educate them about life in America with audio-visuals and guest speakers. The most famous speaker was Eleanor Roosevelt, who took a special interest in the club on her visits to England.

An article appeared in the *Reader's Digest* about the G.I Brides. When it was written, the number of such marriages was a mere twenty thousand. This would grow to seventy   thousand by the following year! In part, the article said:

"...It is no small matter for a young woman to be taken across the sea to live among strangers. The American Red Cross recognizes the problem and the need for instructing the young wives in American ways. One result is a 'G.I. school for brides' in London, the idea of Elsie Celli, a pretty Red Cross worker from Dorchester, Massachusetts. The school now numbers four hundred wives and fiancées. Miss Celli hosts guest speakers, shows movies; unpretentious travelogues about life in our cities, in the country, on the plains, in the nation's capital. Each girl receives a booklet: *A Bride's Guide to the U.S.A.*, prepared by *Good Housekeeping* magazine and the U.S. Office of War Information..." (I still have my copy of *A Bride's Guide to the U.S.A.!*)

Rainbow Corner's ballroom was set up for the lecture with rows of chairs on the dance floor. The usual small tables and chairs were still around its borders. Above them on the walls were well-spaced banners with the name of each state in large, bold letters, where girls could meet who were going to destinations in the same state.

After the program, doughnuts, cookies and soft drinks were served at the little tables. I headed for the banner that said "NEW JERSEY." At this, my first meeting, that banner heralded the very special day when Laurie entered my life. Tall, attractive and elegant in manner and speech, she was to become my role model and closest friend in the following months and years. We were instantly drawn to each other.

"Where does your husband come from in New Jersey, Laurie?" I asked, after we had exchanged names.

She smiled and said: "Oh, you probably won't have even heard of it, it's such a small place--its name is Little Cedar River."

I could hardly believe my ears. All I could stutter was: "Laurie, you're not going to believe this, but I'm going there, too!"

It was reassuring to both of us that we would already have a friend when we reached our new hometown. We never dreamed that this was the beginning of a friendship that would last for the rest of our lives. When I got home, Mom was itching to hear all about the meeting. I told her the astonishing news.

"Well, Bunty, what a surprise! I'm delighted. Laurie sounds like a good friend; now you'll each have one person you already know in America, aside from your husbands. Oh, by the way, I've been busy while you were gone; I finished the alterations on Betty's wedding dress."

I tried on the dress. "Oh, Mom, it fits perfectly, but where's the wedding?"

Al: "WEDNESDAY, SEPTEMBER 12: SENT RADIO MESSAGE TO WIESBADEN WITH REFERENCE TO MY FURLOUGH. NOW I HAVE A GERMAN TUTOR TEACHING ME GERMAN; BETTER THAN JUST A DICTIONARY!"

Bunty: "STILL NO DATE FROM AL FOR HIS FURLOUGH! AGONIZING! LETTER FROM BOB. HE'S WORRIED THAT HE WON'T BE ABLE TO GET A FURLOUGH IN TIME FOR THE WEDDING. SAYS TO GET SOMEONE ELSE FOR BEST MAN. COUSIN LEW SAYS HE WILL BE HONORED.

PICKED UP WEDDING INVITATIONS AND ANNOUNCEMENTS FROM PRINT SHOP. HAD FIRST REAL LETTER FROM AL'S MOTHER."

Railway travel was still tedious in Britain; the trains were now crowded with hundreds of servicemen and women rushing home after the war. Also, continuing fuel shortages meant only one train for every two or three that ran before the war, necessitating more frequent stops. To reach Bishop's Hill from the north of England and from Wales would take the relatives all day, but they happily agreed to attend the wedding.

Auntie Belle said she would be glad to represent the Amiss side of the family. As her wedding gift to us, she volunteered to provide a traditional English three-tier wedding fruit cake, to be made by the bakery owned by her brother in Sunderland.

Cousin Lew and his young wife Dorothy would represent the Ditchfields. Now that Bob might not get a furlough, I had called Lew at the R.A.F. training camp in the north of England where he was now second in rank to the C.O., and had asked him if he would be Al's best man.

"Of course, Bunty, it will be an honor. I have enough clout here at the camp to be able to get away at short notice, so just let me know when, and I'll be there with bells on!"

Al's aunt and uncle in Wales said they would be thrilled to represent his family. All of them were waiting for me to give them a date. And here was I, still wondering if I would ever have one!"

The letter from Al's mother said she had not been well (she later told me that the shock of Al's announcement that he was engaged to be married to an English girl had put her in bed for a week!) The words in her letter were welcoming, but seemed labored; I gathered that she was not comfortable with letter-writing.

Al: "SATURDAY, SEPTEMBER 15:   JUST BEFORE GOING OFF DUTY, THE GREAT INFORMATION CAME THROUGH THAT I'M TO BEGIN MY FURLOUGH TO LONDON ON SEPTEMBER 21ST! HAD TO GET WORD TO BUNTY SO SHE CAN MAKE LAST-MINUTE ARRANGEMENTS. FINALLY

GOT RADIO MESSAGE THROUGH TO LONDON VIA BAD HOMBERG OPERATOR. SO EXCITED I CAN HARDLY THINK STRAIGHT. STILL AWAKE AT TWO O'CLOCK IN THE MORNING. THINKING. PLANNING."

Bunty: "WONDERFUL NEWS! AL IS LEAVING GERMANY ON THE 21ST TO TAKE A BOAT FROM FRANCE TO ENGLAND. ESTIMATED TRAVEL TIME: 5 DAYS. I DATED ALL WEDDING INVITATIONS SEPTEMBER 28." At last, a wedding date! Galvanized into action, I addressed invitations, made phone calls to guests from far and near, also to Lew, Pat, the church, limousine company, florist and caterer.

When I called Elsie Celli to tell her about the wedding date, she said: "Oh, Bunty, of course I'd love to come; you and Al are two of my favorite people--I was the one who brought you together, remember? And incidentally, there's a package here for you from Al's mother in Little Cedar River, New Jersey. I wonder why she sent it to you at this address? Anyway, just stop by when you can, and pick it up."

Wedding gifts began to trickle in. Most were checks, and Al had said his old London buddies had taken up a collection to which Howie and Joe had added when he stayed with them at Wiesbaden. The contents of the package from Al's mother included some lingerie, more conservative than Bob's, but still quite luxurious to my Utility-jaded eyes.

An exquisite crystal vase arrived from a friend of Mom's and a box of elegant stationery from Paul Bates, engraved at the seminary print shop with the strange new name: "Mrs. Albert S. Greene, Jr."

Al: "TUESDAY, SEPTEMBER 18: GOT A RIDE FROM STUTTGART VIA FRANKFURT TO WIESBADEN. WAS TOLD I'LL BE *FLYING* FROM FRANKFURT ON THE 21ST. OH, BROTHER! I TOLD BUNTY TRIP WOULD TAKE FIVE DAYS VIA BOAT FROM FRANCE! HOWIE IS SENDING NEW MESSAGE TO BUNTY TO REMEDY ERROR. HOPE IN TIME. DIDN'T GET MUCH SLEEP ON HOWIE AND JOE'S COUCH; ONLY FELL OFF IT ONCE

THIS TIME. TOO MUCH THINKING! I'M ALLOWED ONLY 35 LBS. OF LUGGAGE. TOSSED OUT SOME STUFF."

Bunty: "HOLD EVERYTHING! ANOTHER MESSAGE FROM AL, VIA THE RADIO ROOMS AT WIESBADEN AND LONDON. YIKES! PLANS CHANGED! AL'S NOT COMING BY BOAT BUT FLYING ON THE 21ST. HE'LL BE HERE THREE DAYS FROM NOW! WE'LL HAVE TO MOVE THE WEDDING UP TO THE 24TH!"

Mom wailed: "Oh, Bunty, whatever will we do?"

I put my arms around her. "Mom, don't worry, everything's going to work out. I'll take care of things." I frantically repeated the performance of notifying everyone--Lew, Pat, guests, church, florist, limo, caterer--to tell them the new date for the wedding. Hardest hit in rearranging their plans were the relatives from Sunderland and Wales, but they rallied well. However, some of the guests had other commitments on the new date--among them my boss, Freddy, and sadly, Elsie Celli. Blossom Brown gladly accepted the invitation to represent Rainbow Corner, as did my new friend Laurie.

Al: "FRIDAY, SEPTEMBER 21: UP AT 7 A.M. LEFT WIESBADEN FOR FRANKFURT. FOGGY. CHECKED IN FOR FLIGHT. NO FLIGHTS OUT TODAY; WEATHER TOO BAD. AM BOOKED FOR TOMORROW. HERE'S HOPING! BUTTERFLIES IN ABDOMINAL REGION. NOT ALLOWED TO STAY AT AIRPORT OVERNIGHT. MISSED TRUCK BACK TO WIESBADEN-- HOPPED A BUS INSTEAD. SPENT NIGHT ON HOWIE AND JOE'S COUCH. RATS! TOSSED AND TURNED ALL NIGHT--FELL OF COUCH TWICE. RATS AGAIN! FIGURED I WOULD CERTAINLY GET A FLIGHT TOMORROW SO DIDN'T TELETYPE BUNTY."

Bunty: "TODAY SEEMED UNENDING. MY HEART TURNED OVER EVERY TIME THE PHONE OR THE DOORBELL RANG. WAITED UP UNTIL 11

P.M. STILL NO SIGN OF AL. HE'S FULL OF SUPRISES BUT THIS ONE IS NO FUN. EXHAUSTED. DECIDED TO GIVE UP AND GO TO BED."

Still listening for the front doorbell, I tossed and turned, alternately fussing at Al for not getting in touch with me then agonizing that he might be lying injured in a hospital or worse; after all, I wasn't yet his "next of kin" so I wouldn't have been notified. If only cellphones had been invented back in 1945, how different things would have been!

Common sense calmed my nerves. I convinced myself: "Don't be so silly, Bunty, you know he's probably en route and has no way of getting in touch, wherever he is. Go to sleep." I said a quick prayer for Al's safety, then slept in exhaustion.

Al: "SATURDAY, SEPTEMBER 22: AROSE EARLY. STILL FOGGY. TOOK OFF FOR FRANKFURT AGAIN. TOLD THAT DUE TO FOG NO FLIGHTS AGAIN TODAY. CAN'T BE SURE ANY BETTER TOMORROW, BUT BOOKED ANYWAY. BACK TO WIESBADEN. DIDN'T TELETYPE BUNTY TO RAISE HER HOPES. PROBABLY A MISTAKE. SPIRITS AT ZERO LEVEL. WENT TO RED CROSS CLUB. GOT OUT A BOOK ON MARRIAGE. WHATEVER WILL BUNTY BE THINKING?"

Bunty: "SPENT THE DAY IN AGONY WAITING FOR AL'S ARRIVAL, BUT STILL NO SIGN. OH, I HOPE HE'S O.K.! OR HAS HE CHANGED HIS MIND AND DOESN'T WANT TO MARRY ME AFTER ALL? I DON'T KNOW WHAT TO THINK! AND WHAT WILL WE DO ABOUT THE WEDDING ARRANGEMENTS?"

Mom was trying to keep my spirits up. "Bunty, dear, if he doesn't come by the twenty-fourth we'll just have the reception and make it into a party, then you and Al can get married quietly, whenever he arrives."

I knew she was doing her best to keep me afloat, but this went over like the proverbial lead balloon! I said: "Auntie Belle, cousin Lew and Dorothy, and Al's aunt and uncle will be arriving tomorrow. You know the old saying, 'misery loves company?' Well, that's just how I feel, and that's what they will be. Some party!" I burst into tears. "Whatever will I tell my grandchildren?" I sobbed.

Al: "SUNDAY, SEPTEMBER 23: THIS IS GETTING MONOTONOUS! LEFT WIESBADEN AGAIN FOR AIRPORT. THIS TIME: SUCCESS! ARMY TRANSPORT AIRCRAFT. TOLD I MUST REPORT MONDAY, OCTOBER 1 FOR RETURN TO STUTTGART. 0800 LANDED AT BIGGIN HILL AIRFIELD IN KENT NEAR LONDON. CHANGED MONEY. HITCHED RIDE TO UPPER WOODSIDE INTO ARMS OF MY LOVE. EXHAUSTED. HIT THE SACK FOR A LONG NAP."

Bunty: "AL ARRIVED SAFE AND SOUND THIS MORNING. PRAYERS ANSWERED. HE BROUGHT ME A BEAUTIFUL LITTLE SHORT-WAVE RADIO AS A WEDDING PRESENT. HIS AUNT AND UNCLE ARRIVED FROM WALES THIS AFTERNOON. AUNTIE BELLE, LEW AND DOROTHY ARRIVED FROM SUNDERLAND THIS EVENING. WEDDING TOMORROW!"

Mom, Dad and I had a mournful breakfast, still having received no word of Al's whereabouts. Mom was close to tears. I thought of the wilted flowers, cancelled limos and confused guests, then could hold back my own tears no longer.

Suddenly, the doorbell rang. Mom dried her eyes. "Oh, that must be the milkman--he's a bit late this morning."

I ran to open the door, and there on the doorstep was Al's duffle bag, and Al standing over it looking haggard and disheveled in his battledress and boots, having hitched a ride down Bishop's Hill with the milkman in his little electric delivery truck. With a bottle of milk in each hand, he grinned wearily at me and said: "I think you ordered two bottles, Miss?"

Our prayers had been answered! I almost collapsed from relief, but instead threw myself into his arms. Tears ran down our faces as we laughed and sobbed together. Grimy, unshaven and bone-tired, Al still looked to me like my knight in shining armor (disguised as James Stewart, of course!)

After greeting Mom and Dad, Al produced a beautiful little short-wave radio from the bulging duffle bag and handed it to me: "Here, sweets, happy wedding!" he said.

I cried all over again and kissed him, tears and all. I thought he would never let me out of his arms, but I didn't care. After serving him a hearty breakfast Mom packed him off to bed, and in a few hours he was in good enough shape to greet his excited aunt and uncle when they arrived that afternoon from Wales.

Later, the house overflowed with the addition of Auntie Belle, cousin Lew, resplendent in his R.A.F. officer's dress uniform, and his pretty wife Dorothy. They had all traveled south together from Sunderland to London by train, then by taxi to Bishop's Hill. Mom and Dorothy rushed around with cups of tea for everyone, while Dad brought Auntie Belle's two suitcases into the dining room. "Jack, put them oop very carefully on't table, there's a good lad," she said, in her north country accent. "Now keep your fingers crossed, all of yoo." She took out her keys and nervously unlocked both suitcases.

A spontaneous cheer went up as the contents of the suitcases were unwrapped from their layers of insulation, to uncover three corrugated cardboard boxes containing the three tiers of the wedding cake, each one larger than the other, nestled where they had been tightly wedged in place in the suitcases by Auntie Belle's underwear and several sweaters. She carefully opened each box, revealing a rectangular fruit cake covered with its traditional coating of marzipan, and over it an outer coating of hard, white confectioner's sugar icing, beautifully sculpted with garlands of roses. All three tiers were miraculously intact, thanks to their professional packaging at the bakery, Auntie Belle's underwear and sweaters, and Lew's expert handling of the suitcases on the train journey from Sunderland. Auntie Belle's soft north country voice said it all: "Ee, I'm *that* glad everything's alright!"

Deep silence fell on the house in Bishop's Hill that night, as its human content slumbered from sheer exhaustion and relief.

Wedding Day with Cousin Lew and Pat

Thank You, Auntie Belle

Married at Last!

Al: "MONDAY, SEPTEMBER 24: AT 11:30 TODAY, BUNTY AND I WERE MARRIED. RECEPTION FOLLOWED. LOVELY TIME. WE'RE SO EXCITED WE CAN HARDLY STAY STILL. BUNTY WAS BEAUTIFUL IN HER WEDDING GOWN--SHE'S ALL I'LL EVER CARE FOR. THE PROMISES WE MADE ARE FOREVER--IT'S WONDERFUL! LEFT AT 2 P.M. FOR THE WHITE HART INN AT GODSTONE. BEAUTIFUL ROOM OVERLOOKING VILLAGE GREEN."

Bunty: "THIS MORNING AT 11:30, AL AND I BECAME MAN AND WIFE. CEREMONY WENT OFF PERFECTLY, SO DID RECEPTION (30 GUESTS.) ARRIVED AT WHITE HART INN, GODSTONE AT 4:30 P.M. PEACE AT LAST!"

I can't remember much of the Church of England wedding ceremony that united Al and me at St. John's church, but I do remember bits and pieces; brief vignettes of the day. Pat looked radiant in her long, rose-pink dress, holding her bouquet of pink carnations. True to tradition, I wore something old: Mom's pearl necklace; something new: Bob's American lingerie; something borrowed: my wedding dress; and something blue: a blue garter supplied by Pat. I picked up my bouquet of red roses and headed with Dad for the waiting limousine.

The pews in the little Romanesque church sanctuary with its whitewashed walls and deep blue carpeting were filled not only with our invited guests, but with many neighbors who had shared with us the terrible days of the air raids that drew us close during the war in the experience of mutual danger.

Dad's hand shook a little as he tucked mine under his arm when the notes of Wagner's march signaled our walk down the aisle. Reverend Throckmorton stood waiting at the altar, prayer book open in his hands. He seemed at least a mile away. I gave my bouquet to Pat, as Al stepped away from Lew to join me at the altar. The vicar addressed us and the congregation, reading from his prayer book the Service of Holy Matrimony, which described marriage, in part, as: "an honorable estate, instituted by God ... not in any way ... to be taken in hand unadvisedly, lightly or wantonly ... but reverently, discreetly, advisedly and in the fear of God."

These words and the promises we made to each other that day stayed with us throughout all the years that followed.

After the ceremony, Al and I signed the marriage certificate in the vestry, then the organ played the familiar strains of Mendelssohn's triumphal wedding march. I walked back down the aisle on the arm of my new husband in his battledress and boots, our hands clinging tightly together. Outside, the photographer was waiting with his tripod set up. He took many photos: Al and me, the wedding party, and then as many guests as could squeeze into the picture--neighbors, friends(including Laurie), and uniforms representing the American Army, R.A.F., American Red Cross, Home Guard, Auxiliary Fire Service and British Overseas Airways Corporation.

Amid a flutter of confetti (no rice--a food item that couldn't be wasted), we walked across the lawn to our reception. In the church hall, the caterers brought out trays of fancy sandwiches and small cakes to the white linen-covered tables. The wedding cake, towering on its stand with each of its three square tiers supported on little columns, waited majestically in front of us to be cut and served.

Cousin Lew tapped for silence on his wineglass, stood up and raised it at arm's length. With the air of a born toastmaster, he declared: "We all know that Rudyard Kipling said: 'East is East, and West is West, and never the twain shall meet,' but Bunty, here, was born in the East in Africa, and Al was born in the West in our erstwhile colonies in America. And if these two hadn't met, we wouldn't all be here today! Let's stand and toast the bride and groom with our wishes for a lifetime of health and happiness together."

More kind words from family and friends brought tears, as I realized that soon I would be leaving these good people forever.

Al: "TUESDAY, SEPTEMBER 25: MARRIED LIFE IS MARVELOUS ALREADY! MR.& MRS. A. S. GREENE AROSE AND WENT DOWN TO BREAKFAST.

TOOK A BUS RIDE THROUGH PRETTY COUNTRYSIDE TO NEAREST TOWN AND BOUGHT ME A WEDDING RING."

Bunty: "NOTHING TO WORRY ABOUT! NOTHING TO HURRY ABOUT! AND IT'S SO NICE TO BE MRS. ALBERT S. GREENE!"
After the wedding I had changed into my new honeymoon suit, but poor Al had nothing to change into; the package containing his dress uniform and shoes to be worn at the wedding was still hung up somewhere in the A.P.O. Back in our room after dinner at the inn, Al had put on a bathrobe and handed over his battledress to a bellboy to be dry-cleaned. Next minute I was in his arms. In his embrace I felt the stress and worry of the past weeks melting away. With my innocence Al was kind and considerate; I enjoyed loving and being loved by this quiet, gentle young man who was now my husband, and with whom I knew I would be happy for the rest of our life together.

Next morning Al's battledress was delivered, dry-cleaned and pressed, in time for a late breakfast. The inn, with its large, swinging sign depicting a white stag with big antlers, fascinated Al, the history buff: "Say, hon', I'll bet nobody in the States could say they spent their honeymoon in a haunted, four-hundred-year-old inn! Listen to this." He read a few excerpts from the guidebook: "The 'White Hart Inn' was built in the fifteen hundreds. Legend has it that Queen Elizabeth the First once stayed here. It was a stagecoach stop--six per day--as they passed through on their way to the south coast.'" Gee, I'm so glad you picked this one, Bunty. The guidebook says that some people claim it even has a ghost!"

I couldn't resist. I said, straight-faced: "That reminds me, sweetheart. Did you hear all that clanking of chains and those eerie footsteps outside in the hallway during the night?"

Al grinned. "No, hon', I slept like a log. Oh, you mean the *ghost*? Well, if it *did* materialize, it had good English manners and skipped visiting us when it saw the 'Do Not Disturb' sign on our door! Who knows, maybe it once had a honeymoon itself! Anyway, my darling, what you probably heard was another guest coming back a bit tipsy from the local pub."

I still think it was the White Hart ghost.

Al surprised and delighted me by saying he wanted to wear a wedding ring. I had deliberately not mentioned it to him because back then in England it wasn't customary for rings to be exchanged at the wedding service; men just didn't usually wear weddings rings. We took the bus through the beautiful Surrey countryside to the nearest town and bought Al a plain, nine-carat gold Utility ring. I put it on his finger and he never took it off.

The days flew by as we exulted in our mutual love. We took walks after breakfast around the village, explored the ancient village church and windmill, fed the ducks in the pond on the village green, and enjoyed delicious meals in the inn's dining room with its old oak-beamed ceilings, gleaming white linen and silverware. All too soon it was time to return to Bishop's Hill.

Al: "SATURDAY, SEPTEMBER 29: TIME SEEMS TO FLY BY! BACK TO UPPER WOODSIDE. PACKED TOP TIER OF WEDDING CAKE IN ITS INSULATED PACKAGING. TOOK UP TO THE A.P.O. IN LONDON AND MAILED TO U.S. FOR FAMILY TO SHARE. TOOK PIECE OF CAKE EACH TO ELSIE CELLI AND BLOSSOM BROWN AT RAINBOW CORNER. SAID FAREWELLS."

Bunty: "WHILE WE WERE IN LONDON WENT AND COLLECTED AL'S RATIONS TO BRING HOME FOR MOM. AL SAID GOODBYE TO ELSIE AND BLOSSOM AT RAINBOW CORNER."

Elsie and Blossom were thrilled with our thoughtfulness in bringing them pieces of wedding cake, in the little white boxes that we had bought to provide a small piece of cake to some of our friends. Tears flowed as the girls hugged Al and said their goodbyes. The emptiness at Rainbow Corner was sad to see, and I was glad when we left and went back to Bishop's Hill. I dreaded saying goodbye to Al. "When will I ever see him again?" I wondered. But once more, I would learn to expect the unexpected from Al Greene.

Al: "MONDAY, OCTOBER 1: AROSE 0600. BREAKFAST. BUNTY WALKED ME TO THE TRAIN STATION. AT 1200 STILL WAITING AROUND IN LONDON AT AIR FORCE DEPOT TO GO TO AIRPORT FOR FLIGHT.

CALLED AND ASKED BUNTY TO COME AND WAIT WITH ME. HAD LUNCH. AT 3:45 WAS TOLD FLIGHT CANCELLED AND TO COLLECT PASS FOR ONE MORE NIGHT. PICKED UP OVERNIGHT PASS. WENT TO AMERICAN EMBASSY AND PICKED UP FORMS TO GET BUNTY ON SAILING LIST FOR THE U.S. BACK TO BISHOP'S HILL. BOB KOPECK HAD ARRIVED! BIT LATE FOR WEDDING!"

Bunty: "ZERO HOUR! AT 7 A.M. WALKED AL TO THE STATION TO GO TO LONDON THEN ON TO U.S. AIR FORCE TRANSPORTATION CENTER. CRIED WHEN WE SAID GOODBYE. HE PHONED LATER ASKING ME TO MEET HIM THERE. TOOK TRAIN TO LONDON. FLIGHT CANCELLED UNTIL TOMORROW. WHOOPEE! STOPPED AT AMERICAN EMBASSY TO GET FORMS I'LL NEED TO GET TO U.S. BACK TO BISHOP'S HILL. SURPRISE! BOB KOPECK IS HERE!"

That morning I said a tearful goodbye to Al at the local train station, then walked back to Bishop's Hill feeling drained and empty. An hour later the phone rang. Al's voice said: "Sweetheart, I've been hanging around here waiting for a flight, but if I don't hear anything by noon they say departure won't be until tomorrow. Hop on a train, come up and wait with me, O.K.?"

My feet flew as I headed back to the train station and joined Al and a milling crowd of G.I.s at the U.S. Air Force Logistics Command depot in London. We treasured a little more time together and waited. At noon, the tinny voice of the P.A. system crackled into life. "All flights to Germany canceled for the day. Overnight passes will be available."

Al put his arms around me so tightly I could barely breathe as we danced around deliriously, while the G.I.s whooped and threw their hats into the air. We ate a soggy sandwich at the depot and waited again. Finally, overnight passes were issued and Al was free to come home with me and return the next day. We went to the P.X. and picked up his rations to bring home, then stopped at the American Embassy. Al registered me on the list for transportation across the Atlantic, and we gathered a small pile of forms to be filled out in order for me to enter the U.S. as a G.I. Bride.

Home again at Bishop's Hill, Al rang the doorbell. We could hardly believe our eyes when it was opened by a grinning Bob Kopeck! A week too late, he had been given his furlough to be best man at our wedding! Bob yelled: "Surprise! Here I am--better late than never!"

Again, I thought of the neighbors. They must have seen me leave with Al early that morning, return without him, then see me leave alone and finally return on his arm later that day. While Al and I were gone, they would have seen Bob, plus duffle bag, being warmly welcomed by my mother, looking a bit stunned. I thought to myself: "Would they have been taking bets on a fistfight on the front walk, when Bob and Al confronted one another for the first time? If they did, they must have been very disappointed to see handshakes and hugs, and the three of us going into the house together, arm in arm. I could just imagine them saying: "But we thought it was only the French who believed in the "ménage a trois'!

Al: "TUESDAY, OCTOBER 2: UP AT 6 A.M. LEFT BUNTY AT 11 A.M. AT DEPOT. NEARLY BROKE OUR HEARTS. A GOOD FLIGHT TO FRANKFURT 4 P.M. GERMAN TIME, THEN TO WIESBADEN. WROTE LETTER TO BUNTY."

Bunty: "AL, BOB AND I SALLIED FORTH TO LONDON TO REPORT TO THE TRANSPORTATION DEPOT. BOB LEFT TO VISIT MR. HIGHGROVE AT HITCHIN. AL'S FLIGHT CALLED AT 11 O'CLOCK. TEARS AND HUGS. FEEL AWFUL."

By now the neighbors must have given up! The three of us left Bishop's Hill early in the morning--arm in arm!

At the Depot, Bob discreetly disappeared to do some errands in London before taking a train to Hitchin to visit his Dad's friend, Mr. Highgrove. My parting from Al was tearful. When he left, I felt weak at the knees and sat down to recover and mop my eyes. Suddenly, Bob reappeared. "Thought I'd check first to see if you were O.K.," he said, setting down his duffle bag and offering me a brotherly shoulder to cry on. He soon had a pretty damp shoulder. He said: "Bunty, after I visit Mr. Highgrove, I've decided to see some of England; this could be the last chance I'll have before I'm shipped back to the States. Hope next time we meet it will be in God's country--Ohio!"

Before we left Bishop's Hill that morning, Bob had hugged Mom and Dad and said: "Well folks, looks like this may be my last trip to England. I want to say thanks, Mom and Pop Amiss, for your kindness and hospitality to me and to Frank. You made such a great difference in our lives when we really needed it."

I didn't see Bob again until a few years later, when Dr. and Mrs. Kopeck invited Al and me to visit the family in Ohio. Seeing Bob and Frank again, and meeting the entire family, was the culmination of our joining hands across the sea in 1944.

At Bishop's Hill our house was quiet again. I wandered from room to empty room. I missed Al terribly, but still had the job I loved, and the next months would fill my life with the new experience of becoming a G.I. bride. And what a story *that* is!

Al: "FRIDAY, OCTOBER 5: 22 YEARS OLD TOMORROW! I'LL PROBABLY BE STATIONED HERE IN WIESBADEN INSTEAD OF STUTTGART. COULD BE WORSE. COMFORTABLE BILLET AND MOST OF THE GUYS FROM LONDON ARE STATIONED HERE. HOW I MISS MY BUNTY! WROTE DAILY LETTER TO HER. BED."

Bunty: "PACKAGE WITH AL'S DRESS UNIFORM AND SHOES THAT HE SHOULD HAVE WORN FOR THE WEDDING ARRIVED, POSTMARKED SEPTEMBER 1! LOOKED OVER PILE OF FORMS WE PICKED UP FROM UP U.S. EMBASSY--GOSH, WHAT A MESS THIS IS GOING TO BE! BACK TO WORK MONDAY."

Birthday cards had become scarce, due to the paper shortage, but I had found one to send to Al. I ached to be near him, and wondered how long it would be before we were together again. Not knowing what to do with Al's package, I decided to wait and see if he wanted me to return it. As I ironed the suntan shirt I muttered: "Well, at least doing this makes me feel closer to him, and I must start getting used to being domesticated. Good practice? Ugh! Me, a housewife?"

I need not have wondered where to begin with the formidable array of forms we picked up from the U.S. Embassy. I would hear from them soon enough, then would begin my near-strangulation in American and British red tape.

It was estimated that about three million U. S. servicemen had spent time in Britain during World War Two. One million had actually been stationed there, and seventy thousand had married British girls. Sadly, according to postwar statistics, it was also estimated that they had left behind roughly twenty thousand illegitimate babies.

As a G. I. Bride, I had become part of a unique phenomenon in the history of World War Two, and also of the United States. Never before in its history had the U.S. Government encountered a female immigrant group of such magnitude--all married to American citizens and all needing to get to the U.S.A. One of the problems in the war-weary minds of the U.S. authorities was what to do with this unprecedented mass of femininity.

There had already been a tactical battle of words between British and American authorities over who would transport the war brides. In effect, the Americans said: "They're *your* women, *you* transport them."

The Brits retorted: "They're married to *your* men, *you* transport them!"

A final agreement had been reached: the Brits would loan some of their troop ships, including the converted *Queen Mary* and the *Queen Elizabeth*, but the Americans would arrange to deliver all seventy thousand brides and their children from all over Britain to various ports, then ferry them across the North Atlantic.

The logistics of such a project boggles the mind, and too many boggled minds can, and did, cause great confusion for the U.S. Army, the American Red Cross, and the war brides themselves.

In the next five months I would be involved with the British Passport Office, the American Embassy, the Personnel Movement Division of the

U. S. Army Transportation Office and the U. S. Army Hospital. Luckily for me, they were all located in London!

Al: "MONDAY, OCTOBER 8: MOVED BILLET FROM TOWN UP THE HILL NEARER TO RADIO STATION. EXCELLENT ACCOMMODATION IN NICE HOTEL. LOOKED UP TENNIS COURT."

Bunty: "BACK TO WORK. CONGRATULATIONS ALL AROUND. SEEMS ODD TO BE SIGNING MY NAME 'IDA GREENE.' ROMANCE MUST BE IN THE AIR: SYD IS ENGAGED AGAIN (IS THIS THE THIRD OR FOURTH TIME?) WENT TO U.S. EMBASSY IN MY LUNCH HOUR TO SEE WHAT IS NEEDED TO SPEED UP GETTING ME TO THE U.S. SEEMS NOTHING CAN BE DONE UNTIL AFFIDAVITS ARE COMPLETED FOR VISA. BOO, HISS!"

I need not have worried about Al's discomfort living an army life; once again he seemed to have landed in the lap of luxury!

Syd was singing "Here Comes the Bride" as I walked into the office. He said: "And 'ere I am, still tryin' to get a gal to the bloomin' altar!"

Scooping me up, he swung me around before setting me down again on my feet. Buzz dashed off to make me a cup of tea, with Bill's silver American Air Force wings shining on the breast pocket of his B.O.A.C. uniform jacket. It was good to leave the quiet house behind in Bishop's Hill and be back among cheerful people in the office. Brad actually smiled and wished me the best, and Freddy looked delighted from behind the pile of unanswered correspondence that was undoubtedly waiting for my return.

The days flew by. Conspicuously absent were phone calls and visits from the U.S. Navy cargo depot characters who had been stationed in London. During the war, their consignments of priority air freight--sometimes by the ton--had consisted of medical and technology supplies essential to the war effort. The hilarious crew and their chatty officer had all been sent home when the depot was disbanded. I smiled as I remembered every one of them calling his home state

"God's Country". I said to myself: "I can just see him now: Ex-U. S. Navy Lieutenant James Truman Oates III, lying on his back with a straw in his mouth in an Iowa cornfield, gazing lazily at the sky--God's Country, of course! I wonder if New Jersey will be God's Country, too?"

At today's lunch hour visit to the American Embassy, I seethed with indignation at the offhanded manner of the clerk in the Transportation Office. "Look, ma'am, you'll just have to wait until you hear from us with your instructions." He gave me a withering look, as if to say: "If I see one more impatient female today I'll throw up!"

I was beginning to suspect that this was only the tip of the iceberg of red tape surrounding my trip to my new home in the U.S.A. That suspicion would very soon prove to be true.

Battle of the Red Tape

Al: "TUESDAY, OCTOBER 9: ALL DAYS PRETTY MUCH SAME ROUTINE. DUTY, CHOW, STUDY, TENNIS, ANSWER MAIL FROM STATES AND BISHOP'S HILL. BUNTY'S LETTERS WONDERFUL."

Bunty: "I CAN HARDLY BELIEVE THE PACKET OF STUFF I RECEIVED TODAY FROM THE AMERICAN EMBASSY! SUCH AN AVALANCHE OF FORMS TO FILL OUT AND SEND BACK AND FORTH BETWEEN AL AND ME. IT'S A GOOD THING WE NUMBER OUR LETTERS--AT LEAST WE'LL KNOW IF A FORM IS MISSING! SENT HIM 'AFFIDAVIT OF SUPPORT' FORMS."

The first onslaught from the American Embassy came in a large official envelope containing a two-sided, legal-sized document called Form 3, plus a wad of other blank forms to be completed . (Years later, I found copies of these documents stored in the battered box with my diaries, still intact, but now yellowed with age.) I stared at the formal wording in front of me: **"Madam,**

Reference is made to your preliminary application for an immigration visa to enter the United States for permanent or indefinite residence. If you desire to travel to the United States as soon as possible, you should now be guided by the visa procedure described below. It is emphasized that the following steps should be taken in the order outlined; steps taken out of turn may confuse and delay the processing of your case.

STEP #1: AFFIDAVITS OF SUPPORT. See attached blank forms, to be filled out by husband and relative(s) in the U.S., assuring their financial support. When received by the U.S. Embassy, a Form 4 will be sent to you stating you are eligible to receive a visa.

STEP #2: TRANSPORTATION. You may apply by mail or in person to the Adjutant General at the American Embassy, London.

STEP #3: BRITISH PASSPORT AND EXIT PERMIT. Next you should apply for these at the British Passport Office in London.

STEP #4: FORMAL VISA APPLICATION, MEDICAL EXAMINATION AND ISSUANCE OF VISA. After completion of steps #1 through #4, the American Embassy will send you a notice to appear at the Embassy for formal visa application and medical examination."

On the following page, the instructions on how to get from #1 to #4 contained sub-divisions whose completion depended on following each step and sub-step consecutively. I was terrified. Then I thought: "Well, Bunty, you can't fight the U.S. judicial system, so you'd better just get started." I worried to Mom: "It could take the rest of my life to get from #1 to #4!" Then the humor of it all made me say: "It reminds of when I read in my childhood about the twelve tasks of Hercules in my encyclopedia! And how about all those sub-divisions?" Somewhat irreverently I broke into song: "Your toe bone connected to your ankle bone, your ankle bone connected to your leg bone, your leg bone connected to your knee bone, now hear the word of the Lord."

I looked again over the list of instructions. "You know, Mom, this time it all looks straightforward enough. Al can do Step #1. I'll do Step #2 as soon as I receive Form 4, after Al has completed Step #1 and sent it back to me to give to the Embassy. Then once I get Form 4, it should be a piece of cake!"

Mom gave me her standard puzzled look. "I'm not sure it's all that simple, Bunty," she muttered, "to me, it's as clear as mud!"

What we both didn't know was that the mud would get much thicker before it disappeared. I sifted through the wad of forms and sent everything to Al that he would need for Step #1.

Bunty: "THURSDAY, OCTOBER 11: DAY OFF (I'LL BE WORKING ON SATURDAY), PAT PRINGLE CAME DOWN FOR THE DAY. SHE'S ENGAGED TO A YUGOSLAV! WENT OUT TO LUNCH, SHOPPING, THEN TO THE MOVIES. WEDDING PHOTOS ARRIVED. ALL GOOD. BEGAN MAILING TH EM OUT."

Pat was temporarily unemployed. When I had first met her she was working for the Americans on the staff of the U.S. Army newspaper *Stars and Stripes*, at the Ministry of Information building in London. The office had closed down when the U.S. forces in the E.T.O began to go home after V-J Day. Today, she looked as radiant as she did in her pink dress when she was maid of honor at the wedding. I hugged her and said: "Congrats, Pat--this engagement of yours is great news, and such a surprise!"

I was puzzled because Pat had never mentioned a Yugoslav boyfriend, but she seemed to be on Cloud Nine. "Oh, Bunty, I'm so happy," she gushed, "his name is Stefan--isn't that a lovely name?"

I waited politely to hear all about Stefan, including his last name, but Pat changed the subject. I was consumed with curiosity; maybe his last name was unpronounceable! In any event, Pat didn't say any more. I didn't ask questions. We spent a happy day together before we went home our separate ways. I never did find out if Pat married her Stefan; we lost touch soon after I sailed for America.

That evening I began sorting, packaging and addressing the wedding photos. I knew family and friends would be expecting them. Now Al's folks would be able to put faces to the names of their newest member's family.

Al: "TUESDAY, OCTOBER 16: WENT WITH HOWIE TO FRANKFURT. POSTWAR JOBS IN GERMANY BEING OFFERED. HE'S GOING TO STAY ON--I'M GOING HOME!"

Bunty: "LETTER FROM AL ENCLOSING COMPLETED AFFIDAVIT FORMS. RUSHED THEM TO U.S. EMBASSY AND WAS TOLD TO SEND THEM BACK TO HIM WITH AN ADDITIONAL FORM 3P WHICH HE HAS TO COMPLETE BEFORE PROCESSING. HE'LL HAVE A FIT! WHAT ARE THEY UP TO? WROTE TO JOAN HOFFMAN, PER AL'S MOM'S REQUEST."
Tears plopped onto the writing pad as I poured out my frustration to Al. Without the affidavits and this mysterious new Form 3P, "Petition for Issuance of Immigration Visa," in which Al would ask for me to be granted a visa, the Embassy wouldn't issue magical Form 4, which would enable me to get a British passport to travel to the U.S.! Back went everything to Germany again. I could just imagine Al's reaction!

Mom watched all this with resignation. Teary-eyed, I said: "Gosh, Mom, Al must love me a lot to go through all of this! They really must be trying hard to discourage G.I.s from marrying foreign girls. But at this end, I'll show 'em my British bulldog spirit and hang on!"

By this time Mom had abdicated from the battle. She just said rather vaguely: "That's my girl!" and went on with her knitting.

Bud Hoffman, another G.I. from Little Cedar River, had married an English girl from Bristol. His mother and Al's were friends at the Little Cedar River Baptist Church. Al's Mom had sent me Joan's address, and asked me if I would write to her, which I did. I wondered if there would ever be a reply!

Al: "MONDAY, OCTOBER 22: RECEIVED 'PETITION FOR VISA 3P FORM' FROM BUNTY. NEED MY BIRTH CERTIFICATE FROM MY MOM. HOPE SHE KNOWS WHERE IT IS! RECEIVED WEDDING PHOTOS OF BUNTY AND MYSELF. TRULY WONDERFUL. MORNING DUTY. NOT MUCH RADIO TRAFFIC. PLAYED TENNIS. CHOW. BED."

Bunty: "HAD A LETTER FROM JOAN HOFFMAN. SHE SOUNDS VERY NICE INDEED."
A new thread was about to be woven into the fabric of my life. Joan's letter sounded friendly. There would be more in our young lives together

in New Jersey, and another friendship that would continue longer than either of us could imagine.

Al: "THURSDAY, OCTOBER 25: MADE INQUIRIES ABOUT GETTING A FURLOUGH TO ENGLAND. NO SOAP. DISCOVERED I AM TO SHIP OUT NOVEMBER 4 WITH MY UNIT FOR REDEPLOYMENT HOME TO THE U.S.! GOTTA DO SOMETHING ABOUT THIS--GOTTA SEE BUNTY BEFORE I GO HOME!"

Bunty: "CHANNEL GALES ARE HOLDING UP MAIL. AWFUL SITUATION! TOOK THE AFTERNOON OFF. LAURIE PICKED ME UP AT THE OFFICE. HAD LUNCH. WENT TO AMERICAN EMBASSY TO SEE HOW TO GET MY PASSPORT. BROUGHT LAURIE BACK TO BISHOP'S HILL FOR TEA." Al's anxiety showed through in his diary entry; he had been trying to get to England before being shipped to the U.S. and had applied for a furlough, which hadn't materialized. My spirits were at rock bottom.

By now, Laurie and I had become good friends at the G.I. Wives Club at Rainbow Corner. Today, she came up to London by train from her home in Surrey, a few miles outside of London. Syd and Brad looked as impressed when she appeared at the office as they had when my erstwhile date Bruce had appeared for the first time in his Royal Navy officer's braid. I fancied I could almost hear a faint wolf whistle and a loud "Wow" from Syd.

After lunch, Laurie and I stopped briefly at the American Embassy to see what I would need to get a British Passport. The surly clerk looked up at me with a glance that said: "Oh no, not this one again!" Aloud, he said: "Before you can apply for that, ma'am, you will need a certified original birth certificate, Form 4P, and a copy of your Travel Orders."

I thought: "What's Form 4P? I certainly don't have that, but at least I can start by finding my birth certificate!"

Laurie and I hopped a train for Upper Woodside so she could really meet Mom, having had only a brief introduction at the wedding. They instantly became friends. Over many cups of tea, Laurie vented her frustration: "It's quite nerve-wracking, you know. I'm *so* anxious to hear from the U.S. Army Transportation Office; I've been married almost a year, and it seems like ages ago that I completed all the forms. But so far there's been no news of any G.I. Bride sailings, even in the future!"

After Laurie left to catch the train home, I asked: "Mom, where's my birth certificate? The American Embassy needs it."

"That's easy, Bunty, I'll go up and get it right away." Mom raced off upstairs to drag out from under her bed the heavy steel strongbox, which had accompanied us every time we went to the air-raid shelter during the war. Slightly out of breath, she reappeared and said: "Here it is, but I'd forgotten that it isn't written in English!"

"Oh dear," I gasped, "I don't know that it will be acceptable, but I'll take it and find out." I looked helplessly at the certificate, which was written in the Buganda Kingdom dialect spoken in the province of Uganda where I was born! I shuddered, but nevertheless not too hopefully took it to the U.S. Embassy the following day in my lunch hour.

The Embassy clerk looked at the certificate as if it would bite him. "Oh, I'm sorry, ma'am," he said, between gritted teeth. "It must be written in English." He gave me a strange look, but made no further comment. I imagined him thinking: "Just as I thought, she's nutty as a fruitcake--now she comes here with what she says is her birth certificate, but it's written in some weird African dialect!" I could almost see him considering a rapid plan of escape if ever I popped up again in front of his desk. Embarrassed, I made a hasty retreat.

I thought: "Wham! Another roadblock!" That evening I wrote to the government office in Entebbe, Uganda, where the certificate had been issued, asking for a certified original of it in English. Once more, I crossed my fingers and hoped for the best.

Al: "WEDNESDAY, OCTOBER 31: RECEIVED ALL BUNTY'S BACK MAIL, BETTER LATE THAN NEVER! TALKED TO MY LOVE ON PRINTER, WONDERFUL BUT TOO SHORT. GETTING READY TO SHIP OUT OF STUTTGART WITH UNIT NOVEMBER 4. TURNED IN EXCESS EQUIPMENT. BEGAN PACKING CLOTHES."

Bunty: "HAD PHONE CALL TO COME TO RADIO ROOM IN LONDON TO TALK ON TELETYPE WITH AL. LOVELY! HE'S TRYING TO GET A FURLOUGH TO ENGLAND. FINGERS CROSSED."

Al had been waiting over an hour to use the teletype machine. His typed words clattered over the teleprinter from Germany: "Hi, darling, I'm trying to get a delay in route from Germany to the U.S. so I can come on furlough to England. Then we can have some time together before I'm shipped home. As it now stands, I'm due to leave Stuttgart on November 4."

I skipped into the house in Bishop's Hill full of excitement. "Guess what, Mom? Al thinks he might be able to get what the Army calls a 'delay in route' and come to England before he goes home!"

Not wanting to dampen my spirits, Mom was still the protective mother. "Now don't get your hopes up too high, dear" she warned, "you know how unpredictable the Army is!"

Disgruntled, I muttered: "Thanks a lot, Mom!"

Al: "SUNDAY, NOVEMBER 4: UP AT 3:45 A.M. CHOW. LOADED INTO TRUCKS. LEFT 0645. ARRIVED FRANKFURT. TRAIN TO MARBURG WITH UNIT, TO AWAIT SHIPMENT HOME. ARRIVED 1330 HRS. ASSIGNED BILLET. NICE ROOM. CHOW. BED 2100. PRETTY COLD."

Bunty: "FINISHED EMBROIDERING TABLECLOTH FOR MOM GREENE FOR XMAS. WONDER WHERE MY HUSBAND IS?"

If only I had known!

Al: "MONDAY, NOVEMBER 5: *AT MARBURG AWAITING EVENTS.* FILLED OUT AND MAILED ANOTHER FORM AND SENT IT WITH MY TRAVEL ORDERS TO BUNTY. IF I SEE ONE MORE FORM I'LL CROAK! THINK I'VE FOUND A WAY TO GET THAT DELAY IN ROUTE! WENT TO ORDERLY ROOM AND APPLIED FOR TRANSFER TO 98TH REPLACEMENT DEPOT IN ENGLAND. TOLD TO COME BACK IN 1-1/2 HRS. APPLICATION READY. SIGNED. WILL TAKE 3 DAYS TO A WEEK TO PROCESS, THEN I'LL SHIP OUT TO ENGLAND FOR A DELAY IN ROUTE. JEEPERS! HOPE IT WORKS! PACKED DUFFLE BAG. MIDNIGHT. BED."

Bunty: "RECEIVED STEP #1 FORMS FROM AL AND TOOK THEM AND MY TRANSLATED BIRTH CERTIFICATE TO AMERICAN EMBASSY. CLERK HAD TOLD ME **A** CERTIFIED ORIGINAL. NOW THEY WANT A *SECOND* CERTIFIED ORIGINAL--JUST ONE WON'T DO. RATS! BLAST THIS RED TAPE--I'M STRANGLING IN IT ALREADY! IN ENGLAND, TODAY IS GUY FAWKES DAY. PEOPLE SETTING OFF FIREWORKS IN BISHOP'S HILL FOR FIRST TIME SINCE 1938. WONDER WHERE AL IS?"

I had no idea where Al could be. I told myself: "Oh, well, Bunty, you might as well resign yourself to the idea of not seeing him until you get to America, whenever that might be. Could be a year from now, the way things are going!"

Today, I once again went to the American Embassy, hoping I had it right this time, clutching the completed wad of forms mailed to me by Al and also my translated birth certificate. The clerk stiffened visibly when he caught sight of me. He looked over my latest batch of documents from Al, and said grudgingly: "I guess these are all O.K. now, ma'am. I'll process them and mail them to Philadelphia. You should receive your Form 4P in a week or two."

I exulted under my breath: "Whew! One half of the Holy Grail is almost in sight! When I have Form 4P, I can apply for an American visa. Then for the other half of the Grail: a British Passport. After that, all I'll need is a ship!"

When I triumphantly produced my newly-arrived English language birth certificate, extracted so painfully from the Dark Continent, the clerk said: "Sorry, ma'am, we need TWO originals of your birth certificate, both certified."

I was stunned. I squeaked: "Couldn't you just make a copy?" By now I was convinced that the clerk, in some sadistic way, was enjoying the whole thing. He drew himself up to his full height and retorted: "No, ma'am. TWO certified originals are what we require."

Furiously, I thought: "Why hadn't he told me that before I sent to Uganda for this one? He had distinctly said 'A certified original'--that's single! And why couldn't he have made a copy?" By this time I knew better than to challenge the U.S. Embassy's procedures, but my fingers itched to swat him with my umbrella, which I kept in my tote bag in case of rain or emergencies. I grated: "Oh, O.K., I'll be back in another week or so."

The first thing I did when I got home was to send another letter to Uganda.

Outdoors that evening, Bishop's Hill was alive with activity. For the first time since before the war, the neighborhood was celebrating one of Britain's favorite holidays--"Guy Fawkes' Day," or "Bonfire Night,"-- to commemorate November 5, 1605, when Guy Fawkes was a participant in the famous Gunpowder Plot aimed to blow up the Houses of Parliament and assassinate King James I of England, while there, in the process. The plotters had designated Fawkes to light the fuse under thirty-six barrels of gunpowder they had smuggled into the basement, then the whole gang would escape across the Channel to Europe in the resulting chaos. Unfortunately for Fawkes, the plot was exposed before he lighted the fuse; he was arrested and executed for high treason.

I remember that before the war, little boys would come to our door pushing a dilapidated baby carriage in which was a dummy stuffed with newspaper and wearing their father's old clothes, to represent Guy Fawkes. They would chorus: "Penny for the Guy, penny for the Guy," and Dad would manage to find not a penny but a silver sixpence to give to each one. In those days before we had air pollution regulations, the "guy" would end up on one of the neighborhood backyard bonfires, as "Guy Fawkes," ceremoniously burned in effigy for his thwarted bad intentions. Parents would join their children dancing around the bonfire, waving "sparklers"--harmless hand-held fireworks--until they fizzled out of sparkle.

For other families, on this first postwar year, big firework displays at public parks kept the children spellbound; those less than six years old had never seen a brighter light outdoors than one on a dimmed wartime flashlight.

Meantime, all I knew about Al was that he was due to be shipped out from Stuttgart with his unit on November 4 to wait for return to the U.S. I could never have dreamed that he had figured out a way to delay the Army's plans, but, as I was learning fast, Mr. Greene was indeed full of surprises!

Al: "MONDAY, NOVEMBER 12: MY TRANSFER TO REDEPLOYMENT CENTER IN ENGLAND AND DELAY IN ROUTE HAS BEEN O.K.'D! I'VE BEEN TAKEN OFF SHIPPING ORDERS TO U.S.A. ALL THE GUYS IN MY UNIT LEFT TODAY. HATED TO SEE THEM GO, FELT TERRIBLY LONELY. I'M THE ONLY ONE LEFT IN THE BILLET! THOUGHT OVER OLD TIMES I'D SPENT WITH THEM. BED."

Bunty: "FREEZING, DAMP DAY. I'VE BROKEN OUT IN HEAT BUMPS AND A COLD IS COMING ON. WROTE TO AUNTIE BELLE TO SAY THAT AL AND I MIGHT COME TO SUNDERLAND, IF HE GETS A DELAY IN ROUTE, BUT DOESN'T LOOK LIKELY."

I felt miserable, but got through the morning at my desk before giving up and going home to bed. Periodically throughout my childhood I had a bout of what Mom called "heat bumps", not contagious, and nowadays known as an allergy rash or hives. Generations of Ditchfields had dubbed their cause "overheated blood," and cured them by concocting a herbal brew called senna tea. The recipe had been handed down like a family heirloom to the present generation. Mom took one look at my itchy blotches and said: "Oh yes, Bunty, you've got overheated blood. I'll make some senna tea, and in no time you'll be as right as rain."

Languishing in bed, my chest rubbed with Vapor Rub to stave off my now-blossoming cold, I pictured the routine. Mom would reach into the kitchen cabinet and pull out a packet of dried senna pods, of which she always had a supply on hand from the chemist's shop ("drugstore" in American English.) In a bowl, boiling water would be poured over the pods, which were then left to cool and "steep" overnight. The murky, brownish liquid which seeped through the pods into the water would be strained into a large pitcher and stored on a cool, tiled shelf in the larder. Those were the days before electric refrigerators had come to British housewives. In the temperate summers, a well-ventilated larder kept food cool enough not to spoil for several days. For the rest of the year the kitchen was frigid; the nearest fireplace was in the dining room (central heating had not yet come to the average middle-class home.)

Senna tea really didn't taste bad at all, and to banish my heat bumps I didn't mind having to drink a small glass of it every day until the supply was all gone. Usually, by that time, so were the heat bumps. I often wondered whether they would have gone of their own accord anyway, but in Mom's mind there was no doubt that senna tea always worked the miracle. To reduce the misery of the itching, Mom plastered bright pink calamine lotion on the angry welts on my skin. Typically, the blotches would become more numerous all over my body, gradually fading away after days of itchy torment.

Al: "TUESDAY, NOVEMBER 13:   FIRST TIME I'VE OVERSLEPT AND MISSED BREAKFAST! WAS AWAKENED BY AN ORDERLY WHO SAID I HAD TO BE READY TO LEAVE IN TEN MINUTES! CHEE, WHAT A MAD RUSH! PULLED OUT OF MARBURG. ARRIVED PARIS AFTER TRAVELING ALL NIGHT IN TRAIN. MOST UNCOMFORTABLE."

Bunty: (Editorial Comment: I was most uncomfortable, too; by this time I was covered with those darn' heat bumps!)

Al: "SATURDAY, NOVEMBER 17: WE'RE AT LE HAVRE. TOTED DUFFLE BAG AND BLANKET TO BOAT, ABOUT 300 YDS. NEARLY KILLED ME-- THEY WEIGH A TON! COMFORTABLE CROSSING ON CHANNEL FERRY. LEFT 1125 HRS. ARRIVED LONDON 0155. TOO LATE TO CALL BUNTY. STAYED AT RED CROSS CENTER FOR NIGHT. GOT TO SLEEP AT 0300."

Bunty: "FEEL O.K. AGAIN. COLD GONE, BUT HEAT BUMPS HAVEN'T QUITE FADED YET. DRAGGED MYSELF TO AMERICAN EMBASSY WITH COPY OF AL'S TRAVEL ORDERS AND SECOND ORIGINAL BIRTH CERTIFICATE JUST RECEIVED FROM UGANDA. MET LAURIE AT EMBASSY AND BROUGHT HER HOME TO TEA. SHE CAME WITH ME TO OUR DOCTOR TO CHECK ON MY HEAT BUMPS."

Al's Travel Orders for his trip home were essential for me to apply for my own Travel Orders for the crossing to the U.S., so I lost no time in getting them safely into my file at the American Embassy. The astonished clerk cringed visibly when he saw me and my calamine-dotted face, but made no comment. I could imagine him thinking: "Here's that same gal again! First she brings me a birth certificate written in some weird African language, then she brings me only one translated original instead of two, and now she's stumbled with her makeup! Just as I thought--nutty as a fruitcake!"

Back at Bishop's Hill, several cups of tea later, Laurie and I walked to the family doctor's office. Thanks to liberal applications of Vapor Rub for my cold , I was fine except for the lingering heat bumps. The doctor looked at them quickly and said: "Bunty, you've done all you can. Just keep up with the calamine lotion; they'll go away soon."

I detected a smile from Mom when we told her. She said complacently: "See, Bunty, the Ditchfield's senna tea is foolproof--it just takes time!"

Neither of us suspected what tomorrow would bring.

Second Honeymoon

Al: "SUNDAY, NOVEMBER 18: SHORT NIGHT AT RED CROSS CENTER IN LONDON! AROSE 0630. BREAKFAST. STORED DUFFLE BAG AT CENTER. TOOK TRAIN FROM VICTORIA STATION TO UPPER WOODSIDE. MY DARLIN' STILL IN BED, LOVELY AS COULD BE. TOOK A BATH, SHORT NAP. DAY FLEW BY. HAPPINESS! EARLY TO BED."

Bunty: "I WAS AWAKENED THIS MORNING AT 8:30 BY SOMEONE BOUNCING ON MY BED--AL! HE HAS AN ELEVEN-DAY FURLOUGH! OH, HE LOOKS SIMPLY WONDERFUL! SPENT THE DAY IN SHEER DELIRIOUS ECSTASY! WHOOPEE!"

I must have suddenly realized how I looked: no makeup, fading heat bumps covered with blotches of bright pink calamine lotion, hair sticking up in all directions. A lingering aroma of Vapor Rub surrounded the bed, where I sat in my disheveled state, shedding tears of joy all over my old

Utility pajamas. I probably thought: "He's never going to look at me again without remembering how awful I look now!"

I need not have worried. Seen through the eyes of love, Al's diary had described me as "lovely as could be!"

Al: "MONDAY, NOVEMBER 19: MOM AMISS PRESSED MY CLOTHES; SHE'S TOPS. BUNTY FEELING BETTER. HEAT BUMPS GONE! SENT WIRE TO AUNTIE BELLE. WE'LL TRAVEL TOMORROW TO SUNDERLAND."

Bunty: "SLEPT LATE IN MY HUSBAND'S ARMS. DIDN'T REALIZE HOW INEXPERIENCED I AM, BUT HE'S SO GENTLE. I LOVE HIM SO MUCH. STOPPED IN AT MY OFFICE. WILL TAKE VACATION TIME UNTIL NOVEMBER 29."

Al and I took the train to London. My boss, Freddy, was surprised and delighted to see Al, who had become a great hit at the office before he left for Germany. He chuckled: "Take as much time as you'll need, Bunty. Now be off, the two of you, and enjoy yourselves."

Al's furlough was celebrated with a Chinese lunch where Bob had taken me in Soho, followed by the incomparable movie "Fantasia," Walt Disney's masterpiece of art and music.

Al: "TUESDAY, NOVEMBER 20: AROSE 6:30. TOOK BUS TO KING'S CROSS STATION IN LONDON. LEFT 9:25 A.M. FOR SUNDERLAND. ARRIVED 4:30 P.M. GREAT SCENERY FROM TRAIN. FIRST TIME I'VE SEEN THE NORTH SEA. SUPPER WITH FOLKS. UNPACKED. VISITED DOROTHY AND LEW DENT. BED."

Bunty: "GOOD SEATS ON ALL TRAINS. HAD TO CHANGE THREE TIMES! ARRIVED LATE AFTERNOON. PHONED DITCHFIELDS. WILL SEE THEM TOMORROW. AFTER SUPPER WE VISITED DOROTHY AND LEW."

Uncle Arthur was waiting for us on the station platform at Sunderland, his short, solid body poised for action as the train drew to a halt. He rushed toward us with hands outstretched, his round face lit up with a smile and eyes dancing with excitement behind their National Health

Service spectacles. His north country accent was quite thick: "Hello, Boonty, and hello, Al, me lad. By gum, it's a rare treat to meet you, lad; I've heard champion things about you from Belle and y're new in-laws in Loondon." He led the way to where his ancient Vauxhall car was parked. "Hop in, you two, and let's awaah. We'll be hoam quick as a flash."

He bundled us and our suitcase into the elderly car, which he had pampered throughout the war on a small spasmodic government petrol ration--a bonus for operating a store that sold food, an essential contribution to the war effort.

The comfortable house next to the store was within easy walking distance of the North Sea shoreline's sandy, rock-strewn beaches. At the door, Auntie Belle greeted us: "Oh, it's that grand seeing you both again. And eeh, what a loovly wedding that was!"

Unruffled and efficient as ever, she was ready for us with "high tea", named for the high farmhouse tables on which a hearty early supper was served to the farmhands in Britain after their long day's labor in the fields. The meat pie, salad and dark brown buttered bread slices made a satisfying meal for Al and me, hungry after our long day's travel.

I couldn't wait to show Al the adjoining "corner shop" full of everything imaginable, with its immaculate stockroom smelling of newly-sliced ham and freshly ground coffee, just as I remembered.

My two young cousins, Audrey and Dorothy, were fascinated by the tall, handsome stranger from America who was now part of the family. Spellbound, they listened to every word he uttered in his American drawl. Audrey tossed her Shirley Temple curls and plopped down on the couch next to him. "Tell us about what it's like in America, Al," she ventured, shyly.

Little Dorothy echoed: "Yes, please, Al," and squeezed in between them. Her hand crept into his.

Al began: "Well, I live in a small town called Little Cedar River, and it's in a bigger place called New Jersey. It's not far from our seashore, but we don't have high cliffs or rocky beaches like you do; just sloping white sandy beaches and sand dunes covered with marsh grass."

"Can we come and see you there?" asked Audrey, resting her head on his chest. Al was having trouble with all this adulation.

Auntie Belle laughed: "Look out, Al, I think you've got yoorself a fan cloob!"

The fan club almost burst with joy when Al told them: "You know, someday when you're a lot older, you girls will come across the ocean and visit us."

This was greeted with squeals of delight. Dorothy was much too young to know why she was squealing, but if Audrey could do it, so could she. Although all of us would see many years and many life changes before it would happen, eventually both girls would see Al's prediction become a reality.

We had promised to call on our best man, cousin Lew, and his lovely Dorothy, as soon as we arrived. There was just enough time for us to walk over to their home for a nightcap before collapsing into bed after our long day.

Al: "WEDNESDAY, NOVEMBER 21: VISITED RUGGED NORTHEAST COAST OF ENGLAND. SO DIFFERENT FROM BEACHES IN SOUTH. VISITED BUNTY'S MOM'S FAMILY. GREAT WELCOME. I'LL NEVER BE ABLE TO SORT THEM ALL OUT!"

Bunty: "AUNTIE BELLE GAVE US A SURPRISE WEDDING PRESENT! WENT TO MARSDEN WITH UNCLE ARTHUR THIS MORNING. THIS AFTERNOON WENT TO VISIT DITCHFIELDS FOR TEA. GREAT NEWS, McKENZIE BOYS REPATRIATED. FAMILY EXCITED TO MEET AL. POOR DARLING, SO MANY NEW NAMES AND FACES TO REMEMBER. EVERYONE O.K. EXCEPT GRANDPA. HE'S VERY ILL."

At breakfast this morning Auntie Belle said: "Boonty, I have a surprise for you." She disappeared upstairs, returning with a large white box, which she gave to me. Opening it, I was flabbergasted to find the most beautiful one of the linen tablecloths she had sent to me to embroider for her, when I had complained of boredom during our wartime two-year exile in North Wales, waiting for our bomb-shattered house in London to be repaired. I had put all the embroidery skills I knew into that tablecloth, and I remember feeling a pang of regret when I sent it back to her! It was still new. Auntie Belle continued: "Remember how beootifully our housekeeper, Mrs. Howland, used to crochet? Well, she made this loovely wide border for the tablecloth and sewed it on. Doesn't it look loovely? I thought you might like it as a wedding present."

I hugged my favorite aunt, teary-eyed and unable to speak. (That tablecloth saw great service over the following years, whenever I treated my American friends to an English tea.)

We climbed into the old Vauxhall, and Uncle Arthur drove us a few miles up the coast, where the North Sea waves crash onto the beaches as cold winds blow them from Denmark to break against the shores of Britain. Uncle Arthur parked the car on the cliff-top road overlooking the beach far below. The limestone sea-cliffs were so high that there was an elevator to take us down to the sandy beach. Worn by the centuries, the cliffs were honeycombed with caves, while jagged rock pillars stood along the beaches, reminders of how much further the cliffs had reached out into the sea before being eroded away.

That afternoon, we took the bus across town for tea at the Ditchfields. The atmosphere was jubilant, not just to see Al and me, but because news had come that Uncle Hal McKenzie's two sons were alive and well in Singapore, after their internment in a Japanese prison camp during the war years. We were sad that Mom's cousin Ernie had been drowned at sea when his ship was sunk during the Battle of the Atlantic, but thankful that he was the only family member to have been lost in World War Two.

Our welcome from Gram Ditchfield and the assembled aunts, uncles and cousins was as warm as ever. I couldn't wait for Al to try their hot buttered toasted teacakes! Al was duly impressed. For once, however, my aunts didn't say "Oh, Bunty, how you've grown," as they had done every year when I was growing up! Al's unassuming, quiet manner charmed them all. I thought: "Well, now they know there's a different kind of American from those rowdy ones they saw early in the war, who turned the town upside down brawling in the pubs and molesting the local girls."

Indeed, in Al they had met a soft-spoken young man with whom I was very much in love, and into whose care they could let me go with confidence.

Al: "THURSDAY, NOVEMBER 22: VISITED GEORGE WASHINGTON'S ANCESTRAL HOME. FASCINATING AND INFORMATIVE. ON TO DURHAM. MASSIVE, BEAUTIFUL CATHEDRAL. GORGEOUS STAINED GLASS. VERY IMPRESSIVE DAY."

Bunty: "AL AND I TOOK A BUS TRIP TO WASHINGTON VILLAGE AND DURHAM FOR THE DAY. DRIZZLY AND CHILLY, BUT SIGHTS NOT TO BE MISSED."

Al and I took off for some sightseeing on our own. Bus service was easily available to take us on our day's pilgrimage.

Five miles away from Sunderland is the village of Washington, home to the manor house where George Washington's forbears lived as land-owning farmers. Restored and furnished as it was in the seventeenth century, the house looked as if the family had just gone out and would soon be back. A reproduction of the famous painting of George Washington crossing the Delaware now hung near a bedroom which had been in use long before he was born.

The ancient city of Durham gave its name to the entire county surrounding it. We followed one of the historic narrow streets up the hill to its crowning glory, Durham Cathedral. With magnificent twin towers, the huge church sits atop a steep bank of the River Wear, here a picturesque stream, which becomes a busy industrial river before emptying into the North Sea at Sunderland. Al recited from his guidebook: "The foundations of the cathedral date back to the year 1093. Described as one of the great architectural treasures of Europe, it is a World Heritage site, unique for the preservation of its early Norman craftsmanship and original Romanesque design."

I was thrilled to share this favorite place of mine with Al. We tagged along with a group of people behind a guide. They stopped when he pointed up at the ceiling: "If you look up, ladies and gentlemen, you will see on the ceiling replicas of the historic coats of arms of leading families in Durham County. The one with three red stars and two horizontal red stripes on a white background belongs to the Washington family. It's said that their descendant, George Washington, proposed it as the subject for the flag of the United States."

Al exclaimed: "Well, I'll be darned! Wait 'til I tell the folks back home!" He was as surprised as the American tourists gazing upwards who had never expected to see the origins of their flag on the ceiling of an old cathedral in England. We found a vacant pew and sat quietly for awhile, soaking up the history that breathed all around us. Diagonal shafts of light streamed through the side windows of the cathedral and the great rose window. Their rays shed little pools of color from the exquisite ancient stained glass onto the rows of huge, carved stone pillars on either side of the nave which held up the soaring roof.

Leaving through the one-foot-thick, weathered oak door, I gripped the heavy iron ring on the replica of the big twelfth-century Sanctuary Knocker with its grotesque lion's head, as I had done every time I had visited the cathedral. Al said: "What are you doing now, hon'? Feel O.K.--a little dizzy, maybe?"

"Oh. no, love, nothing like that," I said patiently, and put on my best tourist guide voice: "In ancient times, before law and order, a wrongdoer could save himself from the screaming mob at his heels by reaching up and holding tight to this same iron ring, to claim sanctuary from the monks inside."

"Well, sweets, I can't imagine what you could have done, and I don't want to know, but how about letting go of that thing and let's go back to the bus."

With my historic bubble punctured, I thought: "He's had enough, and it *has* been a lot crammed into one day." I meekly followed him as we went back down the hill.

Al: "SATURDAY, NOVEMBER 24:   AFTER BREAKFAST WENT TO WALK THE BEACH WITH BUNTY. LOW TIDE. LIVE SEA ANEMONES, TINY CRABS AND FISH LEFT BEHIND BY THE TIDE IN ROCK POOLS. LOVELY THERE. HAD ICE CREAM CONES. GOODBYE TO DITCHFIELDS. LUNCH WITH AUNT HYLDA AND UNCLE LEW. TOUR OF DOCKYARD. WONDERFUL."

Bunty: "STOPPED IN AT DITCHFIELDS. SAID GOODBYE TO GRANDPA. PROBABLY FOR THE LAST TIME. AUNTIE HYLDA MADE LOVELY LUNCH. UNCLE LEW TOOK US AROUND DOXFORDS SHIPYARD. FANTASTIC."

My joy bubbled over that morning as I shared with Al our after-breakfast walk on the beach, bringing back more memories. I was a child again, as we poked into little pools on the rock-strewn sand, discovering tiny sea creatures stranded in them by the receding tide. We walked back along the concrete promenade above the beach, stopping to buy ice-cream cones at the seafront store operated by the Italian family who had come back to reopen it, after their years of detention in an aliens' camp during the war.

On the way to our farewell visit with the Ditchfield's, I took time to share another early childhood memory with Al. Overlooking the beach was a manicured park with a Victorian wrought-iron bandstand, now restored to its former glory, standing just where I had remembered it. I reminisced to Al: "I can almost hear the military brass band playing Strauss waltzes and Sousa's marches, in regimental uniforms with their brightly polished buttons. When I was little, we lived in Sunderland before we moved south to London, and Dad and I sat here on Sunday mornings on folding chairs listening to the concert, to get "out of Mom's hair" while she cooked Sunday dinner."

We walked by the bowling green with its velvety, carefully tended grass. "Here's where I used to watch Grandpa's team competing in bowling tournaments in their white bowling uniforms! Memories!"

After a short walk from the park, we reached my grandparents' home. Gram quietly opened the front door with its stained glass panels and motioned us upstairs to see Grandpa. He was obviously dying, yet he still clung stubbornly to life. Al and I tiptoed to the bed. Grandpa's head moved weakly and he raised his hand a little as Al leaned over him. When Al grasped it, he whispered: "Glad to meet you, son."

I bent to kiss him, remembering the tall, jolly man I had known. I had told Al about the time he bought a "crystal set," one of the first radios. He often accidentally dropped its "cat's whisker" component in the deep pile of the rug, which kept the three of us very young cousins scrambling to find it at regular intervals. And then there was the Christmas dinner when he poured brandy as usual over the plum pudding with its sprig of holly on top. He lit the brandy, which burned with a flickering blue flame through the pudding, but forgot to take out the holly, which caught on fire, causing pandemonium before he calmly snuffed it out with an overturned dessert bowl.

Grandpa whispered: "Hello, Bunty," before dropping back into a deep sleep. Before my next visit to Sunderland he was gone--I cherish his memory.

Auntie Hylda's flushed face showed how she had fussed to produce the delicious lunch, and our hearty appetites showed her how much we appreciated her hard work. Again, Al was touched by his welcome into my Sunderland family.

Sunderland was once dubbed "the largest shipbuilding town in the world," boasting four hundred registered shipyards throughout its long history. Uncle Lew was head of the payroll department at Doxfords, the Sunderland shipyard that was one of England's greatest. Every place he took us he was greeted with "Good afternoon, Mr. Dent." Ignoring his painful back, stooped and bent with arthritis, he walked us around the acres of dockyard, showing us how a ship was built, from the laying of her keel to her launching into the River Wear. Al's diary described it well: "AMAZING PLACE. FROM PRECISION MACHINE SHOPS, CRANKSHAFT SHOP, BOILER MAKER'S SHOP, TO FINANCE OFFICE, EVERY STEP OF THE ORGANIZATION WAS IN THE SAME COMPLEX."

Al and I would never forget Uncle Lew for his gift to us this wonder-filled afternoon.

Al: "SUNDAY, NOVEMBER 25: WHERE DID THE LAST FIVE DAYS GO? TIME TO LEAVE SUNDERLAND FOR TRIP BACK TO LONDON. LITTLE COUSIN DOROTHY WAS ALL READY TO COME WITH US, TALKED HER OUT OF IT SUCCESSFULLY. GOOD TRIP BACK. VERY TIRED. GLAD TO SEE OWN BED AGAIN."

Without a word to anyone, my little cousin Dorothy had packed her small suitcase. She came downstairs as we were leaving, clutching it in one hand. Auntie Belle's voice was soft: "Noo, dear, you cannot go too. You'll joost have to grow oop a bit before you can go and see Al and Boonty in America."

Dorothy looked appealingly at Al. "But you said I can come and visit you!"

Al folded her into his arms. "Yes, honey, but I said when you're a bit older. We're not going back to America just yet, but one day we'll look forward to seeing you there." He put her down gently and she held on tightly to his hand until Uncle Arthur and his wheezing Vauxhall chugged up to the front door to take us to the train station. He grinned. "Oh aye, Al lad, did I ever tell you why they call this car a Vauxhall?"

Auntie Belle and I exchanged apprehensive glances--we knew what was coming!

Al said innocently: "No, I hadn't heard, Uncle Arthur, why do they call it a Vauxhall?"

"Why, lad, it's because those that owns one *valks all* the vay!"

Auntie Belle and I rolled our eyes, but Al doubled up, laughing! Uncle Arthur looked like the cat that swallowed the canary. As I climbed into the wheezing car, he whispered to me: "He's a canny lad, Boonty, enjoys a good laff--see that you keep 'im happy!" As we boarded the train, he thrust a sealed envelope into Al's hand. "This is from me to you, lad." His voice broke as he patted Al's shoulder. "Now awaa, lad, safe voyidge hoame, and mind you take good care of our Boonty."

When we were settled in the train, Al opened the envelope and found two of Uncle Arthur's precious souvenirs of his wartime service: his Air Raid Warden's armband and his British Red Cross pin. I saw the glint of a tear in Al's eye as he put them carefully back in the envelope and into his pocket.

—————— ⚘ ——————

Home to a New World

Al: "THURSDAY, NOVEMBER 29: AT 0900 BUNTY AND I WENT UP TO LONDON. COLLECTED MY DUFFLE BAG FROM RED CROSS CENTER. TOOK TAXI TO WATERLOO STATION. PICKED UP TRAVEL WARRANT. SAID OUR GOODBYES. ARRIVED SOUTHAMPTON. HITCHED RIDE TO REPLACEMENT CENTER NEAR WINCHESTER."

Bunty: "THE DREADED DAY, END OF AL'S FURLOUGH. SAW HIM OFF AT WATERLOO STATION IN LONDON FOR TRAIN TO SOUTHAMPTON. BACK TO WORK."

THE LAST DAYS of Al's furlough flew by and allowed us to relax from our trip north, but the inevitable day of separation had now arrived, and with it my tears. I tried to be thankful for the time we'd had together, and that he had been able to connect with my Sunderland family, then resigned myself to the fact that I wouldn't see him again until I arrived in America. Away from the office madness, and loving every moment of being with Al in Sunderland, I was thinking: "I could get used to this!" But I needed my job, its income, and its power to distract me from frustration until I would be able to sail for the U.S. According to rumors in the G. I. Wives Club and in the newspapers, that could be another year from now!

Al telephoned every day from Winchester, sometimes several times a day. "I'm getting really fed up, sweetheart," he complained, "cooped up here at this depot. How many more games of checkers can I stand? We have to stay here and wait for orders to board ship. Each day a roster of names is called, and so far my name hasn't been on it. Oh, my love, I want you so badly!"

I blew hard on my handkerchief as I put down the telephone receiver. Freddy, Brad, Syd and Buzz discreetly stayed out of my office. As the days went by, I could sense the growing frustration in Al's voice with every phone call, but I was powerless to help.

Al: "TUESDAY, DECEMBER 4: HAVE HAD FLU AND PNEUMONIA SHOTS. BEEN KICKING AROUND HERE NOW FOR FIVE DAYS. NAME NOT CALLED FOR EMBARKATION. GETTING *VERY* FED UP. MISS MY DARLING. REALIZE JUST HOW MUCH I LOVE THAT GAL SINCE WE PARTED. DECIDED TO TAKE TRIP TO SEE HER. NO PASS AVAILABLE. TOOK TRAIN TO LONDON. PICKED UP BUNTY AT OFFICE. CAME HOME TOGETHER."

Bunty: "JUST ABOUT TO LEAVE OFFICE WHEN AL CALLED ME FROM WATERLOO STATION. NEARLY FAINTED WITH ASTONISHMENT! WHAT IS HE DOING BACK IN LONDON? HE DOESN'T HAVE A PASS! WONDERFUL HAVING MY HUSBAND BACK EVEN IF HE IS A.W.O.L.! GOSH, WHAT A SURPRISE FOR MOM!"

Al's frustration boiled over after hanging around for five days, knowing he was only a little over an hour away by train from London. It took me totally by surprise to see him appear at the door of my office, to be greeted with wild cheers from my co-workers and an incredulous look of joy from me.

Between sniffles of delighted surprise at seeing Al again so soon, Mom went into her usual tizzy when she had to find enough rations to stretch for an extra person. (We had remained on rations after the war ended.) But her delight at seeing her new son-in-law overcame any challenges she may have had. Al and I didn't mention he was A.W.O.L.(Absent Without Leave,) not knowing how she would handle another shock in addition to his unexpected arrival.

Al confided to me: "You see, my love, my roommate happens to be married to an English gal, too, but he's still in the depot--didn't want to risk leaving. I've arranged with him to cover for me in case my name is called for departure while I'm here in London."

I suddenly felt cold all over. Al could be in real trouble! But then I rationalized: "Oh well, if it doesn't bother him, I won't let it bother me! I just hope he can pull *this* one off! "

Al: "WEDNESDAY, DECEMBER 5: UP AT 0700. BUNTY AND I RETURNED TO LONDON. AT WATERLOO STATION SAID FAREWELLS. TOOK TRAIN FROM WATERLOO STATION. BACK TO DEPOT AGAIN. ROOMMATE AND I GOT 48 HR. PASSES! THEY BEGIN TOMORROW, BUT WE LEFT TODAY. GIVES US AN EXTRA DAY WITH OUR GALS. CAUGHT SAME TRAIN AS YESTERDAY. WONDERFUL TO SEE BUNTY."

Bunty: "BEFORE GOING TO OFFICE, SAW AL OFF AT WATERLOO STATION ON HIS WAY BACK TO DEPOT AT WINCHESTER. HOPE I WON'T HAVE TO VISIT HIM IN JAIL! HE CALLED AGAIN THIS AFTERNOON-- FROM WATERLOO STATION! HE'S BACK IN LONDON AGAIN, WITH A 48 HR. PASS! IT'S LEGAL THIS TIME--ALMOST. WHOOPEE!"
Although Al's name and also his roommate's were pretty far down on the list, they both knew they were taking the risk that their names would be called for embarkation while they were away from the depot. But, as Mom put it, "the call of the wild" was more impelling to them than flirting with U.S. Army regulations. She added: "Remember, Bunty, you told me when he proposed that Al was full of surprises--well, he still seems to be in high gear!"

With the blessing of all at the office, I took off the next two days from work, and enjoyed what would surely be my last time with Al before we would meet again on the other side of the Atlantic.

Al: "SUNDAY, DECEMBER 9: WHILE ROOMMATE AND I WERE GONE ON OUR PASSES, SURE ENOUGH, OUR NAMES WERE CALLED FOR SHIPMENT! HIS GROUP SHIPPED OUT WITHOUT HIM THIS MORNING; HE HAS TO WAIT FOR NEW ORDERS. MY GROUP STILL HERE--WE SHIP OUT TOMORROW. LUCKEE! CALLED BUNTY. PACKED CLOTHES. HAD FINAL PHYSICAL. PUT COPY OF SHIPPING ORDERS IN MAIL FOR BUNTY."

Bunty: "ZERO HOUR. AL SAILS TOMORROW. I GUESS THIS IS IT! COULDN'T KEEP BACK THE TEARS."

As my tears flowed again, Mom said: "Bunty, this is getting to be a habit! If you don't stop crying, you'll create a high tide here at Bishop's Hill and wash us all away."

I got the message. I blew hard into my handkerchief and stopped crying.

Al: "MONDAY, DECEMBER 10: SCHEDULED TO BOARD SHIP TODAY BUT DELAYED UNTIL WEDNESDAY. NO EXPLANATION."

Bunty: "BACK TO WORK. I HAVE A SECOND NEW ASSISTANT, FIONA CAMPBELL. SEEMS LIKE A NICE GAL. WITH MY INCREASED WORKLOAD SINCE THE END OF THE WAR, SHE'S VERY WELCOME. NOW I HAVE A STAFF OF TWO! WENT TO G.I. WIVES MEETING AT RAINBOW CORNER. LEARNED THAT I DON'T NEED A FORM 4 ANY LONGER, TO GET A VISA! AFTER ALL THAT GRIEF! BUT NOW I CAN GO AHEAD AND GET MY BRITISH PASSPORT. YIPPEE!"

At the office my salary had doubled, but in the time since my last raise my workload had again doubled! My first staff member, Bert, was doing well with the documentation. With the addition of Fiona, I now had help in processing Freddy's increasing load of correspondence.

I was surprised to find myself with a growing staff to supervise! "Not bad, for nineteen years old," I thought, "I hope I can cope!"

Fiona Campbell was a few years older than me--a Scottish girl, pretty, small-boned and petite--her auburn hair tied back with a colored ribbon to match her beige suit. Her long-lashed blue eyes were clouded with some hidden sadness, and she told me her tale of woe in her soft Scottish brogue over a morning cup of tea.

"Ye may be wundrin' a wee bit why I'm here in London instead of up in the Highlands where I belong, Bunty. Och, well, I'm tryin' to start a new life doon here. Someday I want to hae a bit o' fun bein' an airrline attendant and do some globe hoppin' after I settle doon and get yewst to livin' in the south. Eearly on in the war, I married a doctor who was sent over to India in the British Arrmy. The distance between us was too much for him to stay faithful. We had harrsh words and our marriage ended."

In the weeks that followed, Fiona blossomed. She was pleasant and helpful, although still suffering bouts of depression over her failed marriage. As for me, it was a relief to be able to train her so I could delegate some of the routine clerical office work and typing. She gradually adopted these tasks as her own, and enjoyed them with a proprietary air, establishing her value on my little office team.

But the job I loved was taking an equal place to my determination to get myself transported across the Atlantic, now that Al was on his way. News of the demise of Form 4 was great, but when I arrived home from the G.I. Wives meeting I exploded with pent-up indignation.

"Guess what, Mom? The American Embassy has suddenly decided that we don't need that miserable Form 4 to get a visa. To think how Al and I toiled and sweated for two months to get that wretched Form 3P submitted so we could get a Form 4 and a visa, and now I don't need one! All that anxiety and work for nothing!"

Mom looked up from her knitting. "Think of it this way, Bunty," she replied, "it's a victory over the red tape. The U.S. Embassy probably couldn't cope with processing the volume of all those forms pouring in from the G.I. Brides. I'll bet the U.S. Government will end up having to pass a law for you all to get into America more easily!"

She was joking, but she was right! Time would tell that story. Next day I skipped lunch and had my passport photos taken.

Al Sails Home

Al: "WEDNESDAY, DECEMBER 12: BOARDED *U.S.A.T.* (*U.S. Army Transport*) *THOMAS M. KEARNS* AT 0715. PULLED OUT SOUTHAMPTON AT 1100 HRS. SEA CALM. LIBERTY SHIP. CAN ONLY GO AT 12 KNOTS, TOPS. DISTANCE 4100 MILES. SENT A WIRE AND LETTER TO BUNTY.

TRIP TO TAKE 17 DAYS. REMEMBERED THAT TWO YEARS AGO TODAY I HAD BOARDED *AQUITANIA* FOR THE E.T.O."

Bunty: "RECEIVED AL'S SAILING ORDERS IN THE MAIL, ALSO HAD A TELEGRAM FROM HIM TO SAY HE'S SAILING TODAY. WILL SEND ALL MAIL FROM NOW ON TO HIS HOME ADDRESS. COLLECTED PASSPORT PHOTOS IN MY LUNCH HOUR. ARRANGED FOR INCOME TAX REBATE AND SENT FORM TO REDEEM MY SAVINGS BONDS."

"Well, Mom, I feel that I'm really getting somewhere now; there's a break in the red tape logjam at last." I wasn't wasting any time in getting down to the exciting business of preparing for my new life, but it really hadn't dawned on me just how hard it must have been for Mom, seeing me advancing step by step closer to leaving her.

The *Thomas M. Kearns* was a Liberty Ship. Research reveals that these were originally designed by the British, who ordered many from American shipyards to replace cargo ships lost in the Battle of the Atlantic in World War Two. They were so cheap and quick to build that the Americans adopted them for use by the U.S. Merchant Marine. Between the years of 1942 and 1945, an astonishing 2,710 were built. Their life expectancy was five years. My research told me that the *Thomas M. Kearns* was built in 1943, and had taken part in the D-Day landings. By the time Al boarded her she had used up three of her five years.

I thought to myself: "I'll bet she has seen enough tough service to make her a bit rickety. Hope her engine still works O.K.!"

Bunty: "SATURDAY, DECEMBER 15: LAURIE CAME FOR THE WEEKEND. WE WENT UP TO THE BRITISH PASSPORT OFFICE IN LONDON TO DROP OFF MY COMPLETED FORMS FOR EXIT PERMIT, ALSO MY PASSPORT PHOTOS, THEN TO AMERICAN EMBASSY TO DROP OFF AL'S SAILING ORDERS FOR MY FILE. AFTER LUNCH WE WENT TO THE 312TH AMERICAN ARMY GENERAL HOSPITAL FOR OUR VACCINATIONS."

The clerk at the British Passport Office looked over my passport application. I held my breath. After what seemed an eternity, he looked up and said: "Oh, yes, madam, it's all here; your passport will be ready in fourteen days." I danced out of the office, Laurie close behind me. Her husband had already been shipped home, and her formalities had been completed ahead of mine.

The "Holy Grail," the name by which I had dubbed my transportation to the U.S., was getting closer. Form 4 had been wiped out as unnecessary, and the next step--my British passport--would be ready in two weeks! I again felt like Hercules knocking off his many labors, one at a time, except that *my* reward would be that longed-for ship waiting somewhere to take me across the Atlantic.

Laurie brought me down from Cloud Nine. "Well, Bunty, we'd better get over to the hospital and get our vaccinations. That's next on our list for entry into the United States."

I thought, wearily: "One more Herculean labor--ugh!"

Fortified with lunch and rested feet, we took a bus to the other side of London and eventually found the U.S. Army Hospital. Inside, it looked and sounded more like a zoo than a hospital: G.I. Brides, some with howling children, and American servicemen and women preparing to return home, all milling around in the halls and waiting rooms, filling the air with assorted shouts, wails and epithets.

We squeezed through the seething mob to a door above which was a sign marked "Vaccinations", where we were pounced upon by a burly W.A.C. (Women's Army Corps) nurse. She pinched an inch or two at the top of my arm, then like a female woodpecker began a tattoo of small pricks with something that felt more like a blunt instrument than a surgical needle. It was Laurie's turn next. Clutching our vaccination certificates, the two of us fled back to Upper Woodside.

The WAC had warned us not to touch our new vaccinations before a scab had formed, so we slept poorly, worrying that we might accidentally scratch them in our sleep. By next morning, reaction had set in. We could hardly lift our arms: inflamed, swollen, and sporting the results of the WAC's handiwork--two unbearably itchy red welts. That evening we wrote pitiful letters to our husbands, telling them about the sacrifices we were making to get ourselves ready to be shipped into their waiting arms.

Peril at Sea

Al: "SUNDAY DECEMBER 16: WE'RE IN THE MIDST OF A TERRIFIC STORM. SEA IS GETTING ROUGHER, WAVES HIGHER THAN THE SHIP. MY APPETITE ALMOST VANISHED, BUT FORCED DOWN SOME FOOD. THIS 'AFT' PART OF THE SHIP WHERE I SLEEP IS WORST OF ALL. FIRST LIKE AN AIRPLANE, NEXT A SUBMARINE. NOT SEASICK, BUT VERY UNCOMFORTABLE. ROOMATE IS SICK AS A DOG."

Bunty: "LAURIE AND I WENT FOR A WALK IN SPRING GLEN PARK TO TAKE OUR MINDS OFF OUR ACHING ARMS. TOOK SOME PHOTOS. MOM MADE AN ENORMOUS LUNCH. LAURIE LEFT AT 6 P.M. SHE'S SUCH A DEAR, LIKE THE SISTER I NEVER HAD."

It was a good thing that I didn't know until long afterwards what was happening to Al today, tossing around alarmingly in a North Atlantic storm in a small, aging Liberty Ship.

Color film was, at that point in time, almost non-existent. I still look with nostalgia at the black and white snapshots of Laurie and me, that day in Spring Glen Park.

Al: "MONDAY, DECEMBER 17: ROOMMATE SICKER THAN TWO DOGS NOW! SHIP STILL TOSSING WITH STORM. CAN'T GO OUTSIDE SO STAYED IN BED. STORMY WEATHER HAS SLOWED US UP CONSIDERABLY; TRIP WILL TAKE A FEW DAYS LONGER. WANT TO BE HOME FOR NEW YEAR'S EVE."

Bunty: "BACK TO OFFICE. EVERYONE IS RUSHING AROUND DOING SHOPPING AND GETTING READY FOR CHRISTMAS."

By this time I was sure Al would be almost across the North Atlantic. I had no cause to be anxious; he said it would take seventeen days and that I'd receive a cable as soon as he arrived.

In Britain, wartime shortages of food, clothing and just about everything else had not eased. I spent my lunch hour looking in vain for something to buy for Mom and Dad for Christmas. My diary said: "IT'S REALLY HOPELESS!"

Al: "TUESDAY, DECEMBER 18: APPETITE COMING BACK. STILL STORMY. HEARD REPORT THAT TWO U.S. AIRCRAFT CARRIERS DAMAGED IN STORM HAD TO TURN BACK TO SOUTHAMPTON FOR REPAIRS. GLAD NOT OUR SHIP."

Bunty: "HAD A TELEGRAM FROM JOAN HOFFMAN, ASKING ME TO CALL HER URGENTLY. SHE IS COMING TO LONDON TOMORROW FOR HER MEDICAL BEFORE SAILING. WANTS TO KNOW HOW TO GET TO AMERICAN EMBASSY. ARRANGED TO MEET HER TRAIN."
I was looking forward to meeting Joan Hoffman, the G.I. Bride of Al's school friend Bud. She lived near Bristol, about a hundred and fifty miles west of London, and we had been in touch by mail ever since Al's mother had written to ask me to contact her some weeks ago. On the telephone, her pleasant, slightly accented voice sounded very young. I offered to meet her at Paddington train station, take her to the Embassy, then bring her home with me after her medical to stay with us overnight. She quickly agreed, and I arranged to take time off from work to meet her at the Information Desk at the station.

Al: "WEDNESDAY, DECEMBER 19: HAVE 2,935 MILES MORE TO GO. RUMOR IS WE'LL DOCK AT BALTIMORE OR NEWPORT NEWS VIRGINIA. STILL HEAVY SEAS BUT WENT ON DECK. SIGHTED AIRCRAFT CARRIER OFF STARBOARD BOW."

Bunty: "NO SIGN OF JOAN AT THE STATION. TRACKED HER DOWN AT THE AMERICAN EMBASSY. BROUGHT HER HOME TO BISHOP'S HILL WITH ME."

Joan's train arrived on time at Paddington Station. I waited for her at the Information Desk, as we had arranged, but she didn't appear. I waited for two more trains after that. No Joan! Not knowing what to do, I decided to check at the American Embassy. A pretty young blonde, whose face corresponded to the photo she had sent earlier, was coming out of the building. I rushed up to her and said: "Joan? I'm Bunty."

"Oh, Bunty," she said, "sorry. I stopped for a quick lunch then came on here."

I gritted my teeth and said nothing. "Oh well," I thought, "she's very capable--found her way around really well. She didn't need me, after all!"

We headed home to Bishop's Hill. Mom had made a special dinner in Joan's honor. Next morning I took her with me on the bus to London and put her off at Paddington Station to take her train back to Bristol, while I went back to my office. Our next meeting would be in Little Cedar River.

Al: "SATURDAY, DECEMBER 22: SEA'S CALM AGAIN. MAKING BETTER SPEED. APPETITE NORMAL. NOT MUCH CHRISTMAS SPIRIT. MISS BUNTY TERRIBLY."

Bunty: "GRANDPA DITCHFIELD DIED. MOM IS PACKING TO LEAVE FOR SUNDERLAND. MY VACCINATION IS GETTING ME DOWN. HAVE A SPLITTING HEADACHE AND ARM FEELS LIKE A LEAD PIPE."

Dad was home for Christmas. I was glad he could help me to comfort Mom, who was devastated. She and Grandpa had been very close; she was his favorite of the six children in the family. As always, Mom's thoughts were for our welfare, and she gave me a list of possible meals I could make from the rations she had stacked up in the larder.

I was having an unexpected reaction to my vaccination; my temperature was up slightly, and I felt light-headed. It was a relief when Mom began to prepare a few meals ahead of time so I wouldn't have to make them from scratch, which I had never yet been taught how to do.

Al: "TUESDAY, DECEMBER 25: CHRISTMAS MUSIC PLAYING OVER ALL THE SHIP'S LOUDSPEAKERS. WEATHER BRIGHT AND FAIR. GEE, I MISS BUNTY AND MY FOLKS. I CAN JUST PICTURE WHAT CHRISTMAS AT HOME IS LIKE. DINNER HERE ON BOARD WAS PRETTY GOOD. CHRISTMAS DECORATIONS ON TABLES."

Bunty: "DAD AND I SAW MOM OFF FOR SUNDERLAND AT THE TRAIN STATION. I'M HAVING SOME PRACTICE AT BEING A HOUSEWIFE. HOPE I'LL NEVER HAVE A WHOLE HOUSE TO LOOK AFTER! THIS FEELS NOTHING LIKE CHRISTMAS!"
Somehow I got through the day, warming up one of the meals Mom had left for our supper. In my diary nothing was mentioned about any Christmas decorations or exchanging gifts; my words only echoed my own dampened spirits.

Al: "THURSDAY, DECEMBER 27: BEAUTIFUL WEATHER. GULF STREAM. STILL 1,317 MORE MILES TO GO, ABOUT FIVE DAYS MORE. HAVEN'T SHAVED IN 12 DAYS. HAVE QUITE A BEARD! WASHED MY UNDERWEAR. WON'T MAKE IT HOME FOR NEW YEAR'S EVE. BOO!"

Bunty: "BACK TO WORK. WHAT A RELIEF TO GET AWAY FROM THE HOUSE! HOUSEKEEPING MUST BE FUN, WHEN GOOD FACILITIES ARE AVAILABLE AND IT'S YOUR VERY OWN HOUSE, BUT OH BROTHER! MOM REALLY COULD USE SOME MODERN HOUSEHOLD APPLIANCES! SHE'S COMING BACK TOMORROW, THANK GOODNESS."
I was glad to go back to work, to escape the house! I had cleaned up as best I could for Mom's return from Grandpa's funeral, so she would find things "shipshape," as Dad would have said.

Everyone was back at the office, looking a little bleary. Freddy and Brad looked as if they were glad to rest their elbows on their desks. Syd was effervescent as ever in his cockney accent: "Aw, wot a wunnerful time I had," he exulted, "partying wiv me new fiancée. I reely think I'll be getting married this time--my Ivy, she's a reel winner."

Was this Syd's third or fourth engagement? We had all lost track! Brad whispered to me: "I still won't believe it until I hear the wedding bells!"

By now I was wondering when I would get a cable to say Al had arrived in the U.S. I began to worry. What to do? Then I remembered a movie I had seen in which a ship had been insured with Lloyds of London, who kept track of its movements, so I decided to call them and begin my inquiries. The clerk at Lloyds said that shipping was still controlled by the War Shipping Administration, and gave me their phone number. It had taken longer than I thought to get this far, and it was time to leave the office for the day.

Enveloped in gloom, I went home to get dinner for Dad. I thought we had run out of Mom's meals, but I was thrilled when I found one more, lurking in the deeper recesses of the larder. Dad's key clicked in the door, and I ran out to meet him. "Guess what, Dad, we're in luck--one more meal left in the larder! No need to walk all the way to the fish and chip shop and back tonight, after all!"

Al: "FRIDAY, DECEMBER 28: BEAUTIFUL WEATHER. CALM SEA. RUMOR SAYS WE SHOULD DOCK AROUND NOON ON THE 1ST. TOO LATE FOR NEW YEAR'S EVE, BUT STILL O.K. FINISHED LAST CHAPTER OF BOOK I'M READING. PLAYED CHECKERS, BED"

Bunty: "MOM BACK FROM SUNDERLAND. THANK GOODNESS! BACK TO OFFICE, BEGAN SEARCH FOR *U.S.A.T. THOMAS M. KEARNS*."

"Oh, it's good to be back home again," said Mom. "I do so hate sleeping in a strange bed, and it was a very sad time. Most of the family turned up. They all send their love. Did Al get home yet?"

My worried look gave her the answer.

As soon as I had a spare minute at the office, I called the War Shipping Administration. After a few phone transfers, I found a very friendly clerk who had access to the records for Al's troop ship. I asked: "I wonder if you could locate the *U.S. Army Transport Thomas M. Kearns*? I'm sure I would have heard from my husband by this time if the ship had docked. I haven't heard from him, and I'm getting worried."

The clerk must have heard my voice shaking. He replied: "Oh, yes, Miss, I'll be pleased to help you. You can call me every day for news, if you like. Ask for Ron at this extension."

By the second day we were on a first name basis. Ron was very obliging but not very reassuring. "Well, Bunty, it appears that the *Kearns* got off to a late start. She's reported as having struck a submerged object in Southampton Harbor and was delayed two days for repairs. Today's report shows her still on the Atlantic."

I thanked him, but I worried to myself: "An old patched-up Liberty Ship out somewhere on the ocean--I hope she still has all her rivets!

Al: "SATURDAY, DECEMBER 29: 700 MORE MILES TO GO. ANOTHER SUNNY DAY, BUT GETTING COLD. SEA IS BLUE AS COBALT. WASHED MY FATIGUES--THEY STANK!"

Bunty: "AM I GLAD MOM'S BACK! FORTUNATELY DAD AND I MADE IT SOMEHOW WITHOUT HER, AND HE LOOKS WELL FED, BUT WHAT A MISERABLE CHRISTMAS HOLIDAY THIS WAS! VACCINATION NOW COMFORTABLE. MURDEROUS-LOOKING SCAB FORMING ON MY ARM. UGH! PRESIDENT ROOSEVELT HAS SIGNED NEW LEGISLATION FOR WAR BRIDES. WENT UP TO LONDON AND COLLECTED MY BRITISH PASSPORT! HOORAY! WROTE MY DAILY LETTER TO AL."

When Mom returned, so did my good spirits. She barely had taken off her hat and coat before she remarked: "Well, Bunty, you both look great; I think you must have done without me very well!"

"Thanks, Mom, but that's not true; it just convinced me that my future as a housewife is looking less and less attractive!"

"Oh, don't give it a thought, dear," She said with the air of long experience, "you'll get used to it!"

I said nothing.

Meantime, in far-off Washington, D.C., President Roosevelt had signed legislation permitting war brides to enter the U.S. without a visa and to exempt them from going through Ellis Island as immigrants. The medical exam Joan had endured at the U.S. Army Hospital "zoo", which had previously been required before sailing, had also now been waived.

I grumbled to Mom and Dad: "Just think, all we had to go through, wiped out by a stroke of the pen! I really think Eleanor must have put in a good word for us!"

Victory was at hand also at the British Passport Office. My passport was ready for me! I had it in my hot little hand at last!

I had wrestled my way through all the preceding formalities (now mostly unnecessary) and survived; now all I needed was proof of Al's arrival in the U.S., and my Battle of the Red Tape would be over. But where was Al? Ron's report today still said "en route."

Al: "MONDAY, DECEMBER 31: NOT MUCH OF A NEW YEAR'S EVE! WELL, SO MUCH FOR HOPING TO BE HOME FOR NEW YEAR'S. GETTING COLDER OUTSIDE. SIGHTED LAND. SEAGULLS IN LATE AFTERNOON. GETTING EXCITED!"

Bunty: "MET LAURIE IN LONDON AND WENT TO THE U.S. ARMY'S TRANSPORTATION OFFICE AT THE EMBASSY. THEY CONFIRMED NO MORE FORM 4s REQUIRED--NO VISAS NECESSSARY. SHOPPED FOR GLOVES, SLIPPERS AND SWEATERS. NO LUCK! WILL IT EVER BE POSSIBLE AGAIN FOR US TO BUY WHAT WE NEED? AND MORE BAD NEWS, AL'S SHIP STILL ON THE OCEAN."

After another fruitless shopping expedition, I eased my aching feet out of my shoes under the tearoom table as we watched the waitress set a little brown teapot on it. Laurie poured the steaming brew into our cups, and we lingered awhile before taking trains back to our respective homes, tired and discouraged.

If I had been aware that this was New Year's Eve, my diary didn't mention it. The New Year's Eve family parties in Sunderland were no more, since Grandpa Ditchfield had died. Mom, Dad and I stayed up until midnight but without any joyous party of our own. We drank a glass of wine to welcome in the New Year, ate a piece of fruitcake saved from the wedding, and wished each other a Happy New Year, before going off to bed. It didn't occur to me, in my excited anticipation of sailing to a new life in the new year, that Mom and Dad were sharing the sadness of realizing that this would be our last New Year's Eve together.

I thought back across the years of my incredible journey through life so far, and tried to envision the next chapter that lay ahead. There would still be a long way to go, but I was almost on my way. I silently wished Al a Happy New Year, wherever he was, and I hoped he got the message.

Al: "TUESDAY, JANUARY 1:　SEA CALM BUT WEATHER VERY COLD. PACKED EVERYTHING READY TO GET OFF SHIP. SIGHTED FIRST BUOY 1210 HRS. PICKED UP PILOT 1606 HRS. PULLED INTO NEWPORT NEWS AND ANCHORED FOR NIGHT. LISTENED TO ALL RUMORS. PLAYED CHECKERS. EXCITED."

Bunty: "BACK TO WORK WITH A WALLOP! A NEW MEMBER HAS BEEN ADDED TO OUR DEPARTMENT STAFF. RECEIVED A LETTER FROM AL'S MOTHER. SHE'S NOT BEEN WELL. SICK IN BED AGAIN. STILL NOTHING FROM AL."

I called my new friend, Ron, at the War Shipping Administration. The *Thomas M. Kearns* was reported as still en route. "Well, at least she's still afloat," I breathed, gratefully.

At the office, Brad found himself with a new co-worker, an ex-Navy man. Businesses were now expanding and hiring returned servicemen and women; it was looking more and more like peacetime.

The letter from my mother-in-law was what Dad would have called a "moaner". I thought: "She seems to be quite sickly; this time it's been the flu and bronchitis. Poor dear, she must spend a lot of her time in bed. Wonder what she's like?"

Al: "WEDNESDAY, JANUARY 2: AROSE 0745. BREAKFAST. DISEMBARKED 1100. PICKED UP G.I.s FROM ANOTHER SHIP. LOADED ON TRUCKS FOR CAMP PATRICK HENRY. WONDERFUL CHOW, STEAK, MILK, ICE CREAM. SENT CABLE TO BUNTY. ALSO SENT HER A 16-PAGE LETTER BY AIRMAIL. CALLED MOM. TOO TIRED TO UNPACK BAG. SO HAPPY! IT WAS A LONG WAY HOME."

Bunty: "THE WAR SHIPPING ADMINISTRATION REPORTS AL'S SHIP SIGHTED OFF CAPE HENRY. WHERE ON EARTH IS THAT?"
I had fully expected Al to land in New York. Ron reported the *Thomas M. Kearns* was off Cape Henry. In my lunch hour I went to the library and looked up Cape Henry. Al was off the coast of Virginia. Surprised, I asked myself: "What's he doing there? Twenty-one days on that ship already; how much longer to New York?" I would have been surprised to hear that he wasn't going there at all!

Al: "THURSDAY, JANUARY 3: SHOWERED--IT FELT SO GOOD! SHAVED OFF BEARD, FACE FEELS COLD BUT LOOKS MUCH BETTER! BREAKFAST. HAIRCUT. DEPARTED RAILHEAD 2030. TRAVELED ALL NIGHT ON TRAIN. ARRIVED PHILADELPHIA. CALLED MY MOM. ARRIVED FORT MONMOUTH, NEW JERSEY AT 1600. FEEL VERY, VERY TIRED. WROTE BUNTY, BED."

Bunty: "MOM CALLED ME AT THE OFFICE, CABLE FROM AL. HE'S ARRIVED SAFELY. OH, I AM *SO* RELIEVED I COULD (AND DID) CRY. MY

PAYCHECK WAS VERY DECENT THIS TIME, AND WHEN I GOT HOME FOUND MY U.S. ARMY ALLOTMENT CHECK AND A BRITISH INCOME TAX REBATE WAITING FOR ME. WHAT A BANNER DAY THIS HAS BEEN! THINGS ARE REALLY LOOKING UP!"

I was gradually gathering my slender assets into one place so I could bring a lump sum with me to America for our joint bank account. I didn't know about the severe restrictions on the amount of sterling allowed out of Britain. But that was only one of the surprises, both bad and good, awaiting me in the weeks to come.

Al: "SATURDAY, JANUARY 5: BROTHER BILL DROVE MOM AND AMY TO THE CAMP TO VISIT ME. TALKED OVER OLD TIMES. BILL IS OUT OF NAVY AND HAS PLANS FOR A RESTAURANT. FEEL VERY HAPPY ABOUT GETTING DISCHARGED. GET OUT MONDAY."

Bunty: "TOOK MY PRECIOUS CABLE FROM AL TO THE U.S. EMBASSY. THEY HAVE RECEIVED THE FORM CONFIRMING MY VACCINATION. THIS COMPLETES MY APPLICATION FOR TRANSPORTATION FILE; NOW ALL I NEED IS A SHIP!"

I said a grateful prayer of thanks for Al's safe arrival, and remembered to call Ron to thank him for his help in keeping track of the *Thomas M. Kearns*. Al's cable, proof of his arrival in the U.S., and the proof of my vaccination were key documents needed to get me on the list for my own transportation to America. I was glad to hear that a hospital copy of my vaccination certificate was now included in my file. The human woodpecker had done her job well; there was a horrendous scab on my arm that left no doubt of that!

Now that my documentation was complete, my Battle of the Red Tape had been won, but now my battle to cross the Atlantic was about to begin. I felt the emotional tug of two loves pulling me in opposite directions; a loving husband waiting for me stateside and loving parents dreading my departure from home.

Poor Mom. I tried to comfort her as best I could: "Now remember, Mom, with transatlantic air and sea transportation these days we really won't be that far apart, and I'm hoping that you and Dad will be coming to visit us next year. That will give us time to buy a home and be settled in so I can get your bedroom ready!"

Unselfishly, and seeing how concerned I was, Mom did her best to reassure me: "Bunty, darling, I understand. Remember that I left *my* mother as a young bride, to go to East Africa to join your Dad."

What she didn't say was: "But it wasn't for a lifetime."

Al, the Civilian

Al: "MONDAY, JANUARY 7: THREE OTHER GUYS I KNOW FROM LITTLE CEDAR RIVER ARE HERE AT THE CENTER IN N.J.! HOME IS FEELING CLOSER. DREW FINAL PAY. RECEIVED HONORABLE DISCHARGE AND SERVICE MEDALS. ARRIVED HOME. MOM HAD 'WELCOME HOME' TURKEY DINNER FOR ME. PUT ON CIVVIES. STILL FIT ME! MET WITH BOSS AT A.T.& T. JOB WAS KEPT OPEN FOR ME. BEGIN WORK NEXT MONDAY."

Bunty: "AL'S FIRST LETTER FROM THE U.S.A.! SIXTEEN PAGES! MOSTLY DESCRIBING HIS HORRIFIC VOYAGE HOME."
In his letter, Al described in vivid detail the grueling twenty-one days on a small rickety ship at the mercy of the stormy North Atlantic. The ship rode out one of the worst of the winter storms with her engine turned off. I shuddered at Al's description:

"We all wondered if the ship would hold together without breaking apart in the mountainous seas, and worried that the engine wouldn't start up again. She finally limped into Newport News, almost out of food and water, and with seasick G.I.s strewn everywhere. Later I heard a rumor that this may have been the last voyage of the *Thomas M. Kearns*--I wouldn't be surprised! We all wondered if it would have been our last voyage, too!"

Al: "WEDNESDAY, JANUARY 9: OPENED BANK ACCOUNT. AWFUL SKINNY! LOOKED AT MY MODEL A FORD. DOESN'T RUN, BUT ERNIE

SAYS HE CAN FIX IT. NO OTHER CARS AVAILABLE. PLAN TO TAKE TRAIN TO VISIT FAMILY IN PENNSYLVANIA TOMORROW. FIRST STOP, COAL COUNTRY, SHENANDOAH."

Bunty: "AT WORK, TWO NEW ASSISTANTS HIRED TO HELP BRAD AND SYD. WHEN I ARRIVED HOME WHO SHOULD OPEN DOOR BUT PAUL!" Right after the war it was impossible to buy a new car, even if Al had had the money. When he was in high school it took him a year to scrape up enough cash to buy an elderly Model A jalopy, but it had been up on blocks during his two-year absence in the Army, and now it wasn't running. He was desperate for a car to get him to and from his job. His letter went into some detail:

"Ernie Brown owns the Nash auto agency in town. He runs the mechanical end of the business in a fully equipped garage behind the agency; his car-salesman partner takes care of the finances and the showroom. Ernie also owns the two-family house next door to the agency on Main Street that Mom shares with Mrs. Brown, his elderly mother. He's been very kind to me; you'll like him, Bunty. He's going to fix the Model A, and look around for an old prewar Nash for me to buy."

This was the first time Al had mentioned anything about the physical aspects of his home. I was already beginning to feel prickles of uneasiness. My daydream of Al's home, like the one in *Anne of Green Gables*, standing in its own neat acre of lawn with a white picket fence around it, was rapidly fading.

Meantime, in Britain, men and women were being discharged from military service, and were now looking for jobs. B.O.A.C. was looking toward postwar expansion at home and overseas, so hiring was gathering momentum. A fleeting thought crossed my mind: "Well, if something goes wrong and things don't work out for me in America, at least I stand the chance of a good career here, but I'd rather have a career with Al! I wonder what's ahead of me, especially with Al's mother? I guess I'd better start calling her 'Mom Greene'".

It was great to see Paul again, and I must have bored him with the tale of my battle with the red tape and my remote hopes of getting to the U.S. soon.

Al: "FRIDAY, JANUARY 11: TRAIN TO PENNSYLVANIA. FAMILY HERE AT SHENANDOAH ARE FINE. GREAT WELCOME. LEFT THIS AFTERNOON FOR DELAWARE COUNTY TO VISIT AUNT MARY AND COUSIN TOM. STILL IN HIGH SCHOOL, BUT HE'S TALLER THAN I AM NOW!"

Bunty: "JOAN HAS RECEIVED HER 'ALERTING PAPERS' FROM THE U.S. ARMY TRANSPORTATION OFFICE, ANNOUNCING SHE WILL SOON BE SAILING. LAURIE CALLED ME AT THE OFFICE TO SAY SHE EXPECTS TO FLY TO THE U.S. AT THE END OF THE MONTH--TIRED OF WAITING FOR U.S. ARMY TRAVEL ORDERS. SHE INVITED ME TO STAY THE WEEKEND AT HER HOME."

Al's family meant a lot to him. When he was only fourteen, his mother had been widowed when his father died suddenly at the age of forty-nine, leaving her no estate except a small U.S. Navy pension. She was left with four children, three under the age of sixteen. The youngest was born with a heart ailment. She was bedridden most of the time, resulting in costly medical bills until she had died when she was nine years old. With only scant training as a nurse's aide, "Mom Greene" had little hope of raising her family alone. Her relatives had pitched in financially, and she had managed to keep the family together. Bill, the oldest, was never a happy student. To help with expenses, he willingly left high school and went to Pennsylvania to work at the Ford plant located near Aunt Mary, with whom he stayed until he enlisted in the U.S. Navy in World War Two.

Meantime, in 1946 in Upper Woodside, I was "chafing at the bit" to cross the Atlantic. Joan and Laurie, both having been married long before myself, were well ahead of me on the transportation list. Joan's alerting papers brought her a step closer to being able to board a ship; she could now start packing for the journey.

Laurie had become impatient with the U.S. Army Transportation Office. Under pressure from her husband to join him, she had decided to try to book a flight to New York. From my experience working at Airways House, I knew that civilian flights were still in short supply; seats were usually reserved for V.I.P.s with priority. However, there was a stand-by list for passengers who were willing to take their chances and show up at Airways House to wait for a possible last-minute cancellation. Laurie was desperate. She was sold a ticket to New York by Pan American Airways, who used the B.O.A.C. passenger lounge in Airways House for their transatlantic passengers.

Al: "SATURDAY, JANUARY 12: DROVE COUSIN TOM'S CAR. VERY NICE. I'M GREEN WITH ENVY. WENT BY TRAIN TO CAMDEN, N.J. TO VISIT LAST BATCH OF RELATIVES. HOME. ARRANGED WITH NASH AGENCY SALESMAN TO BUY A TRADE-IN 1936 PLYMOUTH COUPE FOR $325. WAS PROMISED IT BY TUESDAY. WILL FIX UP FORD JALOPY AND SELL IT."

Bunty: "ARRIVED AT LAURIE'S FOR WEEKEND TO FIND SHE EXPECTS TO FLY TO NEW YORK TONIGHT!"
When I arrived, as arranged, to spend the weekend with Laurie, I was astonished to find her feverishly packing. Dismayed, I said facetiously: "Going somewhere?"

Laurie paused between folding her underwear and tucking it into odd corners in her suitcase. She said breathlessly: "Oh, Bunty, I've just had a call from Pan American to come to Airways House this evening for a flight to New York! Oh dear, I'm in such a tizzy!" She picked up a piece of paper from her pocketbook and waved it at me. "Look, here's my ticket."

I looked at the ticket. It had no date or flight number. Feeling uneasy, I picked up the phone and called Pan American to confirm that she was on the passenger list for their night flight. I handed the phone to Laurie. She listened for a moment, then put down the receiver.

"Oh, Bunty," she said faintly, "I thought they had me on the passenger list! They said I am not on the list at the moment, but on stand-by, and to come to Airways House in case there is a last-minute cancellation." She turned to me, her voice squeaky with consternation: "But I *do* have a ticket, so I'm going. My husband will be at New York to meet the flight, you know."

I took one look at her worried expression, and quipped: "Now don't get your knickers in a twist, Laurie. I'm going with you."

We rode the commuter train to London and sat in the passenger lounge at Airways House to wait for the shuttle bus that took passengers to Croydon Airport. Laurie looked like a beautiful fashion model, tall and slender, in an immaculate black suit with matching hat, shoes and pocketbook. Wisps of dark hair peeked out from under the brim of her hat, and a flush of pink brightened her lovely oval face with excitement.

The shuttle bus arrived. As each name was called, the passengers filed out through a door leading to the bus; soon we were the only ones left in the passenger lounge. An attendant closed the door. Laurie broke down in a flood of tears. I went to the counter and asked why Laurie's name wasn't called.

"I'm sorry, Miss, "there weren't any 'no-shows'," said the clerk, and she began to close up her counter for the day.

"Laurie dear," I said, putting my arm around her, "you must send a cable to your husband right now to tell him why you aren't on the flight. It will just get to him in time to prevent him from starting off to meet you at New York. Then you're coming home with me. It's best for you not to go home by yourself until you settle down and feel better. We'll contact Pan American in the morning."

Before we left Airways House, Laurie reluctantly sent a cable to her husband, telling him why she wouldn't be stepping off the plane in New York. Next morning we called Pan American to have a definite date put on the airline ticket, but without luck. Realizing that last night's fiasco could be repeated, Laurie got reimbursement for the ticket. She said, disgustedly: "Well, Bunty, I'm through! I couldn't stand another disappointment like that, and bring my poor husband sixty miles to the airport for nothing. Damn that American Army Transportation Corps--they've won after all! I'll wait for a ship!"

Al: "SUNDAY, JANUARY 13: TRIED STRAIGHTENING UP MY ROOM. GOT EVERYTHING SET UP FOR WORK TOMORROW. BIG DAY. GLAD MY SUIT STILL FITS ME."

Bunty: "PAUL STOPPED IN FOR ANOTHER VISIT. LAURIE QUITE FASCINATED TO MEET A ROMAN CATHOLIC PRIEST. I DON'T FEEL TOO WELL."

Paul's visit was a good diversion for Laurie's troubles. His letters were still frequent but seeing him was better, like old times. I was glad to have him meet Laurie, who was by now my best friend. He was thoughtful as he listened to our chatter about trying to cross the Atlantic.

"Listening to you two is like a window into a whole different world for me, you know," he confided. "All I see these days is the seminary, Latin texts and preparations for the priesthood. It's a bit confining, to say the least, but I've decided this will be my life's work. But what a contrast; you both seem to have the world by the tail!"

My attention drifted away, back to our old childhood "gang". "How far apart we've all become," I thought, "my first crush, William, is working in his Dad's office in London as a quantity surveyor; Peter has started his own driving school, giving lessons to a booming generation of new car drivers; and Paul is on his way to ordination as a priest. No more secret codes, Monopoly marathons, homespun radio broadcasts, fishing for tadpoles--but what memories."

Al: "TUESDAY, JANUARY 15: SECOND DAY BACK AT WORK. FILLED OUT FORMS FOR DEDUCTIONS: SAVINGS PLAN, HEALTH INSURANCE, ETC. NONE OF GUYS HERE HAVE BEEN IN SERVICE. HARD TO FIND CONVERSATION. GOTTA LOT TO LEARN ABOUT JOB. LOTS OF STUDY,

TESTS, ETC. COMING UP. GOT MY NEW JERSEY DRIVER'S LICENCE. GLAD ALL FAMILY VISITING OVER. WROTE TO BUNTY, FIRST TIME I'VE HAD TIME TO WRITE HER A DECENT LETTER SINCE I ARRIVED HOME. RECEIVING HER MAIL O.K."

Bunty: "FELT SHIVERY AND DIZZY AT OFFICE. COULDN'T GET WARM. BY MID-AFTERNOON FELT REALLY SICK. CAME HOME AND WENT TO SEE DR. SAYS I HAVE 'FLU' AND ORDERED ME TO BED. NO LETTER FROM AL." My diary recorded that I spent the next four days in bed, with "HARDLY ENOUGH ENERGY OR DESIRE TO EAT, READ, OR EVEN DO ANY KNITTING."

Our family doctor made several visits to the house to see me. (In those days before routine flu shots, this was customary, believe it or not!) The cost of the visits and prescriptions were free, courtesy of the National Health Service.

A letter finally came from Al. I read aloud to Mom the parts that weren't private. Exuding wifely concern, I sympathized: "Poor lamb, he sounds so tired; no wonder he hasn't had time to write. I was beginning to get worried, but what a hectic itinerary he made for himself, starting the day after he arrived home from the Army! He must have traveled hundreds of miles to see his relatives in Pennsylvania and New Jersey! Then he left himself no time to rest up before reporting for work the day after he got back. It makes me feel tired just reading it all!"

Al: "TUESDAY, JANUARY 22: GOT FIRST WEEK'S PAYCHECK, $40.78 CLEAR. WILL GIVE MOM $10 PER WEEK. USE REST FOR BANK AND EXPENSES. OFFERED NASH CAR SALESMAN $325 FOR HIS TRADE-IN 1936 PLYMOUTH COUPE. THINK HE WANTS MORE, CAN'T AFFORD IT. HE'LL THINK IT OVER. OFFERED TO LET ME BORROW HIS CAR UNTIL I GET ONE."

Bunty: "WHEE! FIRST BATCH OF G. I. BRIDES WENT BY SPECIAL TRAIN TO TRANSIT CAMP TODAY, PRIOR TO BOARDING THE *S.S. ARGENTINA*

ON SATURDAY. CALLED JOAN. SHE'S LEAVING FOR CAMP NEXT WEEK! I'LL HAVE TO BEGIN PACKING MY TRUNK! AL HAS RECEIVED HIS FIRST PAYCHECK. WENT TO SEE DOCTOR. WILL GO BACK TO WORK MONDAY."

The news of the start of the G.I. Bride exodus made headlines in the London newspapers as well as across the Atlantic. Joan's voice sounded squeaky with excitement on the telephone: "Guess what, Bunty--I'm leaving for Tidworth Camp next Monday! I can hardly believe it! Bud tells me he went to visit Al. We'll all get together after you and I are both in Little Cedar River. See you soon, I hope!"

Al was pleased with his first paycheck. By 1946 standards it wasn't bad, but could we live on $30.78 per week? Luckily, I didn't see his diary with all the anticipated expenses; I might have unpacked my trunk!

For the G.I. Brides, the logjam of delays had finally broken, but where would I fit into the picture? I decided to find out!

Al: "TUESDAY, JANUARY 29: STUDYING AND TAKING TESTS AT WORK. ROTATING SHIFTS. EVENING AND MIDNIGHT SHIFTS HAVE OVERTIME. WE SURE NEED IT! SOLD MODEL A FORD FOR $80 TO ERNIE'S PARTNER. HE HAS SOLD PLYMOUTH TO SOMEONE ELSE. SAYS I CAN BORROW HIS OWN CAR FOR WORK. I CAN'T CARPOOL BECAUSE THERE'S NOT ALWAYS SOMEONE ON THE SAME SHIFT TO RIDE WITH FROM LITTLE CEDAR RIVER. ERNIE CAN SELL ME A 1937 NASH SEDAN FOR $450. NEEDS REPAIRS BUT HE HAS PROMISED CAR IN 10 DAYS."

Bunty: "LUNCH HOUR VISIT TO SEE THE ASSISTANT ADJUTANT GENERAL AT U.S. ARMY TRANSPORTATION OFFICE AT AMERICAN EMBASSY. FOR *MY* OFFICE AT B.O.A.C. THEY HAVE ADDED A NEW SHORTHAND-TYPIST. NOW I HAVE A STAFF OF *THREE*!"

If only Al had been able to keep his Model A Ford he would have made a fortune by waiting to sell it as an antique, but he needed that $80 badly! In the job that had been held open for him while he was in the Army, he was at the bottom of the ladder as a radioman at an A.T&.T. Overseas Radio Telephone Station that received radio traffic from all over the world and from ships at sea. Located out on the flat coastal marshes of the South Jersey shore, it was a 45- minute commute each way. The men who manned the maze of equipment were responsible for operating and maintaining it in accordance with the company-wide B.S.Ps (Bell System Practices), contained in the large volumes of printed matter at the radio station. The little brick building hummed twenty four hours a day, seven days a week, so there were three rotating shifts: 8 a.m. to 4 p.m., 4 p.m. to 12 midnight, and midnight to 8 a.m. Being "low man on the totem pole," Al had no trouble being assigned "evenings" and "midnights" as often as possible, to bring in the extra few dollars in overtime per week to help us make ends meet, but which would impose a hardship on our home life after I arrived.

Today, on the other side of the Atlantic, I hurried to the U.S. Army Transportation Office at the American Embassy. I needed someone to deal with other than the surly clerk who had processed my completed forms to allow me to be on the transportation list. The signature of the Assistant Adjutant General had been on the first letter I had received, outlining the red tape requirements in pursuit of the now-defunct Form 4.

Dad's advice to me had always been: "Start at the top, Bunty; there's more room up there than down at the bottom." So I put on my best "don't-mess-with-me" look, and told the receptionist that I wanted to see the Assistant Adjutant General. She shrank visibly, as if I had asked to see the President of the United States, then said: "Well, he's very busy, but I'll ask if he will see you."

To my amazement, she was back in a split second and said: "Please follow me." My knees felt as if they had turned to water, as I somehow stumbled down the hallway to the A.A.G.'s office.

The A.A.G. was a handsome young Army officer who grinned and thrust out his hand: "Hi, Mrs. Greene, I'm Lieutenant Mancini. Have a seat." I sat. "Ya know, I married an English gal, too. Trust me, I *do* understand how anxious you must be to join your husband."

He listened as I poured out my fear of having to wait months from now for my Travel Orders. The next words he uttered made me glad I was sitting down: "O.K., Bunty, you bring me a copy of your husband's discharge papers from the Army, and I'll send you your alerting papers two weeks afterwards. How's that?"

My feet hardly touched the ground as I raced back to my office, where another surprise was in store. That afternoon, an assistant to the B.O.A.C. Staffing Officer appeared with a young woman in tow. "Bunty, this is Beryl Short. She's a clerk typist to add to your staff."

Beryl was a brash, bright young thing with an ebullient personality and no apparent cares in the world, in contrast to my depressed but efficient helper, Fiona Campbell. I introduced her to Bert and Fiona. With a disarming smile, Beryl announced: "So glad to meet you. People tell me I have an excellent memory, and I placed third in my shorthand and typing classes at secretarial school, so I'm sure I'll be an asset to this office."

Beryl's precocious statement was greeted by the three of us with a stunned silence. I could almost hear Bert and Fiona thinking: "Wow, I love *me*; who do *you* love?"

I thought about the incumbent Fiona: "I wonder how soon Beryl will lock horns with her? Maybe it's a good thing I'll be leaving after all; I'll bet young Beryl already has her eye on *my* job!"

Beryl proved to be self-assured and competent; she was soon able to take over some of my ever-expanding office workload in areas too demanding for Fiona. Between the efforts of Bert and the two girls, I was now able to end my day without feeling exhausted and deadened by its nonstop demands. And I could hardly believe that I now had a staff of three to call my own!

Beryl's arrival now made a total of six new staff members in our Department since the beginning of the year. We would soon have to move to a larger office. I was experiencing, at first hand, signs of the postwar business expansion in Britain.

Al: "TUESDAY, FEBRUARY 5: LEARNING OPERATION AND MAINTENANCE OF EQUIPENT AT STATION; PASSED ALL TESTS, THANK GOOD-

NESS. ERNIE HAS BEGUN TO WORK ON THE NASH. STILL NEEDS WINDSHIELD AND LOW GEAR IN TRANSMISSION."

Bunty: "AL'S LETTERS NOW ENCLOSE PHOTOS OF LITTLE CEDAR RIVER. PRETTY LITTLE PLACE. BUILDINGS LOOK VERY TEMPORARY, BUILT OUT OF WOOD, NOT OF BRICK OR STONE AS THEY ARE IN ENGLAND."

In 1946 my intended new home, the semirural community of Little Cedar River, had a population of 4,600 people and was sixty miles from the nearest city. I pored over the photo of the picturesque river with a small white-painted gazebo in the foreground. The white-painted wooden buildings in the town looked like dolls' houses; the local bank reminded me of one in a Western movie. I could almost imagine there were hitching posts in front of the stores on Main Street.

"Mom, it looks lovely, but I wonder how I'll cope, without London just a bus ride away?" Remembering my passion for figure skating ongoing from childhood, I added ruefully: "And I'll bet there's no ice rink!"

Mom arranged the photos in a row on the dining room table. "Well, Bunty, you survived the war; you can survive this, too. I'm sure you'll adjust. And remember, you'll have Al and Laurie there with you,"

Al: "SATURDAY, FEBRUARY 9: BUD HOFFMAN CALLED. JOAN IS ARRIVING ON THE *QUEEN MARY* TOMORROW OR MONDAY. LUCKY GUY!"

Bunty: "COPY OF AL'S HONORABLE DISCHARGE PAPERS ARRIVED TODAY, SO I DASHED UP TO LONDON TO GIVE THEM TO THE A.A.G. AT THE U.S. ARMY TRANSPORTATION OFFICE. ANOTHER LETTER FROM AL."

Lieutenant Mancini was having another busy day, now that the ball was rolling with the sailing of the *Argentina*. The Transportation Office buzzed like a beehive; staff members working at fever pitch to cope with the logistics of moving seventy thousand women and their children from Britain to America in the ships available. To my surprise, the receptionist told me the A.A.G. himself would see me again. Once more came the cordial greeting and the invitation to sit. I sat. I handed him Al's papers. While I waited, I mused: "How did I ever get in to see him? Do I remind him of a favorite cousin? Or does he just need a diversion from the pile of papers on his desk? Or maybe he's been a Boy Scout and needs to do his good deed for the day?"

The A.A.G. looked up from checking Al's discharge papers and smiled: "Yes, Bunty, it looks like everything's O.K. I'll mail your alerting papers to you on Monday, then it won't be long before you'll get your sailing date."

I didn't know whether to laugh or cry. It was all I could do to get my wobbly legs to take me out of his office and back to the bus stop. I hoped I wouldn't upset Mom with the news.

Al's letter contained another surprise. Before we were married, Mom had done what she considered to be a mother's duty by giving him a book to read. I had already read it, but Al tucked it away in his duffle bag, and promised Mom he would read it as soon as he could. He mentioned it in his letter: "Hey, hon', I've finally had time to read the book your Mom gave to me before I left England. It's called *Sane Sex Life and Sane Sex Living*. At first I thought she was playing a joke on me, but no, it's serious: frank, explicit and tactful. In my opinion this book would be hard to surpass in its excellence."

I gasped. I had always wondered what Al really thought of that book! Would he ridicule it? Tears of relief came to my eyes as I read reassurance in the familiar handwriting of this loving, gentle man.

Al: "SATURDAY, FEBRUARY 16: CALLED REAL ESTATE AGENT AND WAS SHOWN SEVERAL HOUSES FOR SALE. DECIDED ON ONE OF THEM. NEEDS WORK, BUT LOVELY LITTLE HOUSE. TOOK PHOTOS OF IT TO SEND TO MY HONEY."

Bunty: "MY TWENTIETH BIRTHDAY. NOT A WORD FROM THE ASSISTANT ADJUTANT GENERAL ALL WEEK. I'M FURIOUS! WENT TO THE TRANSPORTATION OFFICE IN MY LUNCH HOUR TO SEE HIM

AGAIN. HE APOLIGIZED FOR BREAKING HIS PROMISE, AND 'PASSED THE BUCK' BY INTRODUCING ME TO MISS WALTERS. SHE IS IN CHARGE OF ALLOCATING ALL THE SPACE ON THE BRIDE SHIPS. I THINK I'VE FOUND THE RIGHT PERSON."

Where were the alerting papers for my sailing date, promised a week ago by my friend (or so I thought at the time), Lieutenant Mancini? I was much more concerned about his broken promise to put those papers in the mail a week ago than I was about celebrating my birthday. Now that I was twenty, I felt old enough to assert myself. I stormed up to the American Embassy and once again the receptionist ushered me in to the A.A.G.'s office. I was about to get an unexpected birthday present.

Lieutenant Mancini looked up from his desk when he saw me in the doorway. "Oh, my God, Bunty," he exclaimed, "I promised you your alerting papers, didn't I? Clean forgot--sorry!" He thought for a minute. "I'll tell ya what I'll do." He turned around to his filing cabinet and pulled out a drawer. "Here's a blank copy of the Sailing Questionnaire form that we send out with the alerting papers. You can sit down right now and fill it out. I'll sign it and hand you over to Miss Walters, my assistant. She allocates all the space on the bride ships; she'll take good care of you." He pressed a buzzer on his desk.

I nearly passed out with surprise! Now I was sure I must remind him of his favorite cousin. Or did he need to record another Boy Scout good deed today?

There was a polite knock on the open office door, and in came Miss Walters. A brusque, well-dressed Englishwoman in her mid-thirties, she had a pleasant face and a kind smile. "Bunty," she said, "I must tell you right now that I can't promise you will sail before April at the earliest, and most probably not until June. The ships are filling up with girls who were on the list long before you."

My face must have registered disappointment bordering on tears. Miss Walters suddenly said: "Look, we're terribly busy today, but come and see me early next Saturday when the office isn't so busy, and I'll see what I can do."

My diary said: "I'M LUCKY--AT LEAST I'LL GET TO SEE HER AGAIN. MAYBE I CAN TALK HER INTO SOMETHING. I'LL HAVE TO PREPARE MY 'CASE'"

I had obviously seen one too many American "private eye" movies!

Bunty: "FRIDAY, FEBRUARY 22: AL'S DONE IT AGAIN! NOW HE'S BUYING A HOUSE! HE SENT SEVERAL PHOTOS. VERY NICE. MAYBE THEY WILL HELP ME WITH MISS WALTERS TOMORROW."

Al's photos of the house were lovely; they showed a little two-bedroom ranch house ("bungalow" to the British,) surrounded by pine trees and a pleasant expanse of green lawn overlooked by an open porch. I trusted Al's judgment about the interior.

I had always believed fervently that my life was in God's hands. To my mind this had been proved, time after time, during those life-threatening days of the war. And now here I was, one day before going to see Miss Walters to plead my case for an early sailing date, and God had hand-ed me my argument with Al's letter! Al had written: "You know, Bunty, I want our home to be in joint ownership, so you will have to sign the sales agreement as well as myself. It's a nice house in good condition and within our price range, but I'm worried that the real estate salesman won't hold it for us for very long."

I said to myself: "If I don't get across the ocean in time to sign those papers, we could lose the house. I'll take the photos and Al's letter with me tomorrow. If Miss Walters has a magic wand, with a little bit of luck she just might wave it for us! Waiting until June for Travel Orders would be horrible!"

Preparations and Goodbyes

Al: "SATURDAY, FEBRUARY 23: HAVE APPLIED FOR A $5,000 G.I. LOAN FOR HOUSE. BROTHER BILL HAS BECOME ENGAGED TO MARJIE McCAFFERTY! CALLS HER A 'SLICK CHICK'! BUD HOFFMAN BROUGHT

WIFE JOAN TO MEET ME. SHE HAS A DISTINCT BRITISH ACCENT! ALL OF US WENT TO VISIT McCAFFERTYS. SHOWED THEM BUNTY'S AND MY WEDDING PICTURES. GREATLY ADMIRED. THEY LOVE MY WIFE. SO DO I--YOU BET!"

Bunty: "WENT TO AMERICAN EMBASSY TO SEE MIS WALTERS. SHOWED HER PHOTOS OF THE HOUSE. SHE SAYS SHE CAN PUT ME ON A SHIP THAT WILL SAIL ON MARCH 19TH! THAT'S ONLY THREE AND A HALF WEEKS FROM NOW! NO WAITING UNTIL JUNE! WHOOPEE! I CAN'T BELIEVE IT!"

Miss Walters looked at the photos Al had sent me, and I read to her the part of his letter about needing my signature for joint ownership of the house. She thought for a moment, then said: "Yes, Bunty, you young folks will need that new home. The ships are filling up fast, but I can put you on one sailing on March 19th. Will that do?"

Would it do? I was speechless. I was even too surprised to cry! I put out my hand and she clasped it. There was no need for words.

In the street outside the Embassy there was a woman selling sweet-scented English violets. Impulsively, I bought three bunches and took them back to Miss Walters. I caught her coming out of her office. I whispered: "Miss Walters, just a small 'thank you.'"

The tears in her eyes, as she buried her face in the sweet-scented fragrance of the purple blossoms, matched my own tears of gratitude.

Al: "MONDAY, FEBRUARY 25: THINGS GOING PAINFULLY SLOWLY. EXHAUSTED ON NIGHT WORK AT RADIO STATION. HOUSE NEEDS APPRAISAL BEFORE LOAN IS APPROVED. HAVE TO WAIT. MAY NEVER GET IT BEFORE BUNTY ARRIVES. ERNIE FINALLY SHOWED ME OLD NASH AMBASSADOR HE WANTS TO SELL ME. BODY IS IN BEAUTIFUL CONDITION. OLD, BUT TOP OF THE LINE. WORTH WAITING FOR NEW PARTS, BUT REPLACEMENTS HARD TO FIND. NEEDS NEW WINDSHIELD. I NEED A CAR SO BADLY!"

Bunty: "GAVE FREDDY A WEEK'S NOTICE AT THE OFFICE. THOUGHT HE WOULD BURST A BLOOD VESSEL, BUT HE'LL GET OVER IT. AL'S LETTER FULL OF WOES OVER JOB, HOUSE, CAR."

My boss had been expecting my resignation, but evidently not so soon. My diary entry continued: "HE WENT AROUND ALL DAY IN A COMPLETE DAZE AND DIDN'T EVEN RECOVER ENOUGH TO TOUCH ANY OF THE CORRESPONDENCE!" Looking at this entry again so many years later I thought it sounded a bit exaggerated, but then I remembered the days of peril we all went through together at the office during Hitler's savage attacks on London with his 'Vengeance Weapons' in 1944: the remote-controlled V-1 "flying bombs" and the indiscriminately-aimed V-2 supersonic rocket missiles. Common danger had developed a close bond of friendship and mutual concern between us that couldn't be forgotten.

Al's latest letter reflected his current problems. He wrote: "These rotating shifts at the radio station are for the birds! I no sooner get used to a week on day shift than I'm working the evening and midnight shifts. I'm tired all the time." The letter went on: "No news from Ernie about repairs for the 1937 Nash. He has ordered parts he needs, but I guess it will take time. I hate to have to borrow cars. But if I take the bus I have to walk one and a half miles on the private road out to the radio station on the marshes every time. Can't find any other car to buy, so I guess I'll just have to wait. Meantime, I may accept Ernie's partner's offer to lend me his own personal car. I'll be a nervous wreck in case I scratch it! Rats!

"The appraiser hasn't given his report on the house yet to the realtor. I guess we'll have to wait for that, too. Civilian life isn't as easy as I thought!"

Al: "THURSDAY, FEBRUARY 28: RECEIVED A LETTER FROM MY LOVE. SHE'S BEEN TOLD SHE WILL BE SAILING FOR U.S. ON MARCH 19TH! I FEEL ELATED AND EXCITED, SO HAPPY I CAN HARDLY KEEP STILL A MOMENT!"

Bunty: "PEOPLE KEEP TAKING ME OUT FOR LUNCH AND TEA. ALL THIS 'GOODBYE' STUFF IS QUITE SAD IN A WAY, BUT I'M SO EXCITED. ALL I NEED NOW ARE MY OFFICIAL TRAVEL ORDERS!"

I thought: "Strange how my life can be such a mixture of joy and sadness: joy for the approaching reality of being with Al, and sadness in realizing that after saying goodbye to so many people I may never see them again."

Bunty: "SATURDAY, MARCH 2: MY LAST SATURDAY 'ON' AND LAST DAY AT B.O.A.C. FREDDY CAME IN AND I HELPED HIM CLEAN UP THE REMAINING CORRESPONDENCE. WE PACKED UP EARLY AT 3 P.M. I'LL SAY OFFICIAL GOODBYES TO OFFICE WHEN I RECEIVE MY TRAVEL ORDERS. LAURIE HAS RECEIVED HERS! LETTER FROM CLEVELAND, OHIO. KATE AND FRANK KOPECK HAVE A BABY BOY!"

My last week at the office was one of turmoil: the retraining of my staff, lunches out, tea parties, goodbyes, tears, laughter. In the midst of it all, Laurie received her Travel Orders for Tidworth Camp.

The Kopecks' birth announcement was a surprise. I had trouble visualizing as a father the glamorous Ninth Air Force aerial gunner I had known, but the letter also said I should write as soon as I arrived in the U.S. Frank Kopeck would remain in touch over the following years until he died, still heartbroken, several years after Kate had passed away.

Al: "WEDNESDAY, MARCH 6: APPRAISAL ON THE HOUSE IS $2,000 LOWER THAN THE ASKING PRICE. CAN'T RAISE THAT AMOUNT EXTRA. HAVE TO GET THE OWNER TO LOWER PRICE IF LOAN IS TO BE APPROVED. REALTOR TRIED TO GET HIM TO COME DOWN IN PRICE, BUT HE HAS REFUSED. IT'S A SELLER'S MARKET. DEAL HAS FALLEN THROUGH. HOW CAN I TELL BUNTY?"

Bunty: "MOM AND I WENT UP TO WATERLOO STATION IN LONDON TO SEE LAURIE OFF FOR TIDWORTH CAMP. SHE SAILS ON THE *QUEEN*

MARY. INCREDIBLE THAT I'LL SEE HER AGAIN SOON, ON THE OTHER SIDE OF THE OCEAN! ARRIVED HOME TO FIND MY TRAVEL ORDERS HAD ARRIVED! I GO TO TIDWORTH ON MARCH 14TH, SAIL ON THE 19TH ON THE SHIP *E.B. ALEXANDER!*"

Laurie's parents were with her on the station platform when Mom and I arrived to see her off for Tidworth transit camp on the specially chartered G.I. Brides' train. At the camp, the brides would await transportation to Southampton to sail on one of the "bride ships", as they had been dubbed.

Dozens of G.I. Brides and their family groups joined those already on the platform. Many girls with toddlers, babies or both, were exchanging hugs and kisses with relatives and friends who would be left behind. For some of them this would be a final goodbye--they knew they could never hope to meet again.

One last hug for her parents, Mom and me, and Laurie joined other girls at the train windows. We waved; the train moved away. Her parents sobbed, and we exchanged one last quick embrace with them before going our separate ways.

When Mom and I arrived back at Bishop's Hill, we found that the mailman had left a large manila envelope while we were away. Struggling to keep my hands from shaking, I opened it, eyes searching under a supply of luggage labels for the most important item. There it was: my Travel Orders! I was to leave Waterloo Station for Tidworth Camp on March 14th. The photos of the house had worked! God bless Miss Walters!

Al: "SATURDAY, MARCH 9: BILL DROVE TO SHENANDOAH TO BRING MOM HOME FROM HER R&R. SHE GOES OFF QUITE OFTEN TO VISIT HER TWO SISTERS, THERE AND AT BOOTHWYN, PA. WILL BE GLAD TO HAVE HER BACK. I'M OUT OF CLEAN SHIRTS AND TIRED OF EATING SANDWICHES! BUNTY LEAVES FOR CAMP ON MARCH 14TH, SAILING ON 19TH. EXCITED."

Bunty: "WENT BY TRAIN WITH MOM TO KINGSWOOD, TO VISIT HELEN AND MRS. HOLLINGSWORTH, BEFORE I LEAVE FOR THE U.S.

A MYSTERIOUS LETTER HAD ARRIVED FOR ME WHEN WE RETURNED, FROM A MRS. MARSH, POSTMARKED WREXHAM."

Mrs. Hollingsworth was my godmother. Mr. Hollingsworth had been stationmaster at Kampala, capital of Uganda, where I was born. With my parents, they were part of the small British community who clung together for social respite in the harsh equatorial climate of Central East Africa. The Hollingsworths had kept in touch with us over the years, after we returned from Africa when I was very young. After he retired, Mr. Hollingsworth brought his wife and daughter back to England and they moved into a grand house in a suburban town on the outskirts of the London area, where they continued the lifestyle they had become accustomed to in Africa.

A uniformed maid opened the door when Mom rang the bell. She took our coats, then stood politely in the background while Mrs. Hollingsworth and Helen came into the front hall to greet us, arms outstretched. I thought I was looking at a movie set in one of those films about generations of an aristocratic family. My godmother was a serene, beautiful woman. She smiled in welcome, standing tall in her black taffeta dress, her white hair coiled in a perfect bun on top of her head. Helen looked forty and spinsterish in her slightly old-fashioned skirt and blouse, but her cheeks were pink with excitement, as if visitors were few.

They hugged us delightedly. In her soft, cultured voice, Mrs. Hollingsworth said: "You may bring us tea in the drawing room, Effie." The maid disappeared and Helen led us through the front hall into the elegant living room.

Mr. Hollingsworth had recently died. Mom and I murmured our condolences. Helen gave me a hug. "Bunty, I can hardly believe you're a married woman! I remember when I was just a young girl in Africa, watching Mummy holding you in her arms when you were christened by the Anglican Bishop of Uganda in Namirembe Cathedral."

I wallowed pleasantly in the deep sofa as Mom, Helen and Mrs. Hollingsworth exchanged reminiscences of life in Africa. Soon Effie reappeared with a large silver tray on which stood an ornate silver tea service and tiered china serving plates adorned with tea sandwiches and little cakes.

This charming goodbye visit, complete with its luxurious English "low tea" (when tea is served on a low table), still lives on in my memory. It was the last time I would ever see the stately woman who was my godmother.

Back at Bishop's Hill there was a letter from a Mrs. Ethel Marsh. I knew her as Ethel Watkins, when we were at school together during my two years as a refugee in North Wales in World War Two, when Mom and I had escaped to Wrexham to wait until the War Damage Commission had repaired the severe bomb damage which had made our home unfit to live in.

With curves in all the right places, blonde hair and blue eyes, Ethel had been the envy of my life and my academic arch-rival at Wrexham Park girls' prep school, and yet we became good friends. Ethel had gone on without me to Bangor University, while I reluctantly came back to London with Mom, after which we lost touch with each other. My school friends Bessie and Maggie had written to tell me that she had met and married an American soldier.

Hearing the news from Bessie and Maggie that I was about to leave England for the U.S. had prompted Ethel to write to me. She was impatiently waiting to sail to New York, then to take the train across the continent to her new home in the western United States. The prep school snobbishness of which we were both guilty showed through her words. Her letter said, in part: "I'll be reporting to Tidworth on the 14th, too! I must say I'm not relishing the voyage in the company of the 'Great Unwashed': those rag-tag members of the G.I. Bride sisterhood. But I hope, Bunty, that we'll sail together! Wouldn't that be something?"

I squirmed at the thought! Ethel wasn't exactly the person whose company I would enjoy as a traveling companion, with that kind of talk! But I said to myself: "Oh well, I'll look for her on the passenger list anyway--but I hope she won't be on the same ship as me!" There was to be irony in Ethel's story, as it unfolded later.

Al: "TUESDAY, MARCH 12: PARTS FOR NASH DUE TO ARRIVE AROUND THE 27TH. LOOKS LIKE BUNTY AND THE CAR WILL ARRIVE TOGETHER. APPLIED FOR A WEEK'S VACATION BEGINNING MARCH 31."

Bunty: "BUSY DAY. CLOSED OUT MY BANK ACCOUNT. ARRANGED BANK DRAFT TO BE SENT TO AL'S BANK IN THE U.S. CHANGED SOME POUNDS INTO DOLLARS. INSURED MY BAGGAGE. WENT TO HAIRDRESSER AND HAD A PERM."

The bus brought me to my branch bank's main office in London to effect the transactions in foreign exchange that the local branch couldn't handle. After insuring my baggage, I found myself on Buckingham Palace Road near Airways House, so I went in to say last goodbyes at the office before checking in for a perm with the hairdresser. I was determined not to let myself "get mushy," as Dad would have said.

The usual mayhem prevailed in the Diplomatic Mail and Cargo Department. I bit my lip and thought: "This is how I'll remember it, and I won't miss it at all. No sentimentality for me!"

I hadn't counted on Freddy's discreet cough as his voice broke when he wished me good luck; or Syd's grip on my hand until I felt it might be permanently flattened; or Brad's mournful face looking even more mournful; or Buzz fingering Bill Bauer's U.S. Air Force wings on his breast pocket, where he had pinned them the day I gave them to him after becoming engaged to Al; or Fiona weeping into her Scottish tartan handkerchief. Despite my best intentions, I broke down and "got mushy."

Al: "WEDNESDAY, MARCH 13: VACATION APPROVED. CHEE, TODAY IS ONE LESS TO WAIT. BUNTY MADE FRONT PAGE NEWS IN THE *ATLANTIC CITY PRESS!* ARTICLE SAYS SHE WILL ARRIVE MARCH 27 ALONG WITH THE SEVERAL HUNDRED OTHER WAR BRIDES ON THE *E.B.ALEXANDER.*"

Bunty: "PAT PRINGLE CAME FOR A SHORT VISIT. SHE'S COMING TOMORROW TO SEE ME OFF! SAID GOODBYE TO NEIGHBOURS. NO TEARS--NONE LEFT!"

Al thought his coworker from Atlantic City was kidding when he told him that his wife had made the front page of the city newspaper, but he believed it when he saw the newspaper article. The flurry of publicity caused by the early G.I. Bride sailings had given the American press a field day, and obviously the local papers weren't going to be left behind!

Excitement electrified every word in my diary. My cabin trunk already had been sent ahead to Waterloo Station; soon the last suitcase was locked and strapped ready for the voyage. Saying goodbye to the neighbors was more difficult than I thought. My diary reported: "BUT I KEPT THE GOOD OLD ENGLISH 'STIFF UPPER LIP.' THE HARDEST GOODBYES WERE FOR WILLIAM'S MOM AND DAD, AND THE COLEMANS NEXT DOOR. BOTH LADIES CRIED BUCKETS, AND I THOUGHT MY HAND WOULD FALL OFF, WILLIAM'S DAD SHOOK IT SO LONG."

I felt I was leaving a vital part of my life behind; I had known most of the neighbors since I was eight years old, and we had gone through the trauma of the war years together in the close bonds of comradeship fashioned by a common danger. Some of the neighbors gave me little goodbye gifts; knick-knacks that I still treasure.

Tidworth Camp

Al: "THURSDAY, MARCH 14: MOM AND AMY WENT TO PHILADELPHIA ON THE TRAIN TO GET SOME THINGS FOR BUNTY'S ARRIVAL. I HAD TO TAKE BUS THEN WALK ONE AND A HALF MILES AGAIN TO RADIO STATION TO WORK. GOT TO FIND AN ALTERNATIVE."

Bunty: "THE GREAT DAY HAS DAWNED! PILED LUGGAGE INTO THE TAXI, BOUND FOR WATERLOO STATION. TRAIN LEFT AT 2 P.M. ARRIVED AT TIDWORTH CAMP AT 5:30. WAS ASSIGNED TO A LARGE BRICK HUT AT FOWLER BARRACKS. SETTLED IN O.K. DINNER: REAL

STEAK, PEAS, POTATOES, THEN CANNED PEARS, ICE CREAM AND COFFEE. SCRUMPTIOUS! STOPPED IN AT RED CROSS RECREATION HALL, AND WHO SHOULD BE THERE BUT *LAURIE!*"

We arrived at Waterloo Station well ahead of the train's departure time. Dad's idea of being on time for a train was to arrive two hours ahead of schedule; needless to say, he had never missed a train in his entire life! The scene on the platform was one of "organized chaos" with G.I. Brides converging on Waterloo Station brandishing their Travel Orders, adding to the complex logistics of the transportation of the largest single immigrant group in United States history.

The train was filling up; one of the special "G.I. Bride Trains" loaned to the U. S. Army to take us to Tidworth Camp, a few miles from the port of Southampton, where we would be "processed" and wait for our designated ship. Mom, Dad, Pat Pringle and Laurie's Mom and Dad were all on the station platform to see me off. I felt very touched that Laurie's parents had come to demonstrate their friendship for me that had developed since Laurie and I had met.

Laurie's Dad seemed very emotional and fidgety. He suddenly broke away and trotted down the platform to the station lunchroom, returning with a brown paper bag which he thrust into my hands. I looked into it and saw two large, fat, sticky buns.

"Just thought you might be hungry on the train, Bunty," he explained. "Good luck, and give Laurie our love when you see her in the U.S."

His simple act of thoughtfulness has stayed in my memory. It was almost departure time. Laurie's Mom gave me a hug and a kiss, and her husband pressed my hand emotionally. As they turned and walked away down the platform they looked back, and waved.

Pat put her arms around me and said: "Now don't forget to write, Bunty. I promise I'll report on everything I know that might interest you about London and what's going on in my life. No wedding bells for me, so far!"

Mom and Dad hugged me, tears flowing. I struggled not to cry, trying to make them feel better about our parting, but when I found a seat in one of the train compartments, I buried my face in the upholstery and sobbed. Sounds of sniffling and nose-blowing came from the five other occupants, but as soon as we had recovered our composure we all began chatting excitedly like old pals.

The train journey passed quickly. At Tidworth station we boarded waiting buses which took us to the transit camp: a huge, sprawling complex at the edge of desolate moorland a few miles from the port of Southampton.

It was late afternoon when a group of us was deposited from the bus in front of a brick hut at Fowler Barracks. I remember a row of army beds on each side of a long, chilly room, and on the wall behind each, just one wire hanger to hold our clothes. The room soon filled up with an assortment of women, some with babies and/or small children. I unpacked my night clothes and tucked them under my pillow. Sitting on the next bed was a cheerful young woman by the name of Dorothy (call me "Dot"), short, dark-haired and dark-eyed, and as round as she was tall. Dot was bound for Raleigh, North Carolina. We shook hands and instantly became friends, but we would have been surprised at that moment to know we would stay in contact for years to come.

We washed up as best we could and walked down to the mess hall for dinner. And what a dinner! My diary's daily inch of space was filled as it itemized the prewar delicacies. After dinner, Dot and I wandered into the Red Cross recreation hall. I blinked hard in disbelief. There, sitting on the edge of the stage, with her long legs dangling, was *Laurie!* How could this be possible, when she should have been almost on the other side of the Atlantic by this time?

Laurie spotted me. She sprang off her perch on the stage and ran down the hall to throw her arms around me.

"I can't believe it's really you, Bunty! Oh, I'll *never* get to America," she lamented, "more than a thousand of us were due to sail on the *Queen Mary* days ago, but she developed some kind of trouble and will have to stay in a Southampton dock until it's fixed. We were all left here at

Tidworth to be divided among the next available ships! I've been reassigned to the *E.B. Alexander*."

I wondered if I'd heard right! I stammered: "Laurie, you'll never believe this, but that's *my* ship! Laurie and I joined hands and danced up and down with joy. My joy was cut short when a horrible thought struck me. I thought: "I wonder if I'll be dumped off the *E.B. Alexander* to make room for one of the girls displaced from the *Queen Mary*?" But then I remembered one of Mom's favorite sayings: "Don't borrow trouble," and decided to let fate take its course.

Al: "FRIDAY, MARCH 15: BEAUTIFUL SPRING DAY. AM BEGINNING TO MAKE SENSE OF THE RADIO EQUIPMENT AT WORK. MY DOG BOBBIE WAS FOUND DEAD. MOM THINKS HE WAS POISONED. I'LL MISS HIM, HAD HIM SINCE HE WAS A PUP. BUNTY AND I WILL HAVE TO GET A NEW DOG AS SOON AS WE HAVE A HOME OF OUR OWN."

Bunty: "DOT AND I WERE RISING AND SHINING AT 6:30, AFTER BEING KEPT AWAKE HALF THE NIGHT BY THREE WAILING BABIES. WENT TO VISIT LAURIE AT HER BARRACKS HUT. HAD A "MEDICAL EXAM." UGH! WROTE LETTERS, THEN WENT TO MOVIES."

"Good morning, Dot." It was getting light outside.

Dot stretched and yawned. "Oh, what a miserable night! We might just as well get up, Bunty, now that we can see what we're doing. Let's get out of here and find some breakfast."

Never having had to share my own comfortable bedroom, I had trouble with this draughty hut where I had to adjust to more than twenty roommates, three of them howling infants. It must have been a nightmare for the poor mothers with very few amenities to make formula or to wash diapers (disposable ones hadn't yet been invented,) but *I* needed a night's sleep, too. Dot and I washed, dressed and left.

Many G.I. Brides have written about these so-called "medical examinations" with a mixture of outrage and amusement. This morning we were told to report to our huts at 10 a.m., take off all our clothes and put on our coats, leaving them open at the front. I suppressed a giggle as I saw my hut-mates lined up by their beds, each one modestly clutching the front of her coat. We shivered as the March chill penetrated the hut while we awaited the examination.

I turned to Dot: "Whatever kind of examination d'you think this can be, Dot? We've already had a medical before we left London."

Dot shrugged, and I heard her teeth chattering. We didn't have long to wait to find out about the examination. A young American army doctor burst through the door of the hut, followed closely by an enlisted man with a clipboard. The girl nearest to the door was visibly rattled as the officer barked at her: "Lift yore arms above yore head, ma'am."

The poor girl looked embarrassed, but obediently raised both arms, losing her grip on her raincoat, which flew open. The officer produced a flashlight and shone it under each arm. He nodded to the enlisted man, who checked something off on his clipboard. The officer then said loudly: "You can put yore arms down, ma'am. Now spread yore legs apart."

The girl flushed, but did as he said. The officer peered into her open coat, shone the flashlight between the girl's legs, nodded again to the clipboard jockey, and said: "Thank you, ma'am. You can button up yore coat now."

The rest of us were aghast at what we had just witnessed, but the two men continued with the same procedure down the rows of women on each side of the hut, obviously looking for signs of insects, or V.D., or both. The humiliation made me feel as if I were one of the "great unwashed" in Ethel Watkins' letter. "Examination" completed, the two men turned on their heels and went back through the door as quickly as they had entered.

Pandemonium broke out in the hut. One furious female voice rose above the others: "The U.S. Army and the American Red Cross will hear about this," she cried. I'm going to see the Commanding Officer as soon as I'm dressed and decent again!"

I said to Dot: "When I tell Al about this, he'll say he was glad he wasn't here or he would have punched them both on the nose. Oh, well, we'll never see any of these people again, so it's not worth wasting our energy complaining. I just hope those two guys will get enough kicks after doing this to a few hundred girls that it'll cure them of ever wanting to look at another woman--at least for awhile!"

Al: "SATURDAY, MARCH 16: GETTING MOM'S HOUSE READY FOR THE GREAT DAY--BUNTY'S ARRIVAL. NEW LINOLEUM ON KITCHEN FLOOR. CLEANED UP BACKYARD AFTER WORK. PAINTED GARDEN SHED. GAVE BILL AND AMY BACK THEIR CLOTHES PARKED IN MY BEDROOM CLOSET WHILE I WAS AWAY."

Bunty: "HITCHHIKED WITH DOT TO COLLECT OUR P.X. RATIONS. VISITED WITH LAURIE. ALL PROCESSING IS NOW COMPLETE. CUSTOMS OFFICERS CHECKED OUR HAND BAGGAGE. I NARROWLY MISSED HAVING ALL MY PERFUME CONFISCATED! WE'RE LEAVING TIDWORTH AT 8 A.M. ON MONDAY!"

Going to the P.X. was like going to heaven after the severe ongoing rationing in England. We collected chocolate bars, lipstick and nail polish like so many Alices in Wonderland.

Customs officers came to our hut and went through our hand luggage that afternoon. I smiled at my diary entry. "All my perfume" consisted of four small bottles, all except one of which had already been opened, therefore not eligible for confiscation. The remains of "Ashes of Roses" and "London Violets" had been birthday presents from my teenage friends William and Peter years ago, and the dark blue bottle of "Evening in Paris" was from my erstwhile friend Arnie at Rainbow Corner, before I knew Al. Most important, the unopened bottle of "Chanel Number Five" that Al had sent me when he passed through Paris on his way to Germany went undetected, lying snuggled under a tube of toothpaste in my cosmetics bag.

Al: "SUNDAY, MARCH 17: HAD TO WORK TODAY. NOT SURE I'M ENJOYING THIS JOB, BUT NOTHING ELSE AVAILABLE IN THIS AREA.

CAR STILL NOT READY. HATE TO KEEP BORROWING. THE NASH IS SO OLD IT'S HARD TO FIND PARTS, SO WILL HAVE TO WAIT. RATS!"

Bunty: "TOMORROW WE SAIL! BOY, WILL I BE GLAD TO LEAVE THE CAMP! FROM THE TALES I'M HEARING, I'M SURPRISED LAURIE HAS SURVIVED BEING HERE FOR EIGHT DAYS."

My ecstasy at the prospect of leaving Tidworth was not only because it would bring me a step closer to seeing Al again, but because of the rumors that had been running rampant among the G.I. Brides.

As we prepared for bed on the day after our arrival, Dot had sounded worried: "I say, Bunty, have you heard a rumor about the P.O.W.s poisoning the hot chocolate?"

The camp was serviced by leftover German and Italian prisoners of war, detained there during the conflict and not yet repatriated to their home countries. They did the cooking and served us good food; we especially relished the rich, delicious real hot chocolate drink, another treat we hadn't tasted for years. However, a wild rumor ran through our huts about the hot chocolate being poisoned, followed by another unsubstantiated one accusing the P.O.W.s of poisoning the babies' formula.

Heeding the rumor, Dot and I avoided the hot chocolate, "just in case." Unfortunately, the rumor about the formula was suspect in the minds of some of the young mothers when, during succeeding voyages, their babies became sick with gastroenteritis after leaving the camp. Tragically, we heard later that some of the babies actually died after becoming violently ill aboard at least one of the bride ships. My heart went out to those poor girls and their babies, and to the G.I. fathers who would share their anguish. I said a prayer of thanks for being spared this ordeal.

Although most of us probably came from average, middle class homes, the G.I. Brides were still a "mixed bag", from all walks of life and levels of society and with many different gradations of intelligence and education. The G.I. husbands were just as much of a mixture, and just as much of a gamble as marriage partners as the girls were for them. I later heard from my friend Maggie in Wrexham, North Wales, that the snobbish Ethel Watkins from our prep school days had sailed away with the "great unwashed", arrived at her new home in the western U.S., and found it to be what she described disgustedly as "a dilapidated cabin clinging to the side of a mountain". In a week she was on her way back to Wales and a divorce.

However, Ethel's experience turned out to be the exception rather than the rule. A generation after World War Two, authors have published statistics from sources such as the National Archives in Washington, D.C., the Public Records Office in London, questionnaires and personal interviews. Surprisingly, the British G. I. Bride divorce rate was found to be below the national average for the United States.

Back at Tidworth Camp, Dot and I were sleepless with excitement.

Ship Ahoy!

Al: "MONDAY, MARCH 18: TOO BAD ABOUT OUR HOUSE. I THOUGHT PRICE WAS INFLATED, ANYWAY. WAS SHOWN ANOTHER HOUSE, BUT WILL WAIT FOR BUNTY BEFORE LOOKING AT ANY MORE REAL ESTATE. RECEIVED CABLE FROM MY LOVE; SHE SAILED TODAY ON THE *E.B. ALEXANDER*. WILL ARRIVE MARCH 27. CAN HARDLY WAIT-- GEEZ, I'M A LUCKY GUY!"

Bunty: "DAY OF GREAT EVENTS! UP AT CRACK OF DAWN TO WASH AND PACK. BREAKFAST AT 7 A.M. TRAIN LEFT TIDWORTH AT 10:30 FOR SOUTHAMPTON. BOARDED OUR SHIP, THE *E.B. ALEXANDER*. SAILED AT 3 P.M. TODAY INSTEAD OF TOMORROW. SENT CABLE TO AL. HAD A WONDERFUL DINNER. WE ALL FEEL GREAT TODAY. I HAVE A COMFY FIRST CLASS STATEROOM WITH THREE OTHERS!"

There was so much to write about the sea voyage and so little space in my diary. I should have kept a separate journal of the voyage, but I was probably too excited to think of it.

A copy of the passenger list was on my bunk. I looked through it for Mrs. Ethel Marsh, but there was no sign of her name. Relieved, I knew nothing more about her until the letter came from Maggie, months later.

As I discovered many years later by reading her history, the elderly 22,000-ton *Edmund B. Alexander* had a fascinating life story. Originally fueled by coal, she was built in 1905 at Belfast, Northern Ireland for a German passenger line, and named *Amerika*. When she was built, she was the largest ship of her kind in the world. She sailed as a passenger liner from 1905 to 1914 between Hamburg and New York. On one of these voyages, on April 14, 1912, the *Amerika* was one of the ships that sent a radio message warning of icebergs in the North Atlantic near where the *Titanic* struck one and sank a few hours later.

Seized by the U.S. upon its entry into World War One and refitted as a troop ship, our ship's name was respelled *America*. She transported more than 40,000 troops to France, then brought another 51,000 back after the war. Subsequently, she sank at her berth in New York (could it have been from sheer exhaustion?), was raised and reconditioned, then sailed as a liner for the United States Lines.

In 1921, she survived a disastrous fire, was rebuilt and sailed again as a liner until 1931. She was laid up for nine years, then refitted as the oil-burning U. S. Army Transport *E.B. Alexander*, named after an American war hero of the 1800s. By 1946, she had again been refitted, and was capable of carrying as many as 904 war brides and 314 children at a time, from Europe to the U.S. Sadly, in 1957 she was sold for scrap. After reading her history, I was rather glad I hadn't known it when I stepped on board!

Reading Al's letter, I was disappointed to lose the house we had hoped to call home. Real estate was at a premium after World War Two, dominated by sellers whose greed drove up prices beyond the reach of many returning G.I.s. However, looking on the bright side, the photos I had brought to show Miss Walters of the little house which would never now be ours, had enabled me to travel to America much sooner than if I hadn't had them--so the house had served its purpose, after all!

On the *E.B. Alexander,* as at Tidworth, no discrimination was shown in assigning accommodations. However, as the voyage progressed there was some sorting out that went on, especially when one bride demanded the removal of one of her roommates after she was found consorting with one of the ship's crew. I thought: "I wonder if it's the same one they found in a field with one of the P.O.W.s that night at Tidworth?"

Because of the last-minute reshuffle, the G.I. Brides from the *Queen Mary,* who had now been assigned to the *E.B. Alexander,* boarded her first. Standing in the long line of girls and their children waiting to board, I watched with envy as Laurie marched up the ship's gangplank. As more and more girls boarded, I struggled with this morbid thought: "Laurie was one of the first to board; I'll bet she will have a wonderful cabin on one of the top decks. By the time it's my turn, I bet I'll be stuck somewhere down in the bottom of the ship with the baggage. Just my luck!"

I was wrong. Poor Laurie. The ship was filled from the bottom up, not the top down as I had presumed, and I was pleasantly stunned to find myself in a first class stateroom already occupied by three congenial roommates! There were two sets of bunk beds, one on each side of the pleasant room. Through the porthole the sun glinted on the calm water of the dock, beyond which could be seen the comings and goings of Southampton's busy seaport. My three roommates had already "bagged" their bunks, and after introductions had been made I climbed the short ladder to the remaining upper one, which turned out to be surprisingly comfortable. I murmured once again: "God bless Miss Walters!"

It seemed like only minutes after boarding was completed that the ship's engines began to throb. I felt their rhythm under my feet, matching my excitement as we steamed slowly out of Southampton harbor, headed west. A gong sounded to call us to dinner. I still have my dining room ticket, now yellowed and battered with age. It reads: "U.S. ARMY TRANSPORT. FIRST CLASS, GREENE, IDA H. STATEROOM 291. PLEASE PRESENT TICKET TO DINING ROOM STEWARD AT FIRST MEAL SERVED AFTER SAILING." This ticket is one of the few souvenirs I have of the voyage.

Seating in the dining room was easy to find, and it began to feel like a luxury cruise, with white-coated waiters floating from table to table carrying trays of delectable foods which I hadn't seen for almost seven years. I spotted Laurie and we sat down together. She was far from happy. "Oh, Bunty," she said, on the verge of tears, "I've been put down in the bowels of the ship where the troops had been crowded together in little airless cabins; there are even some hammocks left down there! It's smelly and hot, too."

I was at a loss to know how to help. The only comfort I could offer was: "Oh, Laurie dear, try not to worry. I'm sure it will be better once we get under way."

At dinner, I thought I had died and gone to heaven! My diary raved: "HAD THE MOST WONDERFUL MEAL!" By this time the *E.B. Alexander* was well under way. I went out onto to the deck after dinner to catch a last glimpse of England through the evening mist. Tears clouded my eyes: tears of regret for leaving the land I loved so much, but also tears of happiness to welcome this voyage bringing me home to Al and the discovery of a whole new world.

Al: "TUESDAY, MARCH 19: MY DARLING IS ON HER WAY! CAN HARDLY WAIT. HAD MY FIRST DAY OPERATING NEW LARGE PIECE OF RECEIVING EQUIPMENT AT RADIO STATION. PAYCHECK $53.79. NOT BAD, INCLUDES OVERTIME."

Life on the Ocean Wave

Bunty: "OOOH! SEASICKNESS IS THE ORDER OF THE DAY! DID O.K. AFTER LOSING MY BREAKFAST. KEPT LUNCH AND DINNER DOWN. SPENT MOST OF THE DAY OUTSIDE ON DECK. FOUND LAURIE THERE--SHE DOESN'T LOOK SO GOOD. WENT TO A MEETING WITH LIEUTENANT HARRIS, SPECIAL SERVICES OFFICER. HE'S PUTTING ON A SHOW. SOUNDS LIKE FUN, SO I VOLUNTEERED."

The food on board was much richer than we had been used to in Britain during the war years; combined with the rocking of the ship as she lurched into the Atlantic, it was a challenge for us new sailors to keep it down! Unable to resist the luxury of fried eggs and bacon, most of us lost our first breakfast. For the rest of the voyage, my diary reported eating all my meals and enjoying them. As Dad would have said: "Well, Bunty, you've found your sea legs. The sea is in your blood, you know."

I believe the sea *was* in my blood. I loved the feeling of being on ship-board. Childhood memories crowded back to remind me of clambering over ships with Dad in the Sunderland docks and of the excitement he transmitted to me as we watched a completed vessel launched into the River Wear.

The promenade deck beckoned me. "There must be sea water in my genes," I thought, "I love the feel of the ocean under me, and the smell of tar on the deck when it is warmed by the sun. I'm sure if I stay away from those greasy fried eggs tomorrow morning my sea legs won't abandon me. When I have time, I'd better look around for Dot and see how she's doing."

As if on cue, Dot appeared, walking briskly around the promenade deck looking decidedly fit as she cast pitying glances at those girls sitting propped up on the deck who were showing all the signs of seasickness.

We greeted each other with a hug. I said: "Glad to see you're looking so well, Dot. I think we both must have found our sea legs."

Dot nodded: "I just hope the weather holds up, Bunty. We still have a long way to go to New York! I feel sorry for all these poor souls sitting around on the deck looking green around the gills. Staying away from those yummy food smells from the dining room would probably be wise, but the motion of the ship doesn't help them either, I'm afraid. Hope we'll be able to stay in the Gulf Stream awhile when we reach it; at least it's smooth sailing out there so that they can recover a bit." She paused and grinned wickedly: "I say, Bunty, how about some lunch?"

Flushed with the undisputed success of our show "*T.S.*" last year at Rainbow Corner, I headed that afternoon for the ship's theater, where a young and energetic Lieutenant Harris was conducting auditions. I thought: "I'll try him out with that old cockney music hall song 'Waiting at the Church' and see what he thinks of it." The lieutenant seemed to like it; I was told to come for rehearsal tomorrow.

Al: "WEDNESDAY, MARCH 20: AMY HAS OFFERED TO LOAN US HER BEDROOM WHEN BUNTY ARRIVES. MUCH NICER THAN MINE, WITH HER NEW FURNITURE, SO I FEEL BETTER. AT WORK LOTS TO LEARN! HAVE PASSED MORE WRITTEN TESTS ON THE RADIO EQUIPMENT. MADE ARRANGEMENTS WITH BOSS TO BEGIN VACATION THE DAY BUNTY ARRIVES. I'LL WORK 4-12 SHIFT, SLEEP A LITTLE, THEN DRIVE BILL'S CAR TO NEW YORK AND PICK HER UP. CALLED REAL ESTATE GUY. TOLD HIM TO KEEP LOOKING."

Bunty: "WE'RE REALLY MOVING INTO THE GULF STREAM NOW WITH A DAY OF BRILLIANT SUNSHINE. TOOK A COUPLE OF PHOTOS ON DECK. SPENT AN HOUR THIS AFTERNOON AT REHEARSAL FOR THE SHOW WE'RE PUTTING ON."

In the Gulf Stream that morning, the North Atlantic Ocean was calm and the sun was warm. I found Dot on the sun deck. I still have the photos we took standing by the ship's rail next to a life preserver ring with *E.B. ALEXANDER* in large letters on it.

I grumbled to Dot: "I wish they had put out some chaise lounges on the deck so we could sit down. I'm dying to get a nice suntan."

Dot looked at me impatiently: "Oh, Bunty, shut up! Did you really think there would be such luxuries aboard an army transport? We're lucky to have a deck to walk on!"

For awhile, Dot and I joined the crowd of girls basking in the brilliant sunshine, sitting on the warm, bare planks of the deck, our backs supported by the nearest vacant surface we could find. Babies were everywhere; one was being wheeled around on the deck in a folding stroller. Some of the girls sat and knitted; others chatted or walked the decks, as Dot and I did on our newly-found sea legs.

On one trip around the promenade deck we ran across Laurie, sitting propped up, surrounded solicitously by her *Queen Mary* friends. She had obviously been, and still was, seasick; her face had a decidedly greenish tinge. Dot and I stopped to talk, but there was nothing Laurie wanted to hear that would cheer her up, so we continued our walk, probably watched with disgust and envy by poor Laurie, as we appeared to be in the best of health.

The American Red Cross and the Army Transportation Corps personnel on board did their best to take care of our needs and to entertain us. The Red Cross girls had their hands full, helping seasick mothers to care for their babies, while for the seasick-free there was a new movie in the ship's theater every night to enjoy.

I was surprised to see the number of G.I. Brides who showed up for the show rehearsal that afternoon in the empty theater. The Special Services Officer, Lieutenant Harris, was young, personable and radiated enthusiasm. He spoke in a loud roar: "Wal, gals, we shore have the makin's of a real good show hyar. Now we'll just run through the things you want to do, and get 'em into some kinda order. How's about y'all get in line and we'll get started, one at a time."

Such talent I hadn't been prepared to see and hear: pianists and singers who could have been successful on the Broadway stage, and dancers who had brought their tap and ballet shoes along and looked as if they had just stepped out of the latest London review.

Viewing all this talent, "cold feet" threatened to send me hurrying out of the room, but I comforted myself with: "Oh well, after I make a fool of myself, I'll never see any of them again and the audience will be scattered all over the U.S.A. without even remembering how awful I was."

By the end of the afternoon we had a show put together.

AI: "THURSDAY, MARCH 21: PACKED UP A 'CARE PACKAGE' FOR MOM AND DAD AMISS. MOM HELPED ME GET CONTENTS. CAKE MIXES, DRIED FRUITS, SUGAR, CANDY, COCONUT, TOWELS. ATTENDED AMERICAN LEGION BAND PRACTICE. MY CLARINET SOUNDS TERRIBLE. NO PRACTICE FOR TWO YEARS. AM GETTING ADJUSTED TO WORK AT RADIO STATION. NEED TO SPEED UP MORSE CODE."

Bunty: "WONDERFUL WEATHER ALL DAY. WENT TO ORIENTATION LECTURE AT 9:30 A.M. VERY INTERESTING TALK ON GOVERNMENT IN THE U.S. THEY ONLY HAVE TWO POLITICAL PARTIES! ATE LIKE A HORSE ALL DAY AND NO REPERCUSSIONS. LAURIE IS FEELING BETTER. HAD TWO REHEARSALS TODAY. SHOW IS SHAPING UP WELL."

Al's 'care package' would be one of many that would be sent to my parents in postwar England; delicacies that were still not available or severely rationed. Dad mentioned in one of their letters that Mom was standing in line for potatoes. Severe shortages continued for several years. Mom wrote ruefully: "We sometimes wonder who won the war!"

On board the *E.B. Alexander* there was a daily lecture available to the G.I. Brides. Thanks to the G.I. Wives Club at Rainbow Corner, I was acquainted with a few of the topics but ready to learn more, especially about there only being two American political parties, compared with the many in Britain's Parliament. And I'd never heard of a "filibuster!"

Laurie was a victim of "big time" seasickness. Having to go down to sleep in the airless spaces below decks didn't help. I sought her out again today, and found her propped up in the same place on the promenade deck. I thought: "Oh, good, she's getting better--she's got her knitting out!" I said: "Laurie, dear, how're you feeling today?"

Laurie grimaced: "Well, Bunty, on a diet of dry rolls, crackers and ginger ale almost from the minute I got on this ship, I must have lost pounds and pounds. I'm wondering if my good black suit will still fit or if it will hang off me when I walk down the gangplank at New York?"

I thought to myself: "She does have a hollow kind of look, but if she's worrying about how she will look in her suit, it's a sure sign she's getting better!"

We talked awhile longer, and by the time I left, her knitting needles were clicking away once more.

The show *G.I. Brides Afloat* was shaping up nicely, under the direction of the effervescent lieutenant. Without any trace of seasickness, I was having fun; all was well with my world.

Al: "FRIDAY, MARCH 22: SPENT MOST OF THE DAY IN ATTIC, WHERE MOM HAD PUT MY CLOTHES WHILE I WAS AWAY. IT'S AMAZING HOW I'D FORGOTTEN WHAT CIVILIAN CLOTHES I HAD. FOUND SPORT JACKET AND SUMMER SUIT THAT STILL FIT, SOCKS, SHIRTS, TIES. NEED NEW PAIR OF PANTS."

Bunty: "THE SHIP RAN INTO A HECK OF A STORM WHICH LASTED ALL AFTERNOON. FELT FINE ALL DAY. ATE LIKE A HORSE, ENJOYED ALL MY MEALS. SAW LAURIE ON DECK BEFORE STORM STRUCK. SHE'S FEELING BETTER, BUT STILL A BIT GROGGY."

I remember going up on deck that morning and finding Laurie propped up again in her usual place. The greenish-yellow tinge had disappeared from her face, although her smile and "hello" sounded rather weary.

I remarked, cheerily: "Good morning, dear; I know you're feeling better all the time now--your knitting has grown!"

After lunch, I went on deck again to have a walk. Laurie had gone, and so had the sunshine; the weather had turned blustery and cold. I pulled up my coat collar and wandered over to the ship's rail to look out over the ocean. The blue sky had turned to gray, reflecting a dark gray sea that made the foamy wake of the ship look even whiter.

Waves were topped with little whitecaps as the ship heaved with the mounting turbulence. This was an exciting new experience. I mused: "If only Dad could be here now! He'd love it. He'd be standing right next to me, enjoying every minute watching the caprices of the Atlantic!" By now I was holding onto the rail with both hands as gusts of wind whipped my face, carrying a salty spray with them. A few moments later I looked aft, and my blood ran cold. Never having experienced a ship wallowing in heavy swells, I was terrified when a wall of water rose higher than the ship, blotting out the sky as we dipped down into what seemed like a bottomless pit in the ocean. I clung to the rail, expecting a huge wave to sweep me away. Just then, the overcast sky and the horizon appeared again as we rose up like a cork on the next swell. Giving up all bravado, I lost no time in scuttling back through the door of the ship's lounge, narrowly missing a surge of girls rushing out to be seasick over the rail.

The storm was short and furious. The *E.B. Alexander* rode it out with her engine turned off. By evening the ship had stopped pitching, the fury of the storm had passed, and we were once more under way.

Bunty: "SATURDAY, MARCH 23: MAYBE CAUGHT A CHILL ON DECK YESTERDAY--OR WERE THOSE RUMORS TRUE ABOUT TAINTED FOOD ON THE 'BRIDE SHIPS'? ANYWAY, I'VE AN UPSET STOMACH. STAYED CLOSE TO BATHROOM ALL DAY! DON'T KNOW WHAT I'D HAVE DONE WITHOUT DOT. SHE KEPT ME COMPANY THROUGH IT ALL. WILL I BE GLAD TO SEE NEW YORK!"

Bunty: "SUNDAY, MARCH 24: FEELING FINE AGAIN! ATTENDED CHURCH WITH DOT THIS MORNING. SPENT AFTERNOON ON DECK WITH LAURIE."

Al's diary had left several days blank, so I presumed he was too busy preparing for my arrival to write!

On board the *E.B. Alexander*, the ship's Chaplain conducted an interdenominational worship service in the lounge. It struck me as very comical the way the whole roomful of people rocked back and forth in rhythm with the ship's motion as they stood to sing the hymns. I couldn't resist whispering to Dot: "Now we know what they mean by 'The Holy Rollers.'" We both burst into a fit of coughing to hide our giggles.

Bunty: "MONDAY, MARCH 25: WE'RE DUE IN TO NEW YORK ON WEDNESDAY! WHOOPEE! SENT A CABLE TO AL. WENT WITH DOT TO SEE THE BABY CONTEST. FINISHED LETTER TO MOM AND DAD. PUT ON OUR SHOW IN THE EVENING. GREAT SUCCESS. WOUND UP AT PARTY IN THE COLONEL'S QUARTERS."

The ship had been my home for a week, and yet I still couldn't believe I would step off her and see Al again. I felt "wobbly" inside as I wrote my letter to Mom and Dad to mail as soon as possible, after I disembarked and could find an airmail stamp.

That afternoon, mothers sat with babies on their laps and toddlers clinging to their skirts, as a panel of "judges" from the Transportation Corps and Red Cross tried to look impartial and official. The small boys were decked out in their best outfits; the little girls had tiny ribbon bows pinned to the scant hair on top of their heads, or ribbon headbands if there wasn't enough hair to pin a bow. Awards went to the "Prettiest," "Chubbiest," "Happiest," "Oldest," "Youngest," etc. In the end, every entry had a prize of some kind, and all the mothers were happy.

Then, in the evening, came the show. It was a smash hit! Again, I marveled at the remarkable amount of talent among the girls on board. I envied those who could play the piano, and particularly the ones who had such beautiful singing voices.

I've often described my singing by saying: "When I open my mouth to sing, a strange noise comes out, but somehow it's usually on key!" The antidote for a not-too-good voice was a cockney accent which offered some camouflage, so I chose a comic vaudeville ballad popular in British music halls in Mom's day in the early 1900s, which has become a classic familiar to the British ever since. Called "Waiting at the Church," this song was familiar to just about everyone in the British Isles, usually included in sing-alongs. It tells the story of a woman from the crowded East End of London, where the cockney accent is prevalent. She gets stood up on her wedding day.

To represent this unfortunate bride, I was draped in a white tablecloth from the dining room as a makeshift wedding gown. Looking dejected as well as rejected, I sang in my best cockney accent:

"There wuz oi, waytin' at the church
Waytin' at the church,
Waytin' at the church.
When oi found he'd left me in the lurch,

Oh, 'ow it did upset me.
All at once, 'e sent me round a note,
'Ere's the very note (waving a large piece of paper)
This is wot 'e wrote:
'Cahn't get away to marry you today,
Moy woife (pause) won't let me!'"

After mopping my eyes with a corner of the tablecloth, I spread my arms to invite everyone, shouting: "Orl right, all together now," and sang the song over again, joined by the audience who belted out the familiar words that reminded them of home. They vigorously applauded themselves (and, I hoped, me). I adjusted the white tablecloth and dragged myself dejectedly off the stage, leaving it for some real talent to follow. When it was over, thanks to the exhausted Lieutenant Harris, the show was pronounced a great success.

True to showbiz tradition, a cast party followed the show. It was held in the quarters of the Transport Commander himself. I tasted champagne for the first time as we celebrated not only the show, but also the voyage taking us to my New World.

Al: "TUESDAY, MARCH 26: TOMORROW'S THE BIG DAY. BROTHER BILL LOANED ME HIS CAR. FILLED IT UP WITH GAS, HAD IT CHECKED OVER. POLISHED IT. LOOKS A LOT BETTER. ORDERED A DOZEN RED ROSES FROM THE FLORIST AND SOME CANDY FOR MY HONEY. CAN HARDLY WAIT UNTIL TOMORROW!"

Bunty: "WE EACH RECEIVED A SOUVENIR CERTIFICATE STATING THAT WE HAD SAILED ON THE *U.S.A.T. 'E.B. ALEXANDER.'* SPENT ALL MORNING GETTING AUTOGRAPHS ON THE BACK OF IT. AFTER LUNCH WE HAD YET ANOTHER UNBELIEVABLE MEDICAL EXAM! WENT TO BED EARLY, READY FOR A BUSY DAY TOMORROW!"
It seemed impossible that the ship had been my home for nine days. All these years later I examined my "Sailing Certificate," now fragile with

age. It had obviously not been designed for the G.I. Brides, but for American troops returning to the U.S. from overseas. On it is printed: "ARMY SERVICE FORCES. TRANSPORTATION CORPS. ARMY OF THE UNITED STATES." On the next line (printed): "NEW YORK PORT OF EMBARKATION." Then, (handwritten): *"Ida H. Greene, London, S.E.19., England." (Printed): "RETURNED TO THE UNITED STATES ON THE SHIP (handwritten) "U.S.A.T., E.B. ALEXANDER." (Printed): WHICH SAILED FROM (handwritten): "Southampton on March 18, 1946."

The back of the certificate is covered with messages and signatures from my roommates and other companions during the voyage. The girls often included the name of the state to which each was going: Kansas, New York, North Carolina, Illinois, California. The signatures include the Special Services Officer, the Transport Chaplain and the Transport Commander. I wondered where they all were now. Tears came when I read the touching farewell written by the Transport Chaplain: "Bunty, may God richly bless you and yours in your new home in America."

At Tidworth Camp, shortly before the voyage, the American authorities had seemed to be obsessed with the physical condition of the G.I. Brides being delivered stateside; ostensibly as part of the immigration requirements, an embarrassing medical exam had ensued. I remembered it vividly, standing naked in my raincoat while the Medical Officer shone a flashlight under my arms and between my legs.

Today on the ship an announcement blared over the P.A. system informing us that yet another medical exam was required before we could disembark! We were again told to take off all our clothes, lie down on our bunks with a sheet over us, and wait for the Medical Officer! My roommates and I were scandalized; how on earth could we need another medical exam? And so soon after the last one? But we all agreed that it was better to comply than risk being detained from getting off the ship at New York. The four of us stripped as modestly as possible. As we ducked under our sheets, I couldn't resist quipping: "Just imagine, girls, this could go down in American history: a whole shipload of women, all lying naked, waiting for one Army officer!"

We were still giggling when the Army doctor arrived, accompanied by a Red Cross nurse, a distinct improvement over the previous clerk with his clipboard. The nurse lifted up one side of my sheet, and the doctor told me to raise my legs and part them. He shone a flashlight over my anatomy. I lowered my legs. The sheet was dropped back over me, and they moved on to one of my roommates. She was livid.

"My husband will hear about this and so will his Congressman," she screamed. She probably realized that nothing would be done about it, but at least she got her indignation off her bare chest!

Laurie and Me

Chicken Country

Beginning a New Life

Al: "WEDNESDAY, MARCH 27: WORKED LAST NIGHT 4 P.M. TO MIDNIGHT. HOME AT 1 A.M. RESTED UP A LITTLE--TOO EXCITED TO SLEEP. PICKED UP ROSES ORDERED FOR BUNTY FROM FLORIST AND BOX OF CANDY. WASHED AND DRESSED. TOOK OFF FOR NEW YORK IN CAR LOANED BY BROTHER BILL. ARRIVED NEW YORK AT PIER 84. COLLECTED FORM STATING THAT BUNTY'S TRUNK AND SUITCASES WILL BE SHIPPED TO MOM'S HOUSE. AT 3:30 P.M. GANGPLANK LOWERED AND BRIDES BEGAN COMING OFF SHIP. UNITED WITH MY LOVE SHORTLY AFTER. WONDERFUL. PHOTOS. DROVE HOME. ARRIVED FOR LATE SUPPER WITH FAMILY."

Bunty: "THE GREAT DAY, AT LAST! SHIP DOCKED AT PIER 84 IN NEW YORK AT 3:30 P.M. AL WAS THERE TO MEET ME. OH, IT'S WONDERFUL TO SEE HIM AGAIN! STOPPED AT A ROADHOUSE ON WAY HOME. DELICIOUS MEAL. ARRIVED AT LITTLE CEDAR RIVER AFTER DARK. AL'S FAMILY THERE TO MEET ME, THEY'RE ALL SIMPLY GRAND. HAD LOVELY LATE SUPPER TOGETHER. WE HAVE AMY'S BEDROOM, FILLED WITH FLOWERS. I JUST CAN'T BELIEVE THAT I'M HERE!"

The ship's lounge was packed with women and children waiting for the double doors to open, to step on the gangplank, and to walk down it onto the New York pier. I hugged my new friend, Dot. "Good luck, Dot, and don't forget to write when you get settled in North Carolina."

"I'll never forget you, Bunty, especially if I ever have an upset stomach! Which reminds me, I'll let you know what the doctor says about this worrisome little lump in my tummy." (Dot wrote later to say how surprised she was to discover she was four months pregnant!)

Laurie raced across the lounge and gave me a hug. "It'll be a madhouse when we disembark, but let's get in touch as soon as we can," she yelled, above the alarming decibels of noise surrounding us from chattering girls and crying babies.

"O.K., I promise," I shouted back.

I reached down for my suitcase handle as the doors opened; girls began to stream through them and down the gangplank to the pier below. From the head of the gangplank I saw Al standing at the foot of it, a dozen red roses like the ones I carried at our wedding cradled in one arm. In his hand was a mysterious brown paper bag. I was already crying, touched that he remembered to bring red roses, when I was enfolded tightly by his free arm. Our kisses held the pent-up longing of the months that had separated us. But a longer embrace would have to wait; we had to move away quickly from the gangplank to avoid being bowled over by the avalanche of G.I. Brides and children pouring down it. Al ceremoniously handed me the brown paper bag.

"It's a surprise present, my love," he said. "I thought you might like to have something you've been longing for."

I peered inside the bag, thinking how extravagant he was to have bought me a new wristwatch, which I really didn't need. Then I looked at him, and saw that mischievous pixie grin of his. Warily, I reached inside the bag.

"Oh, darling, just what I've been dreaming about for six years," I sobbed, and took out a box of licorice candy and a bag of salted peanuts, two of my favorites, which I had often complained to Al that we couldn't get during the war. We laughed, but inwardly I marveled at the devotion of this husband of mine. He had worked the evening shift, arriving home at one o'clock that morning to snatch hardly any sleep before driving from southern New Jersey on the long, traffic-infested highways to New York City. Then he endured what must have seemed hours standing on the pier waiting for me to disembark--and yet he had brought me red roses and remembered my weakness for licorice and peanuts!

A passer-by took a photo for us on the dock with Al clowning and sitting on my lap, and minutes later we drove off in the car borrowed from Brother Bill. After an hour of driving we stopped for a very late lunch at what I called a "roadhouse," (English name for "roadside restaurant.")

I could have written an entire book about my first impressions on American soil, but my diary says just this: "MY FIRST IMPRESSION OF AMERICA IS *CARS!* EVERYONE HERE SEEMS TO HAVE ONE! I'M ABSOLUTELY THRILLED WITH EVERYTHING ! HAD A WONDERFUL SUPPER WITH THE FAMILY BEFORE GOING TO BED."

I was remembering all the cars in my neighborhood in Upper Woodside, up on blocks despite the end of the war, still waiting for gasoline rationing to end. It was almost dark when Al pulled into the driveway of a two story, weathered cedar-shingled house.

If Al's family thought of me as a curiosity they didn't show it. Letters and photos had flown back and forth between us, so we had a chance to get to know each other a little before I arrived. Lined up in the front hall were Al's Mom, tall and heavy-set; his brother Bill, short, beaming and irrepressible; sister Amy, slender and pretty; and Bill's new fiancée, Marjie McCafferty, a little taller than him, but clinging to his hand as if for protection, with a nervous smile. It felt like New Year's Eve at the Ditchfields as I passed down the lineup with its welcoming hugs and kisses. I felt the family's warmth and kindness that first day, and have always cherished it. My new mother-in-law had been the only one I was apprehensive about meeting, but she embraced me in a motherly hug and said: "Well I swan, here's Bunty! Welcome home, and welcome to the family."

I quietly breathed a sigh of relief, and wondered what 'swan' meant. Certainly not the bird I knew!

My new sister-in-law Amy worked as a telephone operator at A.T.& T.'s subsidiary, New Jersey Bell Telephone Company. (This was long before the forced divestiture of the Bell Telephone Companies from A.T.&T.) She was single and lived at home, helping to support her mother. The first thing she had bought with her savings was a beautiful new bedroom set. Unselfishly, she had vacated her room with its lovely furniture for us to use. It was filled with bouquets of flowers from Al's aunts, uncles and cousins, along with welcoming gift cards. I felt loved.

Mom Greene called up the stairs: "Come on down, you two, supper's ready."

Seated at the dining room table, I had the comfortable feeling of being part of the family, as Mom Greene said grace before laden bowls and platters of food were passed from one to the other; quite a different procedure than that at Bishop's Hill, where Mom loaded the plates in the kitchen and passed them through the "serving hatch" into the dining room.

The family's chatter was suddenly interrupted by the loud wailing of a siren outside. As if by instinct, I dived under the table and crouched there in fright.

I heard Bill's voice: "Golly Gee Willikers, what happened?"

Al's head appeared among the assorted knees: "It's O.K., Bunty, there aren't any air raids here--that's our fire whistle!" He helped me back to my seat, and I could envision my new in-laws thinking: "Well, she *does* seem a bit odd, what with her funny accent an' all, but gee whiz, she's finally flipped her lid, poor kid!"

Bunty: "THURSDAY, MARCH 28: THIS MORNING AL'S AUNT MARY AND COUSIN TOM DROVE OVER FROM PENNSYLVANIA AND TOOK AL AND ME ON A TRIP ACROSS BARNEGAT BAY TO THE ATLANTIC SEASHORE. MAILED A LETTER TO MOM AND DAD. MET NEXT DOOR NEIGHBOURS WHO GAVE ME A WELCOME GIFT--TWO BANANAS! SHOPPED FOR A 'TWO-WAY STRETCH.'"

Aunt Mary Booth, Mom Greene's older sister, presided over a late breakfast in the farmhouse-type kitchen. She smiled: "Bunty, Tom and I are going to the shore to buy some fresh fish. Would you like to come with us?"

Thrilled, I nodded. "Yes, please, I can't wait to see absolutely everything!"

The drive in Aunt Mary's Cadillac was luxurious, but I was hardly aware of it, with my nose pressed against the car window, soaking up the unfamiliar scenery as we passed by.

The wooden houses fascinated me. I took my hand out of Al's to point at them, and said to him, "I don't think I've ever seen a house made entirely out of wood before. You'll remember that the ones in England are brick or stone on the outside." I thought to myself: "These houses look so clean and neat, all painted white, charming and beautifully kept, but they almost look temporary, as if they're waiting for someone to come along and rebuild them with something more permanent." Not wanting to seem critical, I kept this impression to myself.

Before us was Barnegat Bay. The great new arching Thomas Mathis Bridge had not yet been built, and we bumped along over the planks of its predecessor, an old rickety wooden bridge spanning the mile-wide water, until we reached the narrow strip of land separating it from the North Atlantic. Suddenly, I glimpsed the vast expanse of ocean reaching to the far horizon.

From the boardwalk bordering the white sandy beach, I looked out on the miles of water I had crossed. Far beyond the breakers was the

empty horizon. I realized for the first time how great a distance now separated me from Mom and Dad.

Al's family were British in origin, so fortunately I didn't have the trauma of some G.I. Brides, who had to adjust to families of a different ethnic
background, language and traditions. Early that afternoon, Al and I visited the next door neighbors, the Baileys, who were also of British origin.
They welcomed me warmly. Mrs. Bailey gave me a bulging brown paper
bag: "Here's a special gift from us to you, Bunty," she said, "we heard you
might enjoy them."

Curiously, I looked into the bag. Wonder of wonders: it contained
two gorgeous yellow bananas! Al must have mentioned to the Baileys
the fact that I hadn't seen a banana for the past six years! I blurted out:
"Oh, thanks so much! You don't mind if I take a bite now, do you?" We
all laughed as my face registered sheer delight in the half-forgotten flavor
that brought back prewar memories.

Mrs. Bailey left the room for an instant and came back with a large,
pleasant woman, comfortably clad in a cotton house dress and apron.

"Bunty, I want you to meet our housekeeper. She's really just like a
member of the family; we couldn't do without her."

The woman smiled and stretched out a motherly hand to me: "I'm
glad to meet you. My name is Ida Norton."

I was taken aback. Another Ida! My family nicknamed me Bunty to
distinguish me from Mom, after whom I had been named Ida. It wasn't a
very common name; I hadn't met any other Idas in Upper Woodside, at
my prep schools--Ravenhurst in London, then Wrexham Park in Wales--
or in college, or even at Airways House. Aside from Mom, in my mind I
thought I was uniquely Ida forever. My bubble of uniqueness burst when
Al had first been introduced to me at Rainbow Corner, and he said: "Well
I'll be! What a coincidence. My mother's name is Ida, too!" Now there
were three of us!

And today, here was the Baileys' housekeeper, another Ida--four of
us! It didn't even end there. When I was introduced to my future sister-in-law's mother, my uniqueness received the knockout punch when

Mrs. McCafferty said: "Oh, how interesting, my name is Ida, too!" Five of us! Now I was just one of a crowd. I thought to myself: "Ida, you'd better go back to being "Bunty"; there's only one of those, at least so far!"

Delighted with my visit to the Baileys, and to register a complimentary remark, I gushed to Mom Greene afterwards: "What lovely people the Baileys are, and I was so surprised to find another Ida next door--such a homely-looking woman!"

Mom Greene's face registered disapproval mixed with incredulity, but she said nothing. It was only after Al and I were alone that he said: "You know, my love, I think you meant 'homey'. Over here, 'homely' means 'ugly'."

"Oh dear," I thought, "imagine 'American English' leaving a letter out of a perfectly harmless compliment and having it mean just the opposite!" But this wouldn't be the last time I would put the proverbial foot in my mouth, as my battle continued with a new language!

Having used up my clothes ration before I left England, I was still desperate for one garment in particular. I decided not to embarrass my new family by having them help me buy underwear. I thought: "It's only a couple of blocks to walk, and I can't get lost when there's only one shopping street, so I'll just go and pick it up by myself." So that afternoon, off I went. Little Cedar River boasted two dress shops, and I ducked into the first one I saw.

A young sales clerk came from the back of the shop with a welcoming smile. "Good afternoon, ma'am, may I help you?"

I answered, "Good afternoon. Would you please show me a 'two-way-stretch?'"

Her smile vanished. "I beg your pardon," she said, "would you mind repeating that?"

Rather impatiently, I repeated: "I would like to see a 'two-way-stretch.'"

She gave me a worried look. "Wait just a minute, ma'am, I'll ask my manager."

She hurried into the back of the store, returning with an older woman. I repeated myself again, explaining with all the patience I could muster that I wanted an elasticized undergarment that stretched in two directions. The two women looked at each other and exclaimed in unison:

"Oh, you mean a *girdle!*"

"Well," said I, with a smile of relief, "where I come from, a girdle is a belt you tie around your waist to close up your dressing gown, which you call a bathrobe, I believe, but if a girdle is what you call a two-way-stretch, it's what I'd like to buy." I emerged from the store victorious, looking much sleeker than I had when I entered it.

Bunty: "FRIDAY, MARCH 29: AL WENT OFF TO CHECK ON THE NASH AND DO SOME ERRANDS. DID QUITE A LARGE WASH THIS MORNING AND IRONED IT ALL THIS AFTERNOON. AL AND I WALKED AROUND TOWN THIS EVENING."

Al went to see Ernie's progress with the Nash, so this morning I decided to begin my duties as a housewife by doing a load of wash. I was uneasy. I fancied that Mom Greene sounded a bit pointed when she had said: "Bunty, do you know how to run a vacuum cleaner?" Piqued by her tone of voice, I had retorted: "Oh yes, Mom's had one almost ever since I can remember!"

Mom had never bothered me with housework, so I had no experience in such mundane matters, least of all washing clothes. With an armful of soiled clothes from the voyage and a white dress shirt of Al's, I staggered downstairs to the kitchen, determined to get them washed and ironed by the end of the day.

Modern electric washers had not yet reached homes in England, so Mom Greene showed me how to use hers. Back then, all they did was wash and rinse. Spin dryers appeared later, and shortly afterwards electric clothes dryers came on the market.

The process took several hours. After being washed and rinsed by the sloshing machine, the garments had to be heaved up in the tub and guided, soaking wet, into the jaws of the waiting electric wringer attached to the tub, which eagerly grabbed each one to feed it through its motorized rollers. Emerging like wrinkled pancakes, they then had to be shaken out and pinned securely to the outdoor clothesline with wooden clothespins. The full clothesline was hoisted into the air and propped in place by a wooden clothes prop, to allow the garments to flap dry in the breeze. Each one dried at a different speed, requiring innumerable trips back and forth to pluck off those that were "ready."

Before she left to do "shopping and errands", which suspiciously took her the rest of the morning and all afternoon, Mom Greene had firmly directed me to remember to starch the collar and cuffs on Al's white shirt and also the front panel containing the buttonholes. She left a bottle of liquid starch and a bowl for me on the table. I poured what I thought would be enough starch from the bottle into the bowl, then gathered the collar, two cuffs and front panel together in my fist and dipped them into it, swishing them around to coat them evenly. On the second swish I realized that all the starch was gone and the collar, cuffs and front panel still weren't thoroughly dampened. I poured the rest of the starch into the bowl, repeated the swishing, squeezed them and hoped for the best.

Staring at me from the table was the bowl, still almost full of liquid starch. With no way to get it back into the bottle, I poured it down the drain in panic and put the bottle in the garbage, hoping my mother-in-law wouldn't miss it before I could buy her a new bottle to replace it.

By lunchtime I was exhausted, but at last there was a pile of dry clothes on the kitchen table, waiting to be ironed. Fortified by a ham sandwich, I was now introduced to the resident electric iron. Words like "steam iron," "wash and wear" and "wrinkle-free" had not yet entered the dictionary. The dried wash had to be dampened in order to be ironed. On the table stood a vinegar bottle full of water with a small metal head on it, perforated to allow water to be shaken out. As each garment was sprinkled, it had to be rolled up tightly to prevent it from drying out again. I looked desperately at the small mountain of rolled-up clothes, turned on the iron, and began to attack it.

I glared down at Al's shirt, spread out on the ironing board. After retrieving it from the floor when it slipped off the board, and burning myself on the thumb, I ironed it, seeing only a few wrinkles disappear as it rapidly dried out again. I was in despair. My first attempt at domestic-ity had been a miserable one, and I went to our room and had a good cry, possessed by homesickness and defeat. Then I fancied I heard Dad's voice in my ear saying: "Come on, Bunty, you can do it: where's your 'British bulldog' spirit?" Feeling better, I pulled myself together and went back to do battle with the damp, rolled-up pile on the table. Al was very understanding, and doggedly wore his shirt with its wrinkled collar when he went back to work.

The air outside was fresh and inviting, so in the early evening Al took me on a stroll around town. At the river's waterfront was a pretty little grassy park, on which stood a white-painted gazebo adorned with a large plaque. I don't remember the exact words, but it read something like this: "HUDDY PARK, IN MEMORY OF CAPTAIN JOSHUA HUDDY, AMERICAN PATRIOT, HANGED WITHOUT TRIAL, 1782." Across the street from the post office was another plaque, erected next to the firehouse. It read: "SITE OF ORIGINAL BLOCKHOUSE. BURNED BY THE BRITISH IN 1782." Embarrassed, I looked the other way!

Research revealed that Little Cedar River's importance in the American Revolutionary War lay not only in its strategic position for shipping, but also because of its salt works. In the 1700s, the only way of preserving food was with salt, which was also necessary in making gunpowder. In the Revolutionary War there were two factions among the Americans: American Patriots, who stood for separation from Britain, and British Loyalists who sided with the British. Both needed salt to preserve food for their fighting men, and fight against each other they did, sometimes brother against brother, father against son!

A blockhouse was a small timber fort built to protect the townspeo-ple and the salt supply warehouses. In 1782, Captain Joshua Huddy was sent to defend the Little Cedar River blockhouse with a small force of Patriots. A much larger force of Loyalists overwhelmed them and burned the blockhouse, along with most of the houses in the village. Huddy was captured by the Loyalists, taken away to be imprisoned, and hanged, thus becoming a Patriot hero.

After learning this piece of American history, every time I had to pass the site of the unfortunate blockhouse and its accusatory plaque on my way to the post office, I found myself guiltily slinking across to the opposite side of the street!

Settling In

Al: "SATURDAY, MARCH 30: STILL WITHOUT A CAR! ERNIE IS WORKING ON IT, BUT PARTS HAVEN'T ARRIVED. WENT OUT HOUSE HUNTING TODAY. BILL LOANED US HIS CAR. SAW SEVERAL HOUSES BUT NONE WORTH CONSIDERING WITHIN OUR PRICE RANGE. AT TONIGHT'S 'WELCOME HOME' DINNER FOR LITTLE CEDAR RIVER WAR VETERANS, BUNTY WAS WELCOMED WARMLY. BROTHER BILL IS TAKING US TO VISIT IN PENNSYLVANIA TOMORROW."

Bunty: "HOUSE HUNTED ALL MORNING WITHOUT SUCCESS. FELT VERY BLUE, DISAPPOINTED AND HOMESICK, SO HAD A GOOD CRY. RECOVERED IN TIME TO GO TO METHODIST CHURCH AND ATTEND VETERANS' 'WELCOME HOME DINNER.' JOAN AND BUD WERE THERE. HAD A WONDERFUL TIME AND GREAT WELCOME."

Once more I knew despair, combined with homesickness. The little house whose photos accelerated my arrival in the U.S. had been sold to another couple. They must have been able to pay the inflated price. Al and I agreed that our stay in Mom Greene's house had to be as short as possible; our first priority was to move into a home of our own. We had also decided that renting was not an option, even if we could have found somewhere to rent. I had yet to learn how to drive a car, so we told the realtor we needed to find a house within walking distance of the town center. But with the postwar scarcity of houses, the chance of finding such a home and being able to afford to buy it was like looking for the proverbial needle in a haystack!

Little Cedar River's churches joined in giving a dinner for their returning veterans, their wives and girlfriends. It was the first time I had gone out socially with Al in his civilian suit, which enhanced his James Stewart personality even more than his army uniform.

Joan and her Little Cedar River husband, Bud, looked so happy. It was the first time I had met him, and I hadn't seen Joan since she stayed with us in London before sailing for the U.S. They had driven to the celebration from northern New Jersey, where they had taken an apartment after Bud decided to use the G.I. Bill to enroll in courses at the college there. Both Joan and I were touched by the welcome given the two of us at the dinner; heartwarming, and a good antidote for homesickness!

I could see something was bothering Joan, so I went with her to the ladies' room to have some privacy to talk. Sounding worried, Joan began: "Bunty, do you have a problem with your mother-in-law?"

"No, nothing specific," I answered, since I didn't want to mention being left with that pile of wash and ironing to figure it out for myself.

"I just wonder if I measure up." Joan's pretty face and blue eyes betrayed her concern. She wiped away a tear with her handkerchief. "Bud's an only child, and I wonder if I'm the kind of girl his Mom had in mind for him to marry. I'm not sure she likes me."

I put my arm around her. "Don't worry, Joan. Bud *chose you*. He is a fine, loyal husband. Things will soon work out."

My own reception by Al's family and friends had been spontaneous and warm. Since my arrival in Little Cedar River there had been only one occasion when I felt resented. Al's sister Amy introduced me to one of the local girls, who wasn't smiling when she observed, with a hint of accusation: "You know, you English girls stole a lot of our American men in World War Two!"

I bristled, but replied sweetly: "But don't forget, your American men stole a lot of British girls!"

Luckily, she smiled, and we ended up as friends.

Bunty: "SUNDAY, MARCH 31: BILL DROVE US TO PENNSYLVANIA TO VISIT MOM GREENE'S FAMILY. LOVELY SCENERY. ARRIVED IN

SHENANDOAH LATE AFTERNOON. AUNT ETHEL MADE US A TURKEY DINNER--DELICIOUS."

Al's two-week vacation was ticking away; it was time to visit his mother's relatives in Pennsylvania. We were up early, bringing our packed suitcase with us to the kitchen where breakfast was already under way. We were still without a car, so Brother Bill had offered to drive us, bringing his fiancée Marjie along. He looked up from his eggs and toast to greet us with one of the typical slang expressions of the 1940s: "G'mornin', kids, glad to see you're 'cookin' with gas' already!"

Soon we were on our way to Pennsylvania. I was glad of the opportunity to get to know Marjie better, as we giggled together while the men toiled to replace the flat tire that happened after our first few miles.

Tuning out Marjie's happy chatter that filled the car, I thought: "How different she is from the girls I've known back in England. The ones I've seen here seem so young and carefree in their 'bobby sox' and 'saddle shoes,' and their pleated skirts that swing out from their legs as they walk. In Little Cedar River, they gather after high school classes with boys in the Sweet Shop on Main Street, with its soda fountain and juke box, to sip Coca-Cola and dance to the latest records. Even sixteen-year-old American high school girls wear red nail polish and lipstick! But if such luxuries had been available to us during the war, our strict school rules would have banned them from being worn in the classroom. As for pleated skirts, 'Utility' ruled them out. British wartime skirts weren't allowed enough material to make even one pleat!

My mind returned to the present. Back then, before Interstate Highways came with built-in rest stops, gas stations and restaurants, the main roads went through one town after another, with a "diner" or two in between. At lunchtime, we stopped at one of these railway carriages converted into a restaurant, and ordered the Blue Plate Special. I gratefully gave up chasing my piece of fried chicken around the plate with a knife and fork when everyone picked theirs up with their fingers. I said secretly to myself: "I'm glad Gram Ditchfield and Mom can't see me now; they would have wondered if they'd brought me up right!" Eating with one's fingers in England (except for fish and chips) was "not done". But what a delightful relief this was!

The sandy pine barrens of coastal New Jersey had long since been left behind, and we had crossed the wide Delaware River by ferry (the big new bridges had not yet been built); another first experience that had me imagining the early settlers in their covered wagons and how they must have looked for shallows where they could ford the river safely.

We came to the foothills of the Appalachian Mountains where the road could be seen for miles ahead until it met the horizon at the top of a hill. The car rounded curves on mountain highways, revealing spectacular views of broad green valleys below, and red barns decorated with their provocative Pennsylvania Dutch "hex" signs. I was enchanted. The car climbed higher and higher.

We now drove slowly through the main streets of coal-mining towns nestled all through the mountains, slumbering in the Sunday sunshine. From the car we could look down side streets crammed with rows of small houses.

Anxious that his new sister-in-law would be properly introduced to her new country, Bill took on the role of tour guide: "You know, Bunty, some of these old towns have mining tunnels far below the houses! Would you believe that in some towns the whole population was housed within a single square mile? The tightly-packed houses were built by mine owners in the late nineteenth and early twentieth centuries whose greed made them rich with a double income from the same piece of land: coal seams below the ground, and rents from the folks living above them in their crowded homes. The mining company proprietors even owned what was sometimes the only store in town, and could overcharge whatever they pleased to miners who had nowhere else to buy. This often caused them to fall into permanent debt. There's a song about it with a line that goes: 'I owe my soul to the Company Store.' No wonder that when the unions came in they were so popular!"

Shenandoah had been such a coal-mining town in its infancy. Al's Grandmother Millard, Aunt Ethel and Uncle Clem, lived in one of the long rows of houses erected on both sides of the street called "shotgun" houses, built with one room behind another and with an exit door at each end. In my new relatives' house the rooms were small, but quite comfortable. At ground level there was a cellar containing a furnace and its supply of coal in a large bin. A short flight of steps up from the sidewalk was an open porch, where the front door led into the parlor. Behind this was the dining room, followed by the kitchen, with the back door leading out of that. The kitchen window looked down on a tiny "yard" with a small, carefully manicured lawn, above which stretched a clothesline suspended on a pulley outside the back door and anchored on a post at the end of the yard. Already one floor above ground level, the wash line could be pulled away from the house as each piece of laundry was pinned on it, then left to flap dry in the brisk mountain breeze. Upstairs were four bedrooms and a bathroom, one behind the other, matching the floor plan below.

The house originally belonged to Al's Welsh grandmother, Amy, after whom Al's sister had been named. When she heard I had lived in Wales for two years while our bomb-damaged house in London was being repaired, she immediately lapsed into fluent Welsh. Unfortunately, I didn't understand a word. Sorry to disappoint her, I murmured rather lamely: "Well, I only learned the Welsh national anthem in Welsh, I'm afraid." So we sang it together, and became friends.

Grandmom Amy Millard was already pregnant with her first child when she and Grandpop Millard emigrated to Pennsylvania in the late 1800s, sponsored by her uncle, who worked in the coal mines near Shenandoah. She loved her young English husband William deeply, and described him with pride as "a tall, good-looking man, his eyes 'blue as the skies' and with rosy cheeks and good health from working outdoors."

Before he met Amy, William had earned his livelihood as a stonecutter, building dry stone walls for the farms near his home in Somerset, in southwestern England. In their new home in Pennsylvania, William took the only job made available to him, as a coal miner. Over the years in the mines his ruddy complexion paled, and he died in his early fifties from "black lung disease," silicosis of the lungs caused by the inhalation of coal dust. As a young widow, Amy took boarders into her home and sold her "Welsh cakes" to support her four children: Mary, Ida, Ethel and William.

I inwardly marveled that this tiny woman with the twinkling brown eyes could have produced three large, strapping daughters, all so much taller and more buxom than herself. Dad would have said they "looked well-fed"--he never used the word "overweight". I wondered if her son would be as large as these three daughters; we had yet to meet Uncle Bill.

Al was his petite grandmother's favorite grandchild; she said he reminded her of her beloved husband. While he was away in the Army she had composed poems, full of loving words of admiration and encouragement, and sent them to him. When I first met Al in England, he had shown me one that he had carried with him in his wallet throughout his time in the military.

Amy Millard's poems were known and loved by the citizens of Shenandoah; a new one appeared every week in the local newspaper for the duration of World War Two. They contained the eloquent thoughts of a woman who passionately loved America and revered its fighting men. She shared her strong religious beliefs, and grew lyrical as in one poem she described the beautiful countryside of "Pennsylvania, Queen of States."

Years later, after Grandmom Millard died, Aunt Ethel gave Al a shoebox containing handwritten drafts of these poems which I compiled into an anthology, typed them and had them bound. Each member of the family received one. Now, they already have been passed on to the next generation.

In Grandmom Millard's day, it was customary for one of the daughters of the family to take on the care of her aging parents, either foregoing marriage to live with them or moving them into her own home when she married. As her two older sisters had long since moved away and married, Aunt Ethel was "elected" by default! She married late; Uncle Clem, a coal mine superintendent, was a widower. They bought Grandmom Millard's house, moved in with her, and now took care of both.

Aunt Ethel was a happy little soul, almost as wide as she was high. She was the epitome of the dutiful daughter and a fanatically dedicated housewife. Keeping every corner of her house spotless, she enlisted the help of Sister Ida every year to do the spring cleaning. Coming home to Little Cedar River exhausted, Mom Greene would complain: "That Ethel! She cleans again what's clean already!"

On my first visit to Shenandoah, Aunt Ethel emerged through a cloud of mouth-watering, aromatic vapor from the kitchen, clad in a short-sleeved cotton housedress. Wiping her hands on the apron enveloping her very ample figure, she hugged Al, Bill and Marjie. When it was my turn, arms outstretched, in her odd, husky voice she proclaimed: "God love you, and here's the latest one of my 'jewels'--welcome, Bunty!"

A lump came into my throat. I wondered if she knew the old hymn Dad used to sing to me when I was a toddler on his lap, but I was too close to tears to ask her:

"When He cometh, when He cometh, to take up his jewels,
All His jewels, precious jewels; His loved and His own...
Little children, little children, who love their Redeemer,
Are the jewels, precious jewels; His loved, and His own."

Aunt Ethel had never been a mother, and in her generous soul she loved her sisters' children as if they were her own. Her sincere words and warm hug put me totally at ease.

We enjoyed a magnificent turkey dinner with all the trimmings, during which we listened, spellbound, as Uncle Clem regaled us with stories of his colorful life. His heavy-set, six foot frame was evenly spread in his chair, which creaked as he leaned back between mouthfuls to talk in his resonant voice with its tinge of American-Irish accent:"Begorra, in the old days before Child Labor Laws came in, I was only nine years old when I had to layve school and went oot as a "coal picker" to help support me family. They slung a sack over me skinny shoulders and me job was to fill it with bits of anthracite coal that I would pick out of the slag heaps next to the big underground coal mines. I'd be given a few pennies for it. I'd come home dog-tired an' achin' all over, but me Ma sure needed the money."

Before we left Shenandoah, Uncle Clem also told us--as he remembered it--some of the early history of the rough-and-tumble town teeming with immigrants from all over Europe. He recalled the turbulence of its crooked politics, the dreaded Molly Maguire gangs, the cheating that went on at the polls with ballots marked illicitly with a piece of lead from a pencil under a fingernail.

Bill and Margie left after dinner, leaving Al and me to stay overnight. I was glad to be in our bedroom which was cooler than the downstairs, overheated from the coal-burning furnace. Hot and sweaty, I gladly peeled off my tweed suit jacket and the hand knitted sweater under it. Now I knew why Aunt Ethel wore a short-sleeved cotton housedress!

Bunty in Wonderland

Bunty: "MONDAY, APRIL 1: AL AND I WALKED INTO SHENANDOAH TO EXPLORE. NOW I KNOW WHAT THEY MEAN BY THE AMERICAN 'MELTING POT'! DID SOME GROCERY SHOPPING FOR AUNT ETHEL AT THE AMERICAN STORE, MY FIRST SUPERMARKET! UNCLE BILL MILLARD ARRIVED TO TAKE US TO HARRISBURG TOMORROW."

AS WE WALKED through the town of Shenandoah, my fascination with this new country grew when I saw a microcosm of the melting pot of America. Shenandoah had been populated by immigrants from Ireland, England, Wales, Poland, and other European countries. Their places of worship told part of their story. There seemed to be a church on every street corner: a Jewish synagogue, churches for Welsh and English Baptists, German Lutherans, Italian and Polish Roman Catholics, Orthodox Greeks and Russians; a mingling of onion domes, spires and bell towers, all reaching skyward.

I was surprised to hear that Shenandoah had produced among its famous sons the Dorsey brothers, Tommy and Jimmy. Al and I had danced to music made famous by the Dorseys' "Big Bands"; along with Glenn Miller, they had been my favorites when I listened on the radio to the American Forces Network in England in World War Two.

Al said: "Remember dancing to some of their music at Rainbow Corner, Bunty? Most of the time I was too busy concentrating on not stepping on your feet to listen to the music."

I retorted: "That's why you kept stepping on my feet, my love!"

He laughed and kissed me.

Before we left for our walk, Aunt Ethel had cornered Al: "Albert, I have a little shopping list for you, if you'll stop by at the American Store your way home."

The nearest thing I had seen to a supermarket in England was the Cooperative Society grocery store in nearby Croydon, where Mom bought most of our weekly wartime food rations.

"Well, Bunty, what do you think?" Al was watching the look of incredulity on my face.

"Oh, everything's so different! Our bacon ration was sliced by the grocer on a hand-operated machine with a handle turning a sharp round blade. There was never as much as a whole pound in our week's ration, and I was astounded when I saw that stack of pound packages of bacon here in the refrigerated display case! Mom used to cut slices of that awful beige wartime National Bread at home; American loaves of soft white bread are already sliced and packaged in tightly sealed plastic wrappers. What a different world this is!"

We were home in time for lunch, and so was Uncle Clem. He again held forth with stories about Shenandoah's turbulent past: "In its early days, it was a hard-livin', hard-drinkin' community full of young sons o' bitches from many of the 'auld countries', competin' despritly for survival, and be gosh, d'ye know, back then those bastards boasted that Shenandoah had the highest number of bars and saloons per capita of popoolayshun in the entire wurrald!"

Aunt Ethel confided to me later: "You know, Bunty, Uncle Clem 'took the Pledge' when he was a young man, swearing off alcohol, but he forgot to swear off swearing!"

She was right--Uncle Clem swore like a trooper! When we were alone, I had whispered to Al: "I don't understand a lot of the words he says; maybe it's just his accent."

Al replied: "No, dear, it's not his accent; just words you've never heard before!"

However, Uncle Clem was a good man with a heart as big as a house, so this personality quirk was silently tolerated by the rest of the family.

The only time anyone remonstrated was when Aunt Ethel burst out with: "Oh, Clarence, watch your mouth!" She only used his "Sunday" name in emergencies.

That afternoon brought the arrival of Al's handsome Uncle Bill, who was what Mom would have called a "matinee idol." When I confided this to Grandmom Millard, she retorted: "I call him my 'male butterfly!'" Many years ago his flitting had been brought to a halt by Aunt Betty, a pretty Shenandoah divorcee with two little girls; she married him and they moved to Harrisburg. This was to be our next destination.

Bunty: "TUESDAY, APRIL 2: UNCLE BILL TOOK US TO SEE UNCLE CLEM'S WORK AT THE COAL STRIPPINGS THIS MORNING. INTERESTING AND IMPRESSIVE. DROVE TO HARRISBURG IN AFTERNOON. MET AUNT BETTY, HER TWO ADULT DAUGHTERS, SON-IN-LAW AND GRANDSON. A FULL HOUSE. DECIDED TO LEAVE TOMORROW MORNING."

Uncle Clem had been fascinated by strip mining when it began in the Shenandoah area. Huge excavating machines, cranes and dump trucks were used to remove tons of earth and rock from the surface in order to reach outcrop coal deposits below. Despite Clem's scant formal education, he was an ambitious lad, eventually finding a job at a strip mine. Over the years he developed an uncanny instinct for recognizing the kind of terrain under which outcrop coal could be found--a valuable talent indeed for the mine owners. He had slowly worked his way up into his present position as superintendent of a coal-stripping operation. It was said he could almost smell coal seams, and he was often called upon to contribute his intuitive powers to verify the calculations of professional engineers trying to locate them.

The coal strippings were terraced across hundreds of acres on the hills surrounding Shenandoah. The size of the equipment used to move the earth and rock covering the seams of coal reminded me of one of those science fiction movies about another world where tiny humans were ruled by oversized machines. I still have a photo of Uncle Clem, Al and me standing alongside a huge dump truck, its outsized wheels towering above our heads.

At Harrisburg, we began to realize how weary we were. Uncle Bill's household sounded deafening to us. Everyone talked at once; I was bombarded with questions, and the din was punctuated with the wails and screams of an overactive two-year-old. After days of whirlwind traveling and constant conversation, we had reached the point of no return. We made our excuses after supper and retreated to the comparative quiet of our bedroom for the night, more than ready to leave next morning.

Bunty: "WEDNESDAY, APRIL 3: TOOK TRAIN TO WEST CHESTER. AUNT MARY BOOTH PICKED US UP AT THE STATION. DROVE TO BOOTHWYN, NAMED AFTER THE BOOTH FAMILY. THIS EVENING COUSIN TOM DROVE US TO WILMINGTON, DELAWARE. SAW A MOVIE, THEN HAD MY FIRST PIZZA."

Mary Millard was the "lady" of the family. She had a natural instinct for learning; when she graduated from high school she went on to nurse's training, eventually becoming a head nurse at Wilmington General Hospital in Delaware, just over the border from Pennsylvania. A tall, brown-eyed beauty, she caught the eye of Doctor Thomas Booth, and before long they were married and settled into the spacious new home the doctor built for his bride at Booth's Corners. His medical office, waiting room and examining room were in an extension to the house on the ground floor.

Cousin Tom told us that the family ancestors had acquired land after they emigrated from England and settled in Pennsylvania, in the days of William Penn. As a result, Doctor Booth was wealthy, not only from his own medical practice, but also the rents from tenant farmers on the hundreds of acres of farm land he had inherited.

Dr. Booth married late in life for those days, and Aunt Mary was also in her forties when she became pregnant. She knew she would have to have a Caesarian section, then a fairly new operation and considered risky. Her pregnancy was about half advanced when early one summer evening her husband was called out on a maternity case.

In those times, a country doctor relied upon his pony and trap to take him to outlying farms rather than on one of those newfangled automobiles that had difficulty navigating unpaved farm roads. It was almost dawn when he was able to leave for home after the delivery. The country roads were deserted under a dark and moonless sky, and the exhausted doctor dozed as the pony trotted homeward through the enveloping warm, velvety night air. Soon he was sound asleep. The doctor's pony and trap were hit by a speeding freight train, at a crossing without warning lights or barred gates to protect them.

Aunt Mary was awakened by the police telling her that her husband had been killed. She had the Caesarean section several months later that brought Al's fatherless cousin Tom Booth into the world.

On this evening in 1946, Tom eased his long legs into the car Aunt Mary had bought for him before he completed high school. Seat belts were not yet used in cars, and bucket seats were reserved for sports cars. The front seat of most cars was a "bench seat" stretching across the entire width of the car. I was tightly wedged between Al and Tom as we sped along the highway to Wilmington. Tom parked near a movie theater with its front canopy illuminated by colored light bulbs. The city of Wilmington was ablaze with neon signs and street lights; the prewar lights of London that I barely remembered were dim by comparison. My diary hailed Wilmington as "A WONDERLAND OF LIGHTS."

The movie must have been forgettable; I didn't even mention its name in my diary. After the show, Tom announced: "Now it's time for an Italian tomato pie. I hope you'll like it, Bunty."

"Well, to tell you the truth, Tom, I don't know what that is. In England we don't put tomatoes into pies," was my lame reply.

"Oh, great, then you'll always be able to say I took you for your very first Italian tomato pie." Tom was pleased to be introducing a new culinary treat to this foreign immigrant, and headed for what would now be called his favorite pizza parlor. The "Italian pie" was so enormous that I couldn't believe it was ordered for only three people! One bite, and I was convinced that Britain should never have interned all those wonderful Italian bakers in World War Two!

In the next few days we met cousins, aunts, uncles and in-laws, as we traveled by train through the beautiful green countryside of Pennsylvania back to New Jersey. Everywhere it was the same; a warm welcome from a loving family. I felt blessed. After the rolling hills of Pennsylvania, I was unprepared for southern New Jersey's pine barrens; miles of ugly, crooked pine trees growing in dry sandy soil. Through the grimy train window the seemingly endless flat, colorless landscape afflicted me with a strong dose of homesickness for England's "green and pleasant land." I buried my head in Al's shoulder and sobbed miserably.

Al gathered me into his arms: "Don't cry, Bunty, you're all tired out from these last few days--so many new people and experiences--and now even the landscape is dismal, and so different from England. But *I'm* still here. Remember me? Soon we'll have a home of our own, and I promise we'll have a nice green lawn and you can plant flowers all around it." He added: "I'll even buy a lawn mower!"

I was so overwhelmed by this comfort that I cried all the harder, but this time my tears stemmed from happiness in knowing I had made the right decision to trust my love to this gentle, humorous, reassuring man.

Arriving back at Mom Greene's, we expected to see our Nash all fixed, ready and waiting in the driveway. There was no sign of it.

A Home of our Own

Al: "SATURDAY, APRIL 6: CALLED ERNIE. CAR STILL NOT READY! THREE MONTHS NOW! HE SAYS THEY WON'T HAVE THE NECESSARY PART UNTIL THE END OF APRIL. CAN'T GO ON THIS WAY, CALLED BILL ENGELMANN. SUCCESS! HIS BROTHER WILL LET ME RENT HIS OLD PLYMOUTH UNTIL NASH IS READY. WILL PICK UP CAR ON MONDAY. ALSO, I THINK WE MAY HAVE A HOUSE!"

Bunty: "HOUSE HUNTED WITH CONSIDERABLE SUCCESS THIS MORNING! IT'S TINY, BUT IT'S CUTE, MODERN AND IN TOWN."

Our latest disappointment about the Nash was offset when we went out house hunting with the real estate lady. She was excited: "I want to show you something that just came on the market this weekend. There are tenants in it, almost through renting until they finish building a home. We can go in, and I think it might be what you're looking for."

I couldn't believe what we were seeing: an attractive small stucco house, newly remodeled in a quiet cul-de-sac of larger homes, just off Main Street and only a few blocks from the center of town. All on one floor, it had a large living/dining room, kitchen, bathroom, two bedrooms-- perfect! Asking price: $5,000. Within our price range!

"Oh, Al, it's so cute, and I can walk to town to shop without worrying about a car!"

Our real estate lady suddenly became businesslike: "If you kids are serious, a five hundred dollar deposit will take it off the market in case someone else should see it and get a deposit down before you do. Also, it will give you time to check out a G.I. mortgage. I won't show it to anyone else until you've had a few days to think it over."

The government had enacted legislation to help returning World War Two servicemen and women to readjust to civilian life. "G.I. mortgages" carried a special low rate of interest and getting one would put the monthly payments within our reach financially. Al wrote the check for five hundred dollars; we crossed our fingers and waited.

Al: "MONDAY, APRIL 8: WENT OUT TO ENGELMANNS TO PICK UP PLYMOUTH. HAD LUNCH. TOOK CAR TO GARAGE TO HAVE IT CHECKED. OIL CHANGE: $1.50, TANK OF GAS: $1.50"

Bunty: "WENT WITH AL TO LOCAL SAVINGS AND LOAN ABOUT A MORTGAGE FOR THE HOUSE. IT WILL BE APPRAISED ON WEDNESDAY. WENT TO ENGELMANNS TO PICK UP A CAR AL HAS RENTED. STAYED FOR LUNCH!"

When Al was on the evening shift, we had half a day's free time before he left for his commute at 3 p.m. That morning, we walked the few blocks to the local Savings and Loan office to make a formal application for a G.I. mortgage loan, pending approval of appraisal of the house. The machinery was now in motion to make our dream come true, but little did we guess how long we would have to wait for this to happen!

Al was rapidly reaching boiling point over the car. Ernie had him convinced that the scarce parts needed to get it in working condition would eventually arrive, and Al didn't want to give up on his luxury Nash Ambassador V-8. But by now he had been three months without transportation, sharing or borrowing cars, expecting any day to have his own. Something had to be done!

Putting down the telephone, Al sounded excited: "Hon', Bill Engelmann's brother Richie will let me rent his old Plymouth until our Nash is in running order! We can go today and pick it up, and we're invited to stay for lunch!"

Meeting the Engelmanns was another step for me in getting to know my new country. Bill Engelmann was one of Al's closest friends all through high school; their mothers were also close friends in the American Legion Auxiliary. Bill's younger brother, Richie, was still in high school, but had a car of his own. He had agreed to loan it to Al until our Nash was in operating condition. Al had insisted upon paying him rent. The local bus took us several miles north of Little Cedar River, leaving us off in front of the Engelmanns' chicken farm.

Olga and Wilhelm Engelmann were among the thousands who fled from Germany in the 1930s during the ascent of Hitler's Third Reich. In the U.S., various organizations had made it possible for these immigrants to establish chicken farms in southern New Jersey, which had the right climate and dry sandy soil for them to be successful. And successful they were. By now, beautiful farmhouses were strung along the ten miles of highway between Little Cedar River and Pinewood, Laurie's new hometown.

Upon arrival in the U.S., the Engelmanns used their savings to buy land. They built one chicken coop where they could live in temporary cramped quarters, and another to house their first batch of chickens. Their business slowly evolved until at last there was enough money to build a house. As I saw it today, their farm encompassed several acres with hundreds of white Leghorn chickens. Chicken coops surrounded the roomy, two story white clapboard farmhouse, with its vegetable garden that supplied the family with produce for the summer, and enough left over for Olga to preserve for the winter.

Both husband and wife still worked long hours, "Willie" doing the heavy work on the farm with the aid of a part-time helper: cleaning out, painting and repairing the coops, and marketing eggs and chickens to wholesalers. Olga raised their two boys while she gathered, sorted and "candled" eggs every day while keeping her menfolk well fed, and the house immaculate. The boys helped out on the farm occasionally for pocket money, but their parents' goal was to assure them of a good education for each to develop his own innate talents.

I had never met German people before, and it was with considerable trepidation that I clung to Al's hand as he knocked on the back door of the farmhouse. It was opened by a smiling, well-groomed woman in a flowered apron, with hair pulled back from a pleasant face, and with a blush of the outdoors in her cheeks. She beamed when she saw Al, and stretched out her arms to both of us: "Comm een, Lieblings, and let me have a goot luk at you. I have made a nice lunch for all of us," she cried, on her way out to the porch from which she yelled in the direction of the chicken coops: "Comm, Vilhelm, lunch is ready."

Mr. Engelmann appeared, a tall man clad in denim overalls and with a denim cap on his head. He took off his boots and hat, left them on the porch, then came in and washed his hands at the kitchen sink. "Velcom, Al, and so this is your little bride from England?" He smiled at me, and shook my hand which disappeared into his large one, still moist from soap and water. "Velcom, Bunty Greene. I bet you are still wondering who she is, but you'll soon get used to your new name. Iss goot to have you here."

From then on, I knew I had nothing to fear, and even thought to myself: "I'll bet there must have been plenty of people like them in Germany during the war who hated the Nazis as much as we did!"

Mrs. Engelmann sat us down at the table in the spotless kitchen, sunshine streaming in through the big windows onto the brightly patterned tablecloth, on which four places had already been set out. She looked at me with a smile: "Ach, little one, tell me about your trip heer on zee ship."

"Well, Mrs. Engelmann, it was pretty rough for a couple of days, but it made me all the happier to get here."

"Goot, dot is 'ow Vilhelm and me thought, too, ven ve came!" She beamed again at us, and busied herself putting lunch out on the table: chicken salad, newly baked bread, butter, potato salad, and something I had never seen before called "coleslaw". I was feeling comfortably full when out came a pot of coffee, and a warm apple pie from the oven. After a piece of pie and coffee with real cream I was ready to burst, but as Mom would have said jokingly: "Oh, don't do that, dear, it's so messy!"

"Richie's car iss all set to go, Al." Mr. Engelmann waved his hand in the direction of the outdoors. "Here's the key, take it ven you're reddy. You didn't need to give Richie any money, but iss goot he find out his brother's best friend is goot businessman!"

Al and I rode home in style in Richie's old Plymouth.

The Americanization of Bunty

Al: "TUESDAY, APRIL 9: BUSY DAY. TOOK PLYMOUTH TO GARAGE TO HAVE IT CHECKED OVER BEFORE EVENING SHIFT. FILLED TANK WITH GAS $1.50."

Bunty: "STILL TIRED FROM OUR TRIP. DID SOME WASH, TOOK BUS TO PINEWOOD AND SHOPPED FRANTICALLY FOR GIFT FOR MARJIE'S BRIDAL SHOWER TONIGHT. STOPPED IN TO SEE LAURIE FOR A FEW

MINUTES TO TELL HER MY TROUBLES. FEEL VERY TIRED. ATTENDED MARJIE'S 'SURPRISE' SHOWER IN EVENING, UNDER DURESS. HOUSE FULL OF PEOPLE I DIDN'T KNOW. VERY LOVELY GIFTS, I'M GREEN WITH ENVY!"

It had only been three days since we returned from our whirlwind tour of Al's relatives; less than a month had passed since I arrived in the U.S. The time change (five hours back from British time), the letdown from the stress of meeting so many new people and also missing much-needed sleep, had all taken their toll. And today came a showdown with my mother-in-law!

Marjie's bridal shower was to take place that evening. When I lived in England a "shower" meant only a sprinkle of rain! When I had asked Al's mother what a bridal shower was she had said: "Oh, it's just a gathering of a bunch of women who sit around while the bride-to-be opens her gifts. Then they all have dessert and go home."

Al was working the day shift, so I had been up at six-thirty to get his breakfast, pack his lunch and see him drive off in Richie's old Plymouth. There was some wash to do, so I did it by hand in the kitchen, rather than cope with the washing machine, which by now I was convinced was out to get me!

Before he left for work, Al had stoked up the coal-burning kitchen stove, and a cheerful aroma of hot coffee was coming from the pot on top of it. Footsteps descending the stairs heralded the arrival of Mom Greene, who was obviously feeling out of sorts. She exuded an atmosphere of gloom as she sat down at the kitchen table.

I said brightly: "Good morning, Mom. The coffee's nice and hot, let me get you a cup." No response. I filled a cup with coffee and set it down in front of her, with the cream pitcher and sugar bowl. Still no response.

I thought: "When she's in this kind of a mood, my best bet is to disappear, and I still have to buy a gift for Marjie, so I'll go up to Pinewood on the bus, buy the gift, and visit with Laurie to get my spirits up."

As soon as I could escape the brooding silence, which I sat through while Mom Greene had her breakfast, I caught the bus to Pinewood.

In one of the gift shops, I found a lovely embroidered linen tablecloth and six matching napkins. I had them gift-wrapped, and wrote a special "Bridal Shower Wishes" card to tuck under the ribbon.

I knocked on the door of Laurie's new apartment, and a few minutes later we were enjoying a cup of tea together.

"Great news, Laurie. We've put a down payment on a little house. I'll be so glad to move; it isn't a bed of roses living with Al's mother, you know, or for her either, having Al and me invading her home. We try to give her a break--we often eat out at a couple of those awful 'Mom and Pop' restaurants in town; $1.50 for a meal that Al says isn't even worth 75 cents!"

"I know, Bunty," she replied. I had to live on my father-in-law's chicken farm when I first came here, and that was pretty stressful until we found this apartment."

"Oh, Laurie, I really dread going to this bridal shower tonight--one more roomful of people I've never met, and I'm so tired."

Laurie thought for a minute. "O.K., all you have to do is to say very sweetly: 'Mom, would you mind taking my gift with you tonight? I'm really very tired, and I need to get to bed early.'"

It sounded fine as I rehearsed it on the bus back to Little Cedar River, but when I tried it out I wasn't prepared for the explosion that followed. Al's mother looked at me, eyes flashing with rage, as she virtually howled: "You *must* attend Marjie's shower, my girl. It's your duty as one of the family." She continued her tirade, warming to her theme with increasing decibels and repeating herself until I thought I might explode, too. All I wanted to do was to crawl into bed and have a good cry. Where was Al when I needed him? He wouldn't be home until five o'clock, or maybe even later, if he had to work late.

Homesickness gripped me for the beautiful rolling green country-side of England, and for the closeness my Mom and I had enjoyed for so many years. I threw myself across the bed and let the tears flow, drifting into an emotionally exhausted sleep and awaking to decide to comply with the summons and go to the shower. Composure regained, I took my only good dress out of the "shiff-o-robe" as Mom Greene called it, and braced myself. The shower wasn't the ordeal I had imagined, and in one respect I should have been grateful to have been forced into going, as the ceremony proved to be good preparation for me two days later.

Al: "THURSDAY, APRIL 11: HOUSE APPRAISED AT $4,500. ASKING PRICE: $5,000. WILL ASK OWNER TO REDUCE PRICE, THEN CAN SWING DEAL."

Bunty: "'OUR' HOUSE HAS BEEN APPRAISED, PRICE TOO HIGH BY $500 BUT COMPROMISE REACHED. WENT TO A BABY SHOWER THIS EVENING FOR WIFE OF ONE OF MEN AT RADIO STATION. HAD A WONDERFUL TIME. DIDN'T GET HOME UNTIL 2 A.M.! THE GALS DECIDED TO MEET ONCE A MONTH."

Nowadays it seems incredible that $500 too much in the price of the house would have made such a difference, but in those days it was obviously a lot of money. At $4,600 the compromise made everyone happy. The sale was in motion!

That evening, Al walked me up the front path of the most beautiful house I'd seen in the U.S.: the home of his boss, whose wife was giving a surprise shower for the first baby expected among the wives of the radiomen who had returned from World War Two to work at the radio station. Al rang the doorbell.

"Oh, hello, Al--don't worry, someone will bring your new bride home. Come on in, Bunty, and meet everyone." Nancy Cooke gently took the gift clutched in my hand, and then my coat.

After Marjie's bridal shower I felt more like a veteran; this time I knew what to expect, so I was prepared with a gift and card ahead of time. Twelve women were already seated in a circle around the beautifully appointed living room which was festooned with pink and blue crepe paper streamers for the occasion.

I sat down on the sofa, and Nancy addressed the assembly: "Girls, this is Bunty Greene, Al's new wife from England. Welcome, Bunty. Now,

girls, I told Charlene I was just having a social meeting for the radio station wives, and gave her a time an hour later than I gave all of you, so
the shower will be a complete surprise for her when she arrives. While
we're waiting, why don't we all get acquainted by telling a little about
ourselves?"

The radio station had been undergoing postwar expansion. Like myself, most of the wives were strangers to New Jersey, some having recently
moved from the New York area. When it was my turn, I said: "Well, I came
here by the scenic route: Africa, then England, and now New Jersey!"

There was a surprised murmur, a short burst of applause, and a circle
of smiles. I thought happily: "That clinched it. I think I'm 'in'--one more
step in the 'Americanization of Bunty' as Al calls it."

The evening accomplished something more than we had expected.
In between the "ooh's" and "aah's" as each baby gift was unwrapped by
an excited Charlene, we decided to get together once a month.

What to call our new club was solved by one of the husbands. "Of
course, you can only be called one thing: 'The Static Club.' That's just
what a roomful of women all talking at once sounds like--the static on the
radio!"

These were the days before FM, and the crackling noise of the in-
terference that marked radio reception was, and still is, called by radiomen "static." So the Static Club we became, and we remained so for
many years until our husbands' A.T.& T. transfers took most of us away. In
contrast to Marjie's shower, time at this one had flown by for me. Nancy
Cooke served a mouth-watering dessert after all the gifts were opened,
and the chatter continued until the wee hours, by which time we were
all firm friends. Al was waiting up for me when one of the girls drove me
home at 2 a.m..

"Hi, hon', how come you could stay awake this long?" he asked,
sleepily.

I felt as fresh as a daisy: "Oh, I guess all the excitement overstimu-
lated me, but don't get any ideas!"

I should have known better; Mr. Greene was always full of ideas, and we found a perfect ending to a perfect day.

Bunty: "THURSDAY, APRIL 18: AMY HAS A CAR! SHE TOOK MOM GREENE TO PENNSYLVANIA TODAY, LEAVING ME AS CHIEF COOK AND BOTTLE WASHER! TRIED MY HAND AT MAKING A MEAL FOR AL AND BILL."

Amy had bought an elderly second-hand car; she was itching to take a trip in it. Mom Greene left with her for a few days at Boothwyn, taking her cooking expertise along. Panic seized me; she had also left behind two hungry working men, and I hadn't yet been entrusted with cooking an entire dinner.

"HORRORS!" I thought. "I've never had to cook a whole dinner before, but thank goodness I have a cookbook. Mom always said: "Anyone who can read, can cook!" A few days prior, Laurie had invited Al and me to her apartment for a meal. She produced a superb chicken dinner, followed by a delicious dessert. I was completely in awe of her cooking, and wondered if my miserable culinary skills would ever match hers. The first test was to come sooner than I had expected!

With a heavy heart I leafed through my "Acme Cookbook". Laurie and I had each bought one at the local grocery store on her first visit to me at Little Cedar River. ("Betty Crocker" had not yet appeared on the culinary scene with her kitchen-tested recipes.) Resigning myself to the inevitable, I became optimistic: "Well, I'd better give it a try; if Laurie can do it, I can do it!"

The "Lamb Chop and Vegetable Casserole" looked easy enough. To give myself plenty of time, I started preparing it before lunch, cutting the vegetables into precise half-inch cubes as directed. With the chops arranged on top, it looked just like the picture in the cookbook. So far, so good! The casserole spent all afternoon in the refrigerator. The recipe said to cook it for an hour, so I took it out of the refrigerator an hour before dinner time and put it in the oven.

An encouraging aroma wafted from the oven as Bill, home from work, erupted into the kitchen. He danced a little jig: "Hi-de-ho-hello! What's buzzin', cousin? How y'a doin', Bunty?" he burbled, giving me a brotherly bear hug.

I thought to myself: "Well, it *sounded* a bit like English!" Not knowing how to respond to his "jive talk", I smiled and said, trying to convince myself: "O.K., thanks Bill. I've had a great day getting acquainted with my new cookbook. Dinner will be ready as soon as Al gets home. How was *your* day?"

Al arrived shortly afterwards. "Boy-oh-boy, something sure smells good!" He sniffed appreciatively.

Triumphantly, I brought the casserole to the table, and they forked the perfectly browned lamb chops off the top and onto their plates. Bill was an accomplished cook, and I was more worried about his reaction than Al's, who probably would have eaten anything I had put in front of him and said it was wonderful.

Bill hovered over his plate and sniffed. "M-mm, smells great! I thought you said you couldn't cook, Bunty. This looks terrif'!" He helped himself lavishly to the gravy and precisely cubed veggies. I watched him lift the first forkful to his mouth and strained my ears, listening hopefully for sounds of satisfaction. All I heard was: "crunch, crunch,"

My heart sank; the veggies weren't cooked! The "Acme Cookbook" hadn't told me that because the casserole had been in the cold refrigerator for so long, it should be brought to room temperature before cooking, or, if not, that it should be left in the oven to cook an extra half-hour! I wanted to die!

Al and Bill did the dishes, (no electric dishwashers in homes yet, in 1946) and their reassuring hugs eventually stemmed my tears and restored my bruised ego. Between sobs, I said to Al: "Don't tell Laurie!"

Forest Fire!

Bunty: "SATURDAY, APRIL 20: SPENT LAST NIGHT ALONE IN THE EMPTY HOUSE. BRRR! SPOOKY. GLAD WHEN AL CAME HOME FROM

WORK AT 1 A.M.! TODAY FIRE SIRENS SOUNDED ALL DAY LONG: FOREST FIRES! AND THE MARSHES AT MANAHAWKIN ARE ON FIRE, TOO!"

It had been an unsettling day--the wailing of the neighborhood fire siren, followed by the clanging of bells and screaming of sirens on the fire trucks as they stormed out of their firehouses into the distance.

Amy had explained it all when it first had happened the previous week: "This is forest fire season, Bunty, here in south Jersey. It happens in the dry weather in spring. Sometimes hundreds of acres of pine forest are burning. Roads and even schools and stores have to be closed because of the heavy smoke, and because nobody knows where the wind will take the fires."

They say everything seems worse at night. The old house creaked and groaned as the spring winds whipped around it in the dark. Al was working the evening shift, from 4 p.m. to midnight. It normally took him almost an hour to get home. Amy and Mom Greene were in Pennsylvania. Bill was out. I checked the doors and windows over and over to make sure I was safely locked in! I was still wide awake when Al came home at 1 a.m., and announced that he had to go back on the day shift, from 8 a.m. to 4 p.m. This meant he had to leave home again at 7 a.m. It would be a short night's sleep, but there was worse to come.

Near Little Cedar River were miles of coastal plain: the New Jersey pine barrens. After the winter, last year's dry underbrush in the forests and dry reeds on the coastal marshes needed very little to set them alight: a spark from a careless cigarette butt, a campfire not properly extinguished, or even a broken piece of glass reflecting heat from the sun's rays, were enough to do the trick. Fanned by winds and fed by the rising sap in the trees, fires raced through hundreds of acres of scrub pine and scrub oak before being brought under control.

I began to worry when Al wasn't home by his usual time at 5 p.m. after working the day shift. Finally, an hour later, I heard the car in the driveway. He burst through the door, coughing and white as a sheet, and threw himself onto a kitchen chair. Alarmed, I quickly poured him a cup of coffee. I quavered: "Poor darling, something terrible must have happened; relax and tell me all about it."

Al was trembling. "Let me calm down first, love, and I'll tell you a story that will make your hair stand on end!"

He drank his coffee, and helped by the warmth of the coal stove the color returned to his cheeks. Wearily, he began: "Well, hon', as you know I was pretty tired, having to switch from the evening shift to the day shift without much sleep, but the scene that morning as I came closer to the radio station had my adrenalin pumping. The wind gusts were tossing sparks across the highway from the forest fires that were already burning, and they had ignited the dry marsh grass around the radio station. By that time I was coughing from the blowing smoke seeping into the car. I parked and ran inside the station. The night shift guys had had a scary night, but conditions worsened, and now all of us were trapped inside the building. The fires swept from the huge MUSA antennas on the marshes toward the station, scorching the garage. We could see the flames licking closer. They were only a few feet away from the walls of the station before the firemen had them under control. There were volunteer fire companies from towns all around, and now I know why they call them 'firefighters.' They sure had a fight on their hands, and thank God they won."

Al continued with his story: "Fortunately, Richie's car wasn't damaged. A little after four o'clock, I somehow got it out onto the highway. We would have been trapped like fish in a barrel if the one-lane access road from the highway to the station had been blocked by the fire. Only the heroic efforts of dozens of fire companies from the surrounding towns and villages, and the grace of God, had spared us."

I listened to Al re-living his ordeal.

"But the nightmare continued. Daylight was fading; thick clouds of smoke drifted across the unlit highway from the forest fires. Crawling along at almost zero miles per hour, I couldn't see which lane I was in, or even where the center line was on the road. The smell of the smoke filled the car. Seemed like hours until I finally drove out of the fire zone. Home never looked better!"

He was still shaking, so I tried to make him laugh with funny stories of my experiences with the fire sirens.

"Remember the first time the sirens went off when I was buying pork chops at the butcher shop? I didn't know that Little Cedar River's volunteer firemen always responded immediately; no matter what they were doing, they just dropped whatever it was and ran to the fire station. That's exactly what the butcher did--dropped my pork chops in the middle of cutting them, and rushed out to the street to jump on the fire truck as it passed by the store on its way to the fire. I ran out of the store after him; we never did have pork chops for dinner that night!"

Al smiled and squeezed my hand. I threw in another funny story for good measure: "You know how the neighborhood siren nearly blows your ears off when it goes into action? Remember the time when I first arrived here from England and we were all sitting around the dinner table when it went off with an ear-splitting blast? It reminded me of our 'Moaning Minnie' air raid siren back home! With that memory still fresh in my mind from the war, remember how I dived under the table and ended up on the floor? I think I almost scared everyone to death!"

The stories evoked a chuckle, then: "Hey, hon', let's go to bed early." Al was back to normal!

American Generosity

Bunty: "MONDAY, APRIL 22: WHAT'S WRONG WITH THE FAMILY? AMY AND MOM GREENE CAME BACK FROM PENNSYLVANIA THIS MORNING AND TOOK ME SHOPPING. DIDN'T LET ME OUT OF THEIR SIGHT! AMY KEPT ME BUSY TIDYING UP THE BACKYARD ALL AFTERNOON. THIS EVENING WENT WITH THEM TO BAPTIST CHURCH. AHA! JOAN AND I WERE GIVEN A SURPRISE KITCHEN SHOWER!"

My sister-in-law had kept me busy all day. There was no time to slip up to Pinewood to see Laurie; she had seen to that! The morning was leisurely and fun. Among the shops on Main Street we browsed in the "Five and Ten Cent Store"--a Woolworth's which reminded me of the one at

Croydon back in England. We bought some odds and ends for my new home. Next, Amy and I helped Mom Greene to shop for groceries and carry them back to the weathered old house.

It had been a strenuous afternoon. After doing yard work with Amy, I was feeling sweaty and tired. I decided to stay in my blue jeans until bedtime, then take a bath, get into my pajamas, and have an early night.

After dinner, Mom Greene looked at me quizzically. "Bunty, you should go upstairs and get cleaned up and changed. Remember, I told you we have to go to the Baptist Church; the ladies in the Missionary Guild are having their monthly meeting, and I've told them about my new little daughter-in-law. They asked me to bring you to the meeting so they could meet you. Amy's coming, too."

"Oh, Lord," I thought, as I trudged upstairs to the bathroom, "another roomful of new faces! But having had one showdown already with Mom Greene, I don't want another--I'm just not up to it! I'll make the supreme sacrifice and get washed and changed; I wouldn't want to upset the whole Missionary Guild by not showing up. And anyway, if Amy's coming it can't be that bad."

When I came downstairs well-scrubbed, wearing a clean skirt and blouse and with makeup newly applied, nobody knew I'd had any other idea in mind, and off we went.

In the church hall was a large group of women sitting in a circle, and I was puzzled when I saw Joan among them. The minute I walked in, they all shouted: "Surprise!" I looked behind me to see who they were shouting at. Then, to my astonishment, they all stood up clapping their hands. It must be me! Adrenalin rush! I wasn't tired any more!

One of the women led me to a chair next to Joan, near a strange contraption that looked suspiciously like a large, round garbage can covered with copious quantities of pink crepe paper. Above it, on a wire arch hung with pink and white streamers, was a lettered sign saying: "WISHING WELL". When they had all finished clapping and had sat down again, someone said to Joan: "Reach into the wishing well, Joan, and find something with your name on it."

Joan brought up a beautifully wrapped package and opened it. Inside was a set of colorful kitchen towels. Everyone gasped, "Ooh!" Then it was my turn. I fished out a package from the "well". Inside was a set of pretty fruit juice glasses. Everyone murmured, "Aah!", and so it went on until two piles of boxes sat on the floor next to Joan and me. I was overwhelmed, sure that I was dreaming the whole thing as I unwrapped one delightful surprise gift after another: kitchen gadgets, tea towels, a cookie jar, place mats with matching napkins, and a set of two exquisitely carved wooden wall plaques with scenes of cottages, one in winter and one in summer.

Next day, when I looked at thirty-seven gifts displayed on the dining room table, I knew I hadn't dreamed it all, and once again I marveled at the loving generosity that these gifts represented. I now knew what an American "shower" meant, but I hadn't expected I'd be on the receiving end of one!

On a trip to the church ladies' room after the shower and dessert, Joan confided to me that she was going to the doctor on Saturday, afraid she might be pregnant. I prayed this wouldn't happen to me--not yet!

I found it a bit disconcerting when I caught the ladies at the shower furtively glancing in the direction of my middle, and I often wondered if Mom Greene had gone to bed in shock for a week when Al announced our sudden engagement, because she was convinced that I was pregnant! "Well," I fretted to Al, "I'm sick of seeing their eyes wander down from my face to my abdomen every time I meet them. I just hope we can make them wait!"

Fortune smiled on us--we were able to have a home, furniture and a bank account before welcoming our daughter, two years later!

Operation Fur Coat

Al: "WEDNESDAY, APRIL 24: BILL LOANED ME HIS CAR. WE TOOK OFF FOR NEWARK, ARRIVED AT IRVINGTON TO VISIT JOAN AND BUD, AFTER A FEW WRONG TURNS. GOOD TIME WITH THE HOFFMANS."

Bunty: "DROVE UP TO NORTH JERSEY TO VISIT JOAN AND BUD HOFFMAN ON OUR WAY TO NEW YORK CITY. HAD A GREAT VISIT. DINNER AND DANCING OUT. STAYED OVERNIGHT AT THEIR APARTMENT."

Al was currently enjoying what he called a "four day weekend" (four consecutive days off, after working two weeks straight.) Today, we were embarking on a mission in New York City, with an overnight stop on the way, to take Joan and Bud up on their invitation when we met at Joan's and my kitchen shower at the Little Cedar River Baptist Church.

When my Mom knew I was going to America to live, she had put aside some of her savings which she gave to me before I left England. Placing an envelope in my hand, she had looked at me very seriously: "Now, Bunty, I want you to promise me you will use this money to buy yourself a fur coat when you get to America. I know they have terribly cold winters there, and I want you to be warm."

I was stunned. I'm sure Mom must have formed her impression of North American winters after watching the frozen wastes in those old movies starring the Royal Canadian Mounted Police. After consulting her world atlas, she was undoubtedly convinced that New Jersey was almost on the Canadian border, and she was determined that her only child should not freeze to death. Every letter from her ended: "Bunty, have you bought your fur coat yet?"

Lurking among the reading materials at Al's radio station was an enormous mail order catalog from a company with showrooms in New York City, offering discount prices to A.T.&T. employees. Al had borrowed the catalog and brought it home for me to see. I spent hours looking over pictures of a mouth-watering array of merchandise, from diamond rings to baby carriages--also a page full of fur coats.

Every day when Al came home from work, he would ask: "Well, Bunty, have you chosen your fur coat?"

At last I had said uncomfortably: "Darling, I appreciate seeing the catalog, but I don't feel right about paying that kind of money for something I've only seen in a picture, or, even more important, that I've never tried on. And how could I know which one to choose from that whole page of gorgeous fur coats?"

"Well, my love, I don't think I can stand any more of your Mom's reminders! New York isn't that far away--let's go and see what's in that catalog!"

"But what will we use for a car? Richie's may never make it!"

"Not to worry, sweetheart, I'll swing a deal and swap Brother Bill's car for Richie's, just for the trip."

So we had called Joan and Bud Hoffman, and arranged to stop overnight with them first. Bud had decided to attend university courses in Newark, taking advantage of the "G.I. Bill" passed by Congress to help World War Two veterans, many of whom were struggling to make ends meet with civilian expenses. He and Joan had an apartment in Irvington, an easy commute.

Al and I were struggling, too, to place our marriage on a firm foundation with the basic necessities. But today, to celebrate our first visit together, the four of us decided to splurge.

Bud said: "I know just the place for us to go--the 'Meadowbrook'--I'll drive us."

Frank Dailey's Meadowbrook was an enormous, imposing building, a short ride from Joan and Bud's apartment. Inside was the largest dance floor I had ever seen, with dining tables surrounding it. A "Big Band" was already playing on the stage, couples were dancing, and the tables were beginning to fill up with diners.

The Meadowbrook had its heyday in the 1930s and 1940s for dining and dancing, becoming celebrated nationally for the Big Bands who played there: Glenn Miller, Artie Shaw, Benny Goodman, Tommy and Jimmy Dorsey, to name a few. Radio programs were broadcast regularly from the Meadowbrook, featuring such singers as Frank Sinatra and Jo Stafford. Al and I danced together for the first time since Rainbow Corner.

"We could have used a dance floor this size at Rainbow," commented Al, huffing a little over the jitterbugging we had just done, "but I wouldn't have swapped this for what we had there, would you, hon'?"

Trying to catch my breath, I just shook my head in reply. However, this evening was for me another once-in-a-lifetime experience to be topped by none other like it. I *had* to write it all down; my next letter home to Mom and Dad was a fat one!

Bunty: "THURSDAY, APRIL 25: SAID FAREWELLS TO JOAN AND BUD. LEFT AT 10 A.M. FOR NEW YORK. SHOPPED FOR FUR COAT, ALSO AN ELECTRIC IRON. AFTER LUNCH, AL TOOK ME TO RADIO CITY MUSIC HALL. MOVIE FOLLOWED BY INCREDIBLE EASTER PAGEANT. WONDERFUL DAY, WONDERFUL HUSBAND!"

Joan was fairly certain in her fears about her pregnancy. I hoped fervently that her coming visit to the doctor would prove they were unfounded. The added expense and responsibility were something she and Bud didn't need right now. But time would tell, and Joan's worries were left behind as we pulled away from our delightful visit; my focus was on our day in the city which was not yet known as "The Big Apple."

In New York, Al successfully navigated his way to a parking garage, and within minutes we were walking into the showrooms at the address on the catalog.

"May I help you, sir?" A sympathetic-looking sales clerk came up to Al, who cleared his throat and said with an air of great importance:

"Oh, yes, thank you, we're looking for a fur coat."

The sales clerk looked quizzically at us, dressed in our casual clothes. Visibly baffled, he was probably wondering whether this young, naïve-looking couple were joking. The thought crossed my mind that he had an uneasy look about him as if he might be thinking Al would suddenly pull a gun out of his coat pocket and say: "Reach, this is a stick-up." However, he nodded professionally and led us into a second showroom packed with racks full of hangers on which were sample fur coats in all shapes, colors and sizes.

I had never seen so many fur coats! Mustering my best "young and innocent" smile, I addressed the sales clerk: "I must confess I'm confused and dazzled by the many different kinds of coats you have, but I'm going to trust your expertise to help me find the one that would be best. I don't have a winter coat, so I need a fur coat that will wear well, not only for special occasions, but to keep me warm every day in winter and to last for many years."

The sales clerk bristled with authority. "Well, madam, the most hard-wearing fur we have is Mink-Dyed Northern Back Muskrat. It's made with fur from the backs of the muskrats, for hard wear, and I suggest a full-length coat rather than a jacket."

I tried on the sleek coat, feeling its enveloping luxury and comfort. For good measure, I tried on a few other types of fur in various styles, but came back to the original one.

"I like this one best, too, hon'," said Al obligingly.

So I ended up with full-length Mink-Dyed Northern Back Muskrat coat. We paid for it in full, and made arrangements for it to be ordered. The sales clerk suggested: "Since you will not need to wear the coat before the colder weather, would you like to have it professionally stored free of charge? You may request it to be shipped at any time you wish."

We thought this was a good idea, and it was specified on our receipt.

Infected with the spending mood, I suddenly suggested: "While we're here, Al, we do need an electric iron!"

The ecstatic sales clerk conducted us to the showroom filled with small appliances, where he made another sale.

Overcome with the thought of all the money we had spent, I said sternly to myself: "You'd better come down to earth, my girl, after being wrapped up in that fur. But on the other hand, 'extravagance demands practicality,' that's what Mom would say. I'll bet she'll be pleased to hear I've bought an iron, too!"

After a quick sandwich we walked to Radio City Music Hall, another larger-than-life experience for me. We joined the long line winding almost to the end of the block. It moved very quickly. People were coming out from the previous show, and soon we were swallowed up in the massive art deco theater. A full-length movie and the recital by Radio City's famous grand organ were followed by the icing on the cake: the annual Easter Pageant, a spectacular stage show that made the ones in London look tiny by comparison.

Maybe I felt a bit smug about owning a fur coat, on the ride back to Little Cedar River, but this must have been how Mom would have wanted me to feel--her gift to me. I said a quick prayer of thanks for a mother who had saved and sacrificed to keep me warm in the "North American blizzards" to come.

The past two days had been like another honeymoon, just Al and me on our own at last. On the way home he was quiet until we were out of the city traffic, and then he said: "Thank goodness, maybe now your Mom's letters won't be so monotonous!"

Meantime, the "Americanization of Bunty" was in full swing. After my encounters with the infamous "two-way stretch" and lately with the phenomenon of American showers, now that duty visits to the family were over Al reckoned it was time for me to meet some of his friends. He was anxious for me not to have further embarrassing occasions, so he briefed me on American customs ahead of time, but soon one was to sneak in that he didn't anticipate.

Earl Clayton and Al were friends in the Sons of the American Legion band. A phone call from Linda, Earl's wife, invited us to join them for dinner at Little Cedar River's only hotel, "The Riverview", whose dining room windows overlooked the wide river with its marina. Earl knew we still had car trouble, so he offered to pick us up for our dinner date.

I wasn't prepared for what happened next. Al and I walked out to where the car was parked at the curb. Earl and Linda stepped out of the car to greet us. Linda said: "So good to see you again, Al," and smiled at me.

Al shook hands with Earl, then introduced me: "Earl and Linda, this is my wife Bunty, the gal I've talked about so much."

Earl took a step forward. "So this is our new little English war bride? Glad to meet you, Bunty."

I thought I was well prepared. In England everyone shook hands with everyone else. Anxious to be a credit to Al with my English manners, I leaped forward with outstretched hand and shook hands vigorously with Earl. Linda recoiled in shock, as if I had attacked the poor fellow. What Al had forgotten to tell me was that, in Little Cedar River etiquette, men shake hands with men, but for women a mere nod of the head is customary.

I sighed to myself: "Out with another English custom and in with Little Cedar River etiquette! It's too late now, but I'll add it to my list of 'do's' and 'don'ts', and I'll get it right next time!"

The meal was magnificent, as was the view, and I hoped our good time together would give Linda time to recover from my handshaking blunder. Later, I sad to Al: "Well, dear, that's one American custom that slipped between the floorboards, but at least Linda and Earl will never forget me!"

Welcome Dinners

Al: "FRIDAY, APRIL 26: BACK AGAIN ON DAY TOUR AT WORK. IT'S MURDER GETTING UP AT 6:30 A.M.! VISITED FOLKS WHO RUN HIGHLAND LAUNDRY. SAW HOME MOVIE TAKEN AT RECENT CHURCH 'DINNER AND SOCIAL' FOR RETURNING SERVICEMEN FROM LITTLE CEDAR RIVER. BUNTY AND I WERE IN THE MOVIE, LARGE AS LIFE. WE SEEM TO BE QUITE PHOTOGENIC!"

Bunty: "AL WENT BACK TO WORK. WE WERE INVITED TO DINNER WITH MACPHERSONS. GORGEOUS HOUSE ON RIVERFRONT--PRIVATE BEACH, SAILBOATS! DELIGHTFUL EVENING."
The phone rang. I heard the soft Scottish burr in the woman's voice.
"This is Heather MacPherson. Is this Bunty Greene? We've heerd that ye've just ar-rived here frae England, and we thought we'd like to get acquainted. Och, I know it's short notice, but d'ye think ye and yoor hus-band could come to dinner toneet? We'd loove to meet ye."

Al was working the day shift, so this was fine. Amy and Bill could fend for themselves!

Jock MacPherson and his wife, Heather, had emigrated from Scotland over a decade before and had established the first laundry in Little Cedar River, a lucrative business which had grown with the town, largely due to their hard work and "canny Scot" business acumen. The Highland Laundry was now the largest in the entire area, and the MacPhersons were now very wealthy. My diary gushed about the beautiful home they had built on the riverfront, overlooking their own private beach with its dock, and several sailboats moored nearby. My jottings proclaimed: "WHAT AN AMAZING HOUSE THEY HAVE--HUGE! LOVELIEST I'VE EVER BEEN IN! SIX BEDROOMS AND EACH WITH A PRIVATE BATH. WOW!"

After showing us the home movie he had made at the Welcome Home social at the Methodist Church when Joan and I first arrived, Jock told us about his "war work". His Scottish brogue grew more pronounced as he spoke: "Och, ear-rr-ly in the war, when I hair-rr-d that British Royal Navy ships came into yon Brooklyn Navy Yard for repairs, I telephoned the Yard and asked if I could bring some of those sailor-boys home wi' me for a wee bit've rest and relaxation on their time off. I'm tellin' ye, I drove up whenever they came in and collected a few at a time, especially those lads frae Bonnie Sco'land. Och aye, to be sure, we felt it was doin' our bit for the war effort and it wa' good to hear that loovely Scottish brogue again! Some o' those brave lads kept in touch with us; truly grateful they were for our hospitality. For Heather and me, t'was a fair treat to give 'em home-cooked meals, let 'em use our beach and boaats on the river and mek sure they had a nice relaxin' time for themselves awa'a from the perils o' the North Atlantic. I dinna ken how many we've had here, but it must've been dozens over the war years."

Bunty: "SUNDAY, APRIL 28: MOM GREENE, BILL AND AMY COOKED A SPECIAL WELCOME DINNER IN MY HONOR. THEY INVITED LAURIE, JOAN AND THEIR HUSBANDS. TURKEY AND ALL THE TRIMMINGS! WENT TO BOARDWALK AT SEASIDE HEIGHTS AFTERWARDS FOR SOME SEA AIR."

My welcome to America continued. This time it was Mom Greene who decided to give a dinner party. Bill and Amy, both expert in the kitchen, helped her with the preparations. An article in the social column of the local paper was titled: "MRS. IDA GREENE SR. ENTERTAINS FOR BRIDE

FROM ENGLAND." I still have the piece of yellowed newsprint listing the names of all of us who sat around the table that day.

I was touched by Mom Greene's thoughtfulness toward me, when she invited my best friends Laurie and Joan and their husbands to the superb turkey dinner with all the trimmings, topped off by one of her spectacular apple pies for dessert. On the spot, I decided not to try apple-pie baking; I would never be able to make a pie for Al "like Mother used to make"-- with my kind of luck, the apples would still be raw!

We were all feeling decidedly full afterwards. Bill said: "How about a trip to the shore? We need to walk this dinner off on the boardwalk!"

We piled into two cars and rumbled across the wooden bridge over Barnegat Bay to Seaside Heights, playground for day trippers from nearby towns and tourists from Philadelphia.

The mile-long, action-packed boardwalk was equipped with a carousel and a large variety of rides: roller coasters, dodgem cars, games stands, a fun house, souvenir shops and booths smelling of exotic eatables I had never seen before.

Strolling along the wooden boardwalk together, licking cones of frozen custard, we were kids again; my previous life in England seemed a million miles away.

Al: "FRIDAY, MAY 3: GOT HOME FROM WORK YESTERDAY TO FIND ERNIE ASSEMBLING TRANSMISSION FOR NASH! OUR CAR IS READY AT LAST! WE DROVE TO CAMDEN TODAY TO GIVE COUSIN BILL PEEL A COPY OF CONTRACT OF SALE FOR HOUSE TO LOOK OVER BEFORE WE SIGN."

Bunty: "NATHANIEL NASH IS READY! HAD A GREAT RIDE TO CAMDEN AND BACK IN HIM TODAY."

Al's second cousin Bill Peel was an attorney, raised in Camden where his mother, Mom Greene's cousin, still lived with her family. He willingly looked over the Contract of Sale for our house and pronounced it legally sound.

"Nathaniel Nash" (dubbed fancifully in memory of Revolutionary War General Nathaniel Greene) performed perfectly; at last we could return the borrowed car to Richie Engelmann. Al added wryly: "before it falls apart! Whew!"

Was it the shock of reaching the end of all those weeks waiting for Nathaniel to be road-ready, or just being weary of writing? Who knows? But from now on there were no more daily entries in Al's diary. For some unknown reason there were dozens of empty pages, with only an occasional notation here and there.

Bunty: "SUNDAY, MAY 5: AUNT MARY HAS APPENDICITIS. BILL AND MARJIE TOOK MOM GREENE TO BOOTHWYN TO TAKE CARE OF TOM WHILE SHE'S RECOVERING FROM HER OPERATION. AMY WORKED TODAY. AL IS ON MIDNIGHT SHIFT FOR THE SECOND WEEK. I'M IN CHARGE AGAIN, UGH!"

Mom Greene was sometimes away for one or even two weeks, and I was once again left with the management of the house. Al, Bill and Amy helped when they could, but I was weary of their erratic work schedules and the unending cooking, housekeeping, washing and ironing. Some days I felt ready to pack my bags and go back to England, but I loved Al too much!

Bunty: "SATURDAY, MAY 11: AL HAS FOUR DAYS OFF! TO CELEBRATE, TOOK A TRIP IN NATHANIEL NASH TO BORDENTOWN TO SEE THE FAMOUS WALKER-GORDON DAIRY FARM. FANTASTIC! IN EVENING WENT WITH TWO OTHER COUPLES TO ASBURY PARK TO A DINNER CLUB. DINED AND DANCED. GREAT DAY!"

Al gave me a hug. "How about getting you out of the house, hon'? Let's take the day off." He was worried about having worked two weeks straight, confining me to managing the housekeeping demands for so long without a break, in Mom Greene's absence. Now that the Nash was in good working condition, we were free!

The pride of central New Jersey, and a favorite tourist attraction, was Borden's Walker-Gordon Dairy Farm: a sprawling complex spread over 150 acres, with 1,500 cows producing more than 24,000 quarts of milk per day. The farm's star attraction was the "Rotolactor," a huge automated milking-platform that could milk fifty cows at a time!

Exhibited at the 1939 New York World's Fair, the Rotolactor had "wowed" the crowds. It continued to do so over the years, attracting thousands of tourists to the New Jersey dairy farm. Cows were washed before stepping onto the Rotolactor. As we watched, the glass-enclosed circular platform slowly rotated until it stopped at a waiting cow. The cow already in the stall was disconnected from the automatic milking apparatus on its udder and stepped out, looking rather relieved, to amble away and let the new one step into the vacated stall. The newly-arrived cow was then attached to the milking machine by an attendant, and the Rotolactor began another rotation. By the time each cow had made a complete rotation on the platform, it had been milked and was released.

On that sunny day in May, we didn't know we were witnessing a vanishing part of New Jersey's history. In another few years the farm was no more; the land it stood on is now occupied by more than three hundred single-family homes! The Rotolactor ended up in the Smithsonian National Museum in Washington, D.C.

That evening we went out to dine and dance at a dinner club in Asbury Park with Al's high school friend Norman Isaacs and his girlfriend, who had brought along another couple. Six people fitted comfortably into Nathaniel's bench seats: three of us in each seat. What a fine ending to a splendid day; I felt human again!

Norman was the first of his friends whom Al had introduced to me when I arrived in Little Cedar River. His father owned a chicken farm on the outskirts of town. The German-Jewish family had fled from Nazi persecution in the early 1930s, helped in their U.S. immigration by a Jewish organization which had enabled them to settle in New Jersey with a means of earning a living.

Norman had a brilliant mind, but the family couldn't afford to send him to college; besides, he was needed to help on the farm. Among his passions was classical music, which was also one of mine. Unlike me, he could play the piano beautifully. Al and I had spent an evening with him when I first came to Little Cedar River, and we listened to some of his classical music collection on his phonograph. Describing that evening, my diary noted: "I HAD ONE OF THE MOST ENJOYABLE TIMES TONIGHT THAT I'VE HAD SINCE I CAME TO THE UNITED STATES. I HOPE AL IS GOING TO LOVE GOOD MUSIC AS MUCH AS I LOVE HIM."

After we finally moved into our own home, we invited Norman to dinner. He arrived carrying a large carton. "It's a belated wedding gift, but I wanted to deliver it when you had your own living room to put it in," he explained.

Excitedly, Al and I unpacked the carton. It contained a radio-phonograph in a classy walnut casing, and enclosed in the package was a recording of Mozart's Fortieth Symphony, my favorite piece of music!

Several years passed. Norman went to California to study farming methods. While there, he met and married Goldie, a lovely girl who was involved in a movement that recruited young immigrants to Israel to work in farming communities there. The young married couple signed up to join a kibbutz, journeying to the new state of Israel via England. I had given them my parents' address, and they ended up staying with them in Upper Woodside for several weeks before leaving for Israel.

My Mom and Dad were enchanted with the vibrant young couple, and, in turn, Norman and Goldie loved the warmth of their welcome as surrogate children during their stay. We all remained in touch for several years, but drifted apart as time went by, due to distance and the diversity of our lives.

Norman and his Goldie were two more ships that passed in the night, but like so many of the others, they had been treasured as close friends while they were with us.

"THURSDAY, MAY 16: MOM GREENE HAS STAYED ON IN BOOTHWYN TO HELP AUNT MARY'S RECOVERY FROM APPENDECTOMY. I WONDER HOW LONG THIS TIME? THERE'S NOT A BITE TO EAT IN THE HOUSE. WENT FOOD SHOPPING WITH AMY AND SPENT ALL MY HOUSEKEEPING MONEY."

Once again, I had been left as "chief cook and bottle-washer". I rationalized: "At least it's getting me used to the career of being a housewife!" Then I thought, angrily: "I know my Mom had neglected my housekeeping training back in England, but this is too much!"

I remembered wistfully my career at B.O.A.C. I would have loved to do secretarial work here in the U.S., but there was no opportunity for such a position in Little Cedar River. In those days, the town was too small to host a major business employer; the chance of a job such as mine was non-existent. I was left with the choice of shift work as a waitress, or waiting on customers at the local jewelry store.

Al said: "Forget it, sweets, you're doing just fine at home."

So it was back to the stifling kitchen; the crazy hours for meals; the temperamental vacuum cleaner; the vindictive washing machine and that sinister black coal stove! I wondered if I would ever escape.

Bunty: "SUNDAY, MAY 19: AL AND I DROVE TO SHENANDOAH FOR GRANDMOM AMY MILLARD'S BIRTHDAY CELEBRATION. DELICIOUS TURKEY LUNCH AND ENORMOUS BIRTHDAY CAKE."

What a welcome break! The morning four-hour-plus drive through the Pennsylvania mountains was magical, just Al and me and Nathaniel--at last a car we could call our own. I looked out at the now-familiar scenery as we drove slowly higher and higher up the winding mountain roads.

I was captivated by the scenery: "What a lovely sight it is, Al, with the mountain laurel coming into bloom on the hillsides; they're all covered with pink blossoms. No wonder mountain laurel is the state flower of Pennsylvania! It's so beautiful, it takes my breath away."

Al quipped: "Well, don't let it take all of your breath away, my love, you'll need plenty left to talk to all those folks at Aunt Ethel's. There's likely to be a mob scene up there."

A full house awaited us in Shenandoah. Most of the family members were present, as well as several of Grandmom Millard's friends. Aunt Ethel provided a magnificent buffet lunch, and those who couldn't get around the dining room table ended up with plates on their laps. The old lady presided over the proceedings like the family queen that she was, blowing out all the candles on her birthday cake without any help.

We had to drive back to Little Cedar River the same day, so Al could work the day shift the next morning. My following day's diary entry was a yelp of protest: "MADE AL'S BREAKFAST, AMY'S BREAKFAST, BILL'S LUNCH AND EVERYBODY'S SUPPER. WASHED A PILE OF DISHES FOUR TIMES TODAY--AWFUL!"

Bunty: "THURSDAY, MAY 30: MEMORIAL DAY. AL APPEARED IN THE MIDST OF THE PARADE, PLAYING HIS CLARINET WITH THE SONS OF THE AMERICAN LEGION BAND, AND LOOKING EXCEEDINGLY FED UP. HAD LUNCH, ALSO SUPPER, AT THE LEGION HALL."

Since his return home, Al had taken up some of his prewar routine again. An old high school diary recorded his determination to play the clarinet in the Sons of the American Legion band, noting frequent rehearsals in the American Legion Hall. At the urging of Mom Greene, he began practicing again shortly after I arrived in Little Cedar River.

"I simply can't stand it," I wrote to Mom and Dad, "after a few notes, there comes this dreadful shriek or squeak, and then he stops and begins all over again. It seems to happen at about the same place each time. I'm running out of things to do out in the backyard!"

I remembered that in England, on November 11--the date of the Armistice ending the First World War in 1918--two minutes of silence were observed all over Britain at the eleventh hour on the eleventh day of the eleventh month of the year, to honor the memory of the servicemen and women who died defending their country. Church services on the nearest Sunday were dedicated to their memory, and wreaths were laid at war memorials in cities, towns and villages. This date was also called "Poppy Day." Ex-servicemen sold lapel pins in the shape of small red paper poppies, to support charities helping those of their comrades in need; a reminder of the color of the red blood that was shed among the red poppies blooming on the killing fields of Flanders and throughout Europe during World War One and now during World War Two.

The American Memorial Day was a new experience for me. It officially shared the same commemorative purpose as Britain's Armistice Day, with parades and wreath-laying. It also signaled the beginning of the summer season with Memorial Day picnics. This was also the day when Little Cedar River ladies brought out their white summer shoes, pocketbooks and hats, and put away their winter ones.

Mom Greene called it "Decoration Day" because she traveled every year the fifty miles to Camden cemetery to decorate her husband's grave with flowers, even though he hadn't died in a war.

Al was reluctant to march in the parade, but the band needed clarinets, so he was persuaded. The practicing was excruciating to listen to, but when the great day came, there he was, marching down Main Street with his fellow Sons of the American Legion. "Miserable" is not a strong enough word to describe the look on his face, but I clapped and cheered as he went by, waving my small Stars and Stripes flag for good measure. I liked to think there was a new spring in his step as he marched on down Main Street.

Little Cedar River produced quite an impressive parade for such a small town. After the uniformed Boy and Girl Scouts, followed by the Cubs and Brownies, came a line of shiny volunteer fire trucks; then the volunteer First Aid Squad with their new ambulance, recently bought with donations from the local populace.

There were four marching bands: the Little Cedar River High School band with its prancing drum majorette, cheer leaders and baton twirlers; the Sons of the American Legion band bravely playing, but as if they wished they had had a few more rehearsals, and, lastly, two borrowed bands: cadets from the Admiral Farragut Naval Academy across the river, and an Army band from nearby Fort Dix, each with a small contingent of uniformed marchers.

The music and uniforms were an added excitement for the flag-waving small fry squatting on the curbs. Sitting on folding chairs or standing behind them, people waved flags, clapped and cheered. Through all the resulting pandemonium it was impossible to hear Al's clarinet. I was most grateful, and probably so was he!

The ladies of the American Legion Auxiliary, of which Mom Greene was currently president, provided buffet lunch sandwiches and salads for the occasion. Any leftovers were stored, and several families, including our own, enjoyed them for our supper. My diary ungraciously noted: "BUT IF I NEVER SEE POTATO SALAD AGAIN, IT'LL BE TOO SOON!"

Summer in South Jersey

Bunty: "SATURDAY, JUNE 1: NEVER EXPERIENCED SUCH A HOT DAY! AL AND I DROVE TO PHILADELPHIA TO SHOP FOR FURNITURE. PRICES NOT BAD AT FIRST DEPARTMENT STORE VISITED, BUT FURNITURE IN OUR PRICE RANGE WAS CHEAP AND AWFUL-LOOKING. GOOD STUFF TOO EXPENSIVE. BOUGHT A PAIR OF SANDALS AND SOME SOCKS. CAME HOME VERY TIRED."

BEFORE ANYONE HAD heard of global warming, back in the homeland I had recently left people were known to faint from the heat, and it made newspaper headlines, if the temperature rose over seventy-five degrees Fahrenheit. It was already almost eighty on this hot June day of my first summer in the U.S., when we set off for Philadelphia. I was excited.

I had chatted to Al about the furniture I'd already seen in some of the local homes we had visited: "The most popular styles of furniture I've seen so far are called 'Early American' or 'Eighteenth Century' and everyone seems to have either one or the other. I still like modern furniture best, though!"

Al sighed: "As long as it's good quality and comfortable, I don't mind what style it is, hon'. You just go ahead and get what suits yourself. Now that we have transportation, I think we should spend a day or so looking around the big city furniture stores; how about a trip to 'Philly?'"

A hot, damp breeze blew in through the rolled-down windows as Nathaniel was again pressed into service. This was before cars were air conditioned, so they were suffocating boxes full of hot air in summer. It grew hotter as we drove to Philadelphia, almost sixty miles inland from Little Cedar River.

We realized that because Al was still near the bottom of A.T.& T.'s financial ladder, it would be a challenge to find decent furniture with our limited finances. What we saw in our price range was ugly and cheap-looking. After a discouraging day in the city, we drove home feeling hot, grimy, tired and despondent.

Testing Boundaries

Bunty: "WEDNESDAY, JUNE 5: DROVE UP TO JOAN AND BUD'S VIA POINT PLEASANT WHERE WE BOUGHT A SUMMER CARPET. WENT TO A FURNITURE SHOWROOM NEAR NEWARK, WHERE WE BOUGHT A MODERN SOFA AND MATCHING UPHOLSTERED CHAIR ON SALE. NICE. THEY WILL BE KEPT IN STORAGE UNTIL WE GET INTO OUR NEW HOME. DINED OUT WITH JOAN AND BUD. GREAT DAY."

We had seen Joan and Bud a few days before, when they came down to Little Cedar River to see the doctor and visit Bud's folks. We mentioned that we were beginning to shop for furniture.

Bud's face lit up. "Oh, there's a terrific furniture showroom up by where we live; come on up and we'll take you there."

` So today we were on our way fifty miles north, to pick up Joan and Bud. On the way, we stopped at a store in the small shore town of Point Pleasant, where we found a serviceable, cheap summer rug for the living room to absorb the sand brought in on feet coming from the beach, and to save wear and tear on the second-hand wool rug that I had found advertised in the local paper.

Joan and Bud guided us in Nathaniel to a well-stocked furniture store, where we saw a prewar modern-style upholstered armchair and matching sofa we could afford, on sale. They were a famous brand, comfortable for Al's long legs, with clean uncluttered lines, good quality springs and upholstery. I could hardly wait to see them in our new living room.

My diary noted: "JOAN IS BEGINNING TO 'SHOW' A LITTLE, HERE AND THERE," remembering when Bud cleared his throat in the car and sang: "Junior's Busting Out All O-o-ver," parodying the famous Broadway ditty. The three of us groaned. Yes, Joan was definitely pregnant!

We were to become more involved with this pregnancy than we could have imagined. Bud was an only child, cherished by a rather possessive mother. The doctor had told her she had a "heart condition." Fearing repercussions to her health if upset, her husband and Bud "walked on eggs" to avoid stress at all costs, bowing to her wishes and in general making sure that she suffered as little exertion and strain as possible. Without consultation, she had placed Joan's pregnancy and the delivery of her first grandchild in the hands of the old family doctor, who, we discovered, had already delivered the greater part of the population of Little Cedar River over the years. Mrs. Hoffman planned to have Joan stay with her during the last few weeks of her pregnancy and again to recuperate when she came out of the hospital, after the baby was born.

Joan had other ideas, however. She didn't fancy staying with her in-laws or having the "O.F.D." handling her pregnancy and delivery. She severely displeased her mother-in-law by choosing a younger doctor. Bud and his father held their breath, but luckily Mrs. Hoffman's heart didn't miss a beat.

Having the same opinion of the "O.F.D." ourselves, Al and I recommended the young general practitioner we had chosen, who had recently arrived in Little Cedar River from New York with good credentials and a happy manner, to set up a practice in our growing postwar town. Joan and Bud liked him from their first meeting, and were soon making the monthly prenatal trek from north Jersey to see the doctor of their choice and to visit the prospective grandparents. At that point in time, Little Cedar River had no hospital. The baby would be born at the nearest hospital, in Pinewood, to please Bud's mother.

On their next prenatal visit, Bud dropped Joan off at Mom Greene's to visit with me while he visited with his parents. Visibly upset, she burst into tears. "Oh, Bunty, I'm so miserable," she wailed. "I just can't stand the thought of staying with Bud's mother for two weeks before the baby's due and again after it comes, but what can I do?"

She sobbed into her handkerchief as she sat on Mom Greene's sofa and poured out her troubles. My sympathy for her overflowed. I sought out Al in the bedroom. "Al, dear, surely we'll be in our own home by the time the baby is due, and we'll have two bedrooms. Do you think we could rescue her?"

"Oh, O.K., love, we'd better put her out of her misery; let's tell her it'll be fine."

I threw my arms around him and told Joan she could come and stay with us; a huge leap in faith, since we didn't yet have our own roof over our heads!

Joan and Bud went home that day happier than when they arrived.

Bunty: "TUESDAY, JUNE 11: LAURIE AND I TOOK THE BUS TO NEW YORK WITH GREAT ANTICIPATION, TO ATTEND A RADIO STUDIO BROADCAST. TERRIFIC! FOUND OUR WAY AROUND JUST FINE IN THE CITY. DIFFERENT FROM LONDON, BUT WE DIDN'T GET LOST ONCE! BOUGHT VERY NICE GIFTS FOR TWO WEDDINGS. SPENT $21.50."

Laurie and I spent as much time visiting each other as we could fit into our schedules: shopping together; going to the beach on the big Pinewood Lake to sunbathe or swim; boosting each other's spirits when they were at low ebb.

On rainy days, we would switch on the radio and listen to some of the daytime programs. In those days everyone listened to the radio; television was in its infancy and hadn't yet reached the average American home. We had several favorite programs, one of which was the popular radio show "Daily Dilemmas," originating in a New York City studio. The Master of Ceremonies routinely invited the radio audience to apply for tickets to the show.

One rainy morning, I had taken the bus as usual from Little Cedar River to Pinewood and had arrived at Laurie's apartment, dripping wet.

Laurie said cheerfully: "I've just put the kettle on, and we'll have a nice cup of tea, dear. Take off that wet coat and hang it up on the shower rail in the bathroom to dry. Let's listen to 'Daily Dilemmas.'" She added, with a touch of mystery: "I have some great news for you."

I groaned to myself: "Oh Lord, she's pregnant! First Joan, and now Laurie. I hope it won't be me next--not yet!"

Laurie set out two cups and brought in the steaming teapot and a plate of cookies. "Guess what, Bunty?"

Unable to keep my thoughts to myself, I burst out: "I know what--you're pregnant!"

"No, nothing silly like that; I've sent away for two tickets to 'Daily Dilemmas'. What d'you think of that?" She looked at me expectantly.

"Thank heavens you're not pregnant! We all need a little time to get used to this new country without plunging into motherhood, if we can help it. But the radio show is in New York. How will we ever get there?" I asked.

"Oh, the bus for New York that goes through Little Cedar River stops at Pinewood. You can get on at Little Cedar River and I'll get on here. It'll take us right into Manhattan."

She put into my hand a copy of the letter she had written to apply for the tickets. A few days later, I heard her exited voice on the phone: "Bunty, hold on to your hat; we're going to New York on the eleventh!" So here we were this morning, on the bus for our sixty-plus-mile trip into the city.

I don't remember details of the show, but I do remember the screaming audience, the boisterous Master of Ceremonies and the scantily clad showgirl holding up signs saying "Laugh", "Applaud", "Boo", etc.

After the show, we decided to explore our surroundings. As expatriated Londoners, this was a chance for us to prove that we were city girls at heart. The fact that there was no language barrier made things easier, although sometimes when we asked directions we could have used an interpreter! But it was exhilarating to be in a big city again, temporarily escaping the boundaries of the cramped, small-town lifestyle that was now ours.

We found an "automat" cafeteria for lunch, then walked to the Fifth Avenue stores to shop for two wedding presents: one for Amy's best friend, and the other for a girl Al had dated from time to time before going overseas. When her wedding invitation had come, I waved it in front of Al and announced: "Roberta has invited us to her wedding! I'm so glad she found a sailor while you were away!"

He gathered me up in a hug: "I never really knew her that well, my love; I only took her out a couple of times, not even to my high school prom--I couldn't spare the money to rent a 'tux.'"

The New York stores yielded better-than-satisfactory gifts for the two prospective brides. I felt quite extravagant spending more than twenty dollars of Al's hard-earned money all at one time, but then twenty dollars was a lot of money, almost half of a good weekly wage in Little Cedar River in 1946.

Laurie and I returned to rural south Jersey exhausted but triumphant; we had conquered New York on our own and come back intact!

Al: "WEDNESDAY, JUNE 12: WE NOW OWE $4,600 TO THE SAVINGS AND LOAN ASSOCIATION FOR A TWENTY-YEAR MORTGAGE. HOPE TO PAY IT OFF IN EIGHT YEARS OR SOONER. DEED TO PROPERTY WILL NEED TO BE RECORDED; WILL TAKE ANOTHER MONTH OR SO! YIKES, WILL WE EVER GET INTO THIS HOUSE?"

Bunty: "UP BRIGHT AND EARLY. AL AND I WENT TO THE LAWYER'S OFFICE TO SIGN THE TITLE DEED FOR OUR HOUSE. MET THE SELLER FOR THE FIRST TIME, SHE'S A SHREWD OLD GAL, AND NOT SYMPATHETIC AT ALL. TENANTS IN HOUSE STILL FIRMLY IMMOVABLE." The house was ours; we now had the title deed. Legally, we could demand that the tenants vacate; they still showed no sign of being willing to budge. Our lawyer drew up a thirty-day notice for them to leave, but said that even if we brought suit against them if they didn't move, it wasn't worth the hassle or the court costs.

"Oh well, at least we have a roof over our heads at Mom Greene's," I thought, "I'll just have to stop whining about it and wait until the tenants leave. Surely their new house will be finished soon! And the rent will help with the mortgage payments."

If I had had the foresight to realize it, I was getting invaluable training in my new career! Mom Greene's frequent and unpredictable visits to her sisters were a blessing in disguise. How could I learn more about American women at close range than with Amy and her girlfriends? And how much better could I learn to cook than with Bill there to help me? What better preparation for becoming an American housewife could I have?

Bunty: "SATURDAY, JUNE 15: BREAD AND BUTTER ARE TO GO UP IN PRICE ON MONDAY. THERE PROBABLY WON'T BE A SHORTAGE OF BUTTER NOW--I'LL BET PEOPLE WILL SWITCH TO MARGARINE INSTEAD! AL AND I WERE INVITED TO DINNER AT McCAFFERTYS'."

There had been a few postwar food shortages lingering in the U.S. Sugar was rationed when I first arrived; I had to get a ration book although there was no shortage of sugar, as far as I could see. Butter, however, was evidently still in short supply.

One of the first things I noticed about "Al, the Civilian" was that he loved butter. In fact, when I first saw him slather it on his morning toast, I thought to myself: "My gosh! He likes a little toast on his butter!" Hearing that animal fats are bad for our health, and noting that butter was much more expensive than margarine, both nuggets of information convinced me that I could safeguard Al's health and stretch my ten-dollar-a-week housekeeping allowance by switching to margarine.

Marketeers succeeded in making margarine look more like butter with an ingenious do-it-yourself gimmick. I wrote to Mom and Dad: "Getting margarine to look like butter is great fun. In its natural state it's a dirty white color, and comes in a sealed plastic pouch with a little bright orange-colored bubble in one corner. The trick is to pinch the pouch to break the bubble, then squeeze the coloring out into the white stuff. You just keep squeezing and massaging the whole pouch in your hands until the contents are completely blended into a pale yellow. Then you put the pouch in the fridge until the margarine hardens, slit it open, put the marge in the butter dish, and it looks just like butter!"

I could imagine a radio newscaster saying: "More and more thrifty housewives will be kneading their plastic pouches all over America, resulting in a glut of unsold butter on the market."

After Memorial Day, summer had gradually begun in this vacation area around us. Al and I spent most of our leisure time out of doors with other young people our age, including Marjie's sisters and their friends. I remember well our first invitation to dinner at the McCaffertys'.

Jake McCafferty was a large, muscular Irishman with thinning red hair and a weather-beaten face, creased and tanned by years of winter winds and summer suns. He had a flourishing business as a building contractor. When I had first arrived in Little Cedar River, I had seen his name, "J. McCAFFERTY" on the side of a big red excavating machine as it rumbled through town on its way to dig a hole somewhere. Little Cedar River was beginning to enjoy a postwar building boom; homes and commercial buildings were going up after stagnating in the war years. Jake's business was riding high. He would probably have liked to paint "McCAFFERTY AND SONS" on his equipment, but he and his wife had produced four daughters, so he would have to be content with handing over the business someday to four sons-in-law.

Al and I walked up to the front door of the McCaffertys' home in the elite section of town near the Little Cedar River Courthouse. A large, open porch with Victorian "gingerbread" curlicues and white wicker furniture fronted the stately old white clapboard house. Its spacious two stories were surrounded by carefully-tended lawns that led from the back of the house down to the river, where there was a raised wooden dock with several boats tethered to it.

We were welcomed into the living room by Ida McCafferty, whom I had already met at the Baptist Church kitchen shower, and in whose dedicated spiritual nurturing her four daughters had been raised. Tall and well-spoken, demanding but with a plentiful supply of humor, she was the ideal mother for her time. She offset Jake's rough-and-ready presence;

his booming voice softened when he came indoors, and today he had changed his clothes for dinner!

The meal was beautifully prepared and delicious, enhanced by lively conversation. Jake's adoration of his family was quite obvious as they talked and laughed together around the dining room table. After dinner, the girls took us to the basement "playroom". Furnished with old but comfortable furniture arranged for conversation, the room could easily accommodate the friends of all four girls, with space to spare. There was a ping- pong table, a dartboard, and a juke box with a supply of records. Jake was known to be a "horse trader," sometimes accepting something other than money in payment for his work. Apparently the juke box was one of his acquisitions. Fascinated, I asked Marjie how it worked.

Before putting a record in it and pressing the button she said: "You know Bunty, you're a heck of a lot more enthusiastic about the juke box than our elderly minister, old 'Fire and Brimstone'. He called it 'an instru-ment of the Devil' and said that dancing is 'the work of the Devil.' He's annoyed Mom so much that she's going to switch her membership to the church down the street!"

Bunty: "FRIDAY, JUNE 21: AL TOOK ME TO ATLANTIC CITY. WHAT A BEAUTIFUL DAY OUT! NO WONDER THEY WROTE A SONG ABOUT IT. BROUGHT HOME SOME SALT WATER TAFFY FOR THE FOLKS."

Now that we had a car, Al punctuated my life with exciting new experienc-es; this time Nathaniel took us fifty miles south to Atlantic City. We walked along the boardwalk crowded with vacationers and immortalized in the popular song: "On the Boardwalk, in Atlantic City." I looked up its history:

"The first boardwalk in the United States, it had been expanded each time it was renovated after being built in 1870. Now four and a half miles long, it is a forty-foot wide expanse of herringbone-patterned wood planking. . ."

When I first saw the boardwalk, a row of ostentatious, glitzy casinos had not yet replaced the elegant hotels, boutiques and other little shops along its border. On the boardwalk between them and the beach, some summer sightseers were being pushed along the boardwalk in odd-look-ing wicker "rolling-chairs", each mounted on a frame with wheels and topped with a canopy.

At one of the candy stores, we stopped to watch a machine making "salt water taffy", stretching out the chewy confection that threatened to cement human jaws together with every bite and to lift fillings out of every vulnerable tooth. We brought a box home for the family. My diary amusingly recalled: "THEIR EFFORTS TO AVOID LOCKJAW WITH THE SALT WATER TAFFY KEPT THEM QUIET ALL EVENING!"

Bunty: "SATURDAY, JUNE 22: ROBERTA HAINES'S WEDDING. VERY PRETTY INDEED. I CRIED, AS USUAL. HOT DAY. AFTERWARDS AL AND I CHANGED AND HEADED FOR THE BEACH."
Roberta was a beautiful bride. Compared with my wartime wedding, this one was much more elaborate. Everything was color-coordinated, from the pretty bridesmaids' gowns to the decorations at the reception, all intended to complement Roberta's stunning dress; a delight to my Utility-oriented eyes.

I routinely wept at weddings. Al took my hand in his: "Remember last September, love? You didn't cry then, if I remember rightly."

I recalled that, at our wedding, how awesome it was to hear the sol-emn words of the Sacrament of Holy Matrimony, read from the Church of England prayer book by our Vicar. Between sniffles, I whispered back to Al: "I was too scared to cry!"

He laughed softly and squeezed my hand.

I thought to myself: "Could our wedding have really happened less than a year ago?"

The bride and groom left the church in a blizzard of confetti and rice. My thoughts drifted back again to my own wedding day: "I remember some confetti but no rice--it was still rationed, if you could find it at all. The quantity they threw at this bride and groom could have made enough rice pudding for my whole neighborhood!"

Roberta tossed her bouquet for some lucky girl to catch and become the next bride. This was a new custom to me. Also, there were many differences between our wedding reception and this one; not the least was the wedding cake. Expecting to see a traditional English fruit cake with its marzipan coating and crunchy confectioner's icing, I was surprised by this American wedding cake. It was like an English sponge cake, light and airy, with soft, foamy icing that melted in the mouth. I muttered to Al: "These Americans, they have to do everything differently from the Brits, but I'll confess that this cake is probably a lot easier to digest!"

Al grinned: "But the top layer couldn't have been boxed and sent overseas to the in-laws like ours. Chalk one up for the British on that score!"

The day was stifling hot; not a breath of air came in through the wide-open windows at the reception. In those days before air conditioning, Little Cedar River's summer climate was almost the same inside as out of doors; electric fans merely served to distribute the heat and humidity fairly evenly inside the room. Unaccustomed to anything close to this in England, I felt myself wilting, and I tugged at Al's arm. He took one look at my scarlet face and damp, straggling hair and made our excuses to Roberta's parents. We rushed home, replaced our sweaty clothes with bathing suits and headed for the beach.

The township of Little Cedar River owned a private ocean beach next to its commercial neighbor, Seaside Heights. There was no gaudy board-walk here, only faint smells of the food concessions if the wind blew in the wrong direction. The soft, cream-colored sandy beach offered ample space to spread out beach blankets and to erect beach chairs and umbrellas. It stretched far back from the ocean, ending with a border of grassy sand dunes at the edge of an uncluttered private parking lot. Admittance was free for Little Cedar River residents. Badges could be picked up each summer at the Town Hall, to be checked at the beach by two of the town's own lifeguards when they came down to stretch from keeping vigil on their high perches.

At the beach, a refreshing breeze was blowing. The sand sloped innocently into the little ripples at the edge of the Atlantic Ocean. But, a few feet out, under the water gathering itself into breakers, there was an undertow often powerful enough to drag a swimmer into deeper water; a terrifying prospect for me, whose swimming experience was limited to a few strokes in the shallow end of an indoor pool.

I watched Al dash into the water and dive into the incoming breakers, breathing a sigh of relief when I saw him bob up again in the calm stretch of water beyond. I relaxed in the comfort of the warm, dry sand, remembering the last holiday I had with Mom and Dad before the war. I thought: "The English Channel was never like this wild ocean. But I'll take this beautiful sand any day over that English beach full of pebbles!"

On some days, however, even this beautiful beach had its down side. In England in summer there had been tiny stinging flies called "midges". In New Jersey there were bigger and better mosquitoes, but even worse were the large biting flies called "green heads." Whenever a land breeze blew out from the marshes, thousands of these green-headed monster flies swarmed over the sunbathers on the beach, taking small chunks out of their skin and coming in a close second to the infamous Jersey Mosquitoes in their lust for human flesh. The only option was to pack up and go home. There were times when not a soul was on the beach and the two lifeguards were left to battle the insects alone. But today the breeze was coming from the ocean, and not a fly was in sight.

Al finished his swim. I was waiting for him with a dry towel and put it around his shoulders as he began to shiver.

"I'm wondering if I'll ever have the courage to go beyond those breakers, Al?"

"Well, don't forget, dear heart, I've been swimming in the ocean since I was a kid, but even out there where it looks like calm water you still have to be a strong swimmer to cope with the currents. I'll feel better if you'll stick to the bay or the river if you want to swim."

In south Jersey there were plenty of swimming places other than the ocean: quiet coves on Barnegat Bay; Little Cedar River and its spring-fed creeks; lakes and rivers in the state parks. This was my kind of water, shallow and calm, where my feet could still feel the bottom!

These creeks, lakes and rivers were often bordered by groves of swamp cedar trees. Roots of the cedars made the water brackish, deadly to my new white bathing suit, which emerged on first contact stained with indelible brown streaks. Now I knew why everyone wore a dark bathing suit! As soon as I could afford it I bought a new suit, a lovely shade of dark brown; nobody would even notice if it got darker!

Hot and Humid!

Bunty: "MONDAY, JUNE 24: UP EARLY TO DRIVE TO PHILADELPHIA FOR ANOTHER FURNITURE SHOPPING ATTEMPT. BOUGHT A BEDROOM SET, GATE-LEGGED TABLE, BOX SPRING AND MATTRESS FOR OUR NEW HOME,"

"It's now or never*,*" I panted. "I don't think I can stand another trip in this heat."

Al retorted: "Well, we need something to sleep on, my darling, so we must come up with a bed, or at least a mattress! And you know the city stores are the only ones where we'll find any choices or a price we can afford. One thing's for sure," he observed, looking cool and composed in contrast to my sticky restlessness, "we won't be tempted to waste time window- shopping on those hot sidewalks."

The unaccustomed summer heat was affecting me more than I could have anticipated. The hot, humid air blowing on me through Nathaniel's open window was suffocating on the long drive to Philadelphia. Unhappily, I dripped perspiration and felt even hotter when I looked at Al, who appeared to be conditioned to this appalling heat and relatively unaffected by it.

He was right; when we arrived we didn't waste any time. We broke all records finding the remaining furniture we would need for our new home in the one big store we hadn't tried last time: Wanamakers.

As we stepped into Wanamakers we heard organ music. Al said:

"They must have known we were coming, Bunty, welcoming us with a record of 'Let Me Call You Sweetheart'."

But it wasn't a recording. Following the sound of the music, we found ourselves gazing in awe at what--the encyclopedia later informed us--had once been the largest operational pipe organ in the world. It had been built for the St. Louis World's Fair in 1904, designed by a George Ashdown Audsley. When John Wanamaker purchased it for his new Philadelphia department store, it took thirteen freight cars to move it, and two years to complete its installation there. By 1930, the number of its pipes had been expanded to an incredible 28,842!

Al and I almost forgot why we had come into the store as we stood spellbound, listening to this 'king of instruments'. We finally tore ourselves away and arrived in the furniture department to discover an affordable beautiful modern walnut bedroom set and also a suitable box spring and mattress. Our bedroom was now completed. For a house without a dining room, we found a gate-legged table that could be opened up in one end of the living room when we entertained dinner guests. A convertible couch that pulled out into a double bed for our second bedroom completed our spending spree. All our purchases would be put in storage and delivered when we wished.

A gas stove came with the house. A new refrigerator, kitchen table and chairs had already been ordered locally from Little Cedar River's one small hardware store. The house already had Venetian blinds; new curtains and drapes could wait! Now all we needed was to take possession of our home. But when? It was a good thing that we couldn't even guess!

Bunty: "TUESDAY, JULY 2: JOAN AND BUD ARE VISITING HIS PARENTS. WENT OVER TO SAY HELLO. JOAN IS HAVING 'MOTHER-IN-LAW TROUBLE,' SO SHE CAME BACK WITH US TO RECOVER."
From time to time my diary reported: "Joan is having mother-in-law trouble" or "Laurie is having father-in-law trouble." In this first year in the U.S.,

sharing our problems--real or imagined--helped all three of us to adapt to our new lives, resulting in enduring friendships that would last all our days.

Bunty: "THURSDAY, JULY 4: A NATIONAL HOLIDAY FOR INDEPEN-DENCE DAY, BUT JUST ANOTHER WORKING DAY FOR MY POOR HUSBAND ON THE EVENING SHIFT. BILL, MARJIE AND AMY WENT TO AUNT MARY'S. THEY DROVE MOM GREENE HOME, FOLLOWED BY TWO MORE CARS WITH AUNTS, TWO COUSINS, ONE UNCLE AND GRANDMOM MILLARD."

On my first July Fourth holiday in the U.S., I had at least expected a pic-nic; instead three carloads of relatives arrived!

That morning, Amy, Bill and Marjie had driven to Boothwyn for a fami-ly picnic lunch at Aunt Mary's. Uncle Clem, Aunt Ethel, Grandmom Millard and a cousin Ann somebody, had traveled from Shenandoah to join them. I wistfully imagined them enjoying a family picnic without Al and me, in the shade of Aunt Mary's gigantic hickory tree.

Al was still a "low man on the totem pole" at the radio station, so he had to work the evening shift on the holiday. At 3 p.m. he went off to work and I stayed home alone in the hot, airless house, stripping down to my bra and panties to try to keep cool. By afternoon, either I was getting used to the oppressive heat or my near-nudity made me more comfort-able; I began to feel better. I ate a solitary soggy sandwich, curled up in a living room chair with the book I'd been reading.

Suddenly, I heard cars pulling into the driveway. I realized to my horror that my clothes were upstairs! As I heard the relatives noisily spilling out of the cars, I made a leap into the kitchen and snatched the red and white checkered tablecloth off the kitchen table. By now they were pouring in the front door, calling my name! I hastily draped the tablecloth around me, clutching it at the back with one hand to keep it closed, and went into the living room to greet them. There were a few strange looks, but I gave everyone a one-armed hug, asked to be excused, and backed up the stairs. It took me longer than I anticipated to wriggle my perspiration-soaked body into a blouse and shorts, and shouts of "Bunty, come on down!" floated up from the living room. I could just imagine what they were thinking: "Well, she's a bit strange, but she'll soon get used to us!"

My diary recorded: "THE HOUSE IS OVERFLOWING! WE WERE ALL STILL TALKING WHEN AL ARRIVED HOME FROM THE EVENING SHIFT AT 1 A.M. WE TALKED FOR ALMOST ANOTHER HOUR! THIS WILL BE A SHORT NIGHT'S SLEEP!'"

Bill was spending the night at the McCaffertys', leaving his double bed available, but that still wasn't enough accommodation. My diary doesn't mention where the extra relatives slept that night; it will always remain a mystery. Grandmom Millard in a sleeping bag? No way! But just imagining it was good for a private giggle!

Early the following morning, the sleep-starved retinue had departed and the house was quiet again. With one of his quirky grins, Al observed: "Well, Bunty, here's something for us to remember when we get our own home: there's only one way to convince family not to stay too long--make sure there's a shortage of beds!"

Bunty: "SATURDAY, JULY 20: NEVER THOUGHT IT COULD BE THIS HOT AND HUMID! COOLED OFF IN McCAFFERTYS' BOAT ON BARNEGAT BAY. HEAVENLY!"

The heat wave continued. Earlier that week, I looked at Al's world atlas. "Al, do you realize that Little Cedar River is almost on the same latitude as Madrid in Spain?" The Mediterranean-like summer heat and humidity robbed me of energy, as well as generating what seemed like gallons of sweat. All I wanted to do was to get undressed, flop onto the bed and stay there. With a flash of insight, I remarked to Al: "No wonder the Spanish need all those siestas!"

Al reminisced: "Hey, Bunty, talking about climate, remember the joke the G.I.'s in England used to tell about the English climate? It went like this: 'Oh, brother! This rainy weather is terrible; would you believe it, one of our guys overslept last week and missed the English summer!' But don't worry, sweets, you'll soon get acclimated to our summers. We call these our 'dog days'."

"What do 'dog days' mean?" I asked.

"Gosh, I don't know--maybe because it's so dog-gone hot!"

We laughed, but my curiosity was so unbearable that after Al went to work that day I walked, clad in as little as was decently possible, to the public library, and looked up "dog days." I read that the name goes back to Roman times, when the hottest weather was associated with with Sirius, the brightest star in the constellation of Canis Major, the "Big Dog." The Romans blamed the hot, sultry days of July and August on Sirius because then the dog star could be seen shining in the sky at sunrise--so they called them "dog days."

Relief from this particular dog day came when brother Bill invited us to join Marjie's sisters and friends on McCaffertys'big sea skiff, for a cruise in the cool breezes on the water.

When Al and I arrived at the McCaffertys' dock on Little Cedar River, the skiff was being loaded with life jackets, picnic coolers and thermos jugs. Brother Bill put on his nautical cap, a souvenir of World War Two when he had served in the U.S. Navy in the Pacific. He called out: "All aboard and cast off."

Nine of us piled into the boat and sat down facing each other across its open deck, shrugging into life jackets as the motor erupted with a roar. Marjie stayed on the dock to slip off the skiff's mooring rope, throw it on the deck and then jump on board. On the open deck, the sun on my face and a blessedly cooling breeze were just what I needed after a fitful night's sleep in a stifling bedroom. As we moved into the river, Al point-ed out to me some landmarks I had only seen from the car. Gathering speed, the boat raced toward Barnegat Bay, passing a summer camp with a crowd of waving children. We waved and shouted "Hi" as we sped by.

In what seemed like only a few minutes, we were out of the river and into the mile-wide expanse of the bay separating the mainland from a narrow peninsula, beyond which stretched the Atlantic Ocean. We were suddenly in a refreshing new world of blue sky and blue water, crowded with boats of all shapes and sizes sailing in flagged channels. The beach-es along both sides of the bay were crowded. The children frolicking at the water's edge reminded me of that last seaside vacation with Mom and Dad in 1939, before World War Two changed our lives forever.

I could hardly believe my eyes when I saw several men standing out in the bay near a flotilla of children in small sailboats called "prams." The water came barely to the tops of the men's hip-length rubber waders!

Al explained to me: "The Bay is part-fresh and part-salt water from the river and the ocean at Barnegat Inlet. It's shallow, except for the channels that have been dredged for the big boats."

"Yes, but what are those men doing standing out there? What on earth are those long poles in their hands?"

Al chuckled: "Those are clam rakes, and the men are clamming; raking in the soft bottom of the bay for clams. They'll probably sell their catch to the tourists when their buckets are full. By the way, Bunty, you haven't tasted clams yet, have you? That's another treat for you to look forward to."

I took his word for it; shellfish and I had not yet established a successful friendship, landlubber that I was from suburban London. Privately, I wondered if would have the courage to eat something that lived in the mud!

Bill steered the skiff along the boat channel to Barnegat Inlet, several miles down the coast. In the distance was Barnegat Lighthouse. I asked Al about its history.

"Bunty, you're not going to like this story. They hadn't built Barnegat Lighthouse when it happened, but the ground it stands on is a historic site. The Revolutionary War was technically over, but hatred remained between those two American factions: the Loyalists and the Patriots. Many of the defeated American Loyalists in southern New Jersey had taken refuge in the pine barrens.

"In 1782, a small British ship carrying an expensive cargo of tea from the Netherlands went aground off Barnegat Inlet, and a group of victorious American Patriots plundered the wreck, working all day to bring ashore as much of the cargo as they could. An informer among them tipped off a rival group of Loyalists. Under cover of darkness, they came to Long Beach and found the Patriots sleeping on the beach, near where the lighthouse is now, exhausted from their day's salvage work. The Loyalists killed them as they slept and took the valuable tea. This incident is called 'The Long Beach Massacre.' There's a historical marker over by the lighthouse commemorating the murders. We'll take a ride to go see it someday."

Bored with Al's story, our shipmates chattered away, exchanging jokes, family stories and local gossip. Marjie had just finished talking when the skiff began to heave up and down alarmingly.

"Not to worry, Bunty," she reassured me, "it's only the wake of that big fishing boat that just passed us."

I looked back to see the cause of the upheaval disappearing in the opposite direction. We continued to rock, as boat after boat left its rippled wake behind for us to bounce around on. After awhile, Bill decided we'd had enough of the rough stuff. Turning the skiff around, he headed back to Little Cedar River, where he cut the motor in a small cove.

"Time for lunch, anyway," he announced. Let's see what goodies Mom McCafferty has put in our picnic coolers."

I suddenly realized how ravenously hungry I was. In minutes, sandwiches and salads were whipped out of the picnic coolers, and paper cups were filled with iced tea poured from the thermos jugs.

The recollection of that wonderful picnic on the boat, anchored in the calm blue water of the little cove fringed with beach plum bushes, with a cloudless sky above, remains etched on my memory. "Another first experience to add to the growing list," I thought, "and another story to write to Mom and Dad and to enter in my diary tonight. I never knew there was this kind of living!"

Bunty: "TUESDAY, AUGUST 6: SPENT THE DAY IN PHILADELPHIA WITH AL AND MOM GREENE BUYING ODDS AND ENDS FOR THE HOUSE. ON THE WAY HOME, BOUGHT BASKETS OF PEACHES. I'M GOING TO LEARN HOW TO CAN THEM!"

The heat wave had temporarily broken with violent thunderstorms and an influx of cooler air. Mom Greene was always ready for a day out, so we took her along to "Philly" for the day, to buy a list of kitchen and bathroom accessories not found in Little Cedar River's hardware store or its Woolworth's "Five and Ten."

Along the homeward highway we passed miles of fruit farms, their trees heavy with crops of peaches, apples and pears. Baskets full of fruit were for sale at their roadside stands. Mom Greene had been watching the road intently for her favorite fruit stand to come into view. After the city traffic had thinned out and we were approaching the pine barrens, she turned to Al: "Albert, I want you to stop at the next fruit stand and I'll get a basket of peaches for canning."

"Aha," I thought: "that's something I'd like to learn how to do! I wonder how she would respond if I asked her to teach me?" I asked tentatively: "Mom, would you mind if we bought a basket for ourselves, too, and would you, perhaps, show me how to can them?"

"Sounds like a good idea to me," she said, with a bright smile, "then you can help me can mine, too."

For the rest of the way home, the car was filled with the musty aroma of ripe peaches, and I wondered if I would ever survive my canning lesson.

Peaches, Beaches

Bunty: "FRIDAY, AUGUST 9:   SPENT THE WHOLE DAY WITH MOM GREENE CANNING PEACHES. DON'T THNK I'LL EVER DO *THIS* AGAIN!" As I came down to breakfast, Mom Greene was bustling around in the warm, sunlit kitchen. She was a tall, strong woman, her large figure covered by a voluminous cotton house dress and apron, her hair caught up off her neck with an army of hairpins. She must have been up at dawn, by the look of all the pots and instruments laid out for the day's canning activities.

The coal stove was already hot. On its black iron surface stood a large soup kettle full of simmering syrup, next to another large pot full of hot water. Next to that was an even larger pot with handles, coated with dark blue enamel. A formidable metal rack stood on the floor by it, looking like some kind of torture instrument. I asked what it was.

"Oh, that's a canner, Bunty, you'll soon see it in operation."

I thought: "'Operation' is a good word for it, by the look of that collection of knives laid out in a row on the table!"

On the floor by the kitchen table, the two baskets of peaches stood expectantly, like helpless, inanimate victims waiting to be attacked. Their eventual destination was obvious: on a picnic table that had been brought into the big kitchen for the occasion were two rows of newly-washed quart jars, standing next to a dish holding their lids.

Mom Greene looked at my shorts and crisply ironed blouse. "Here's one of my aprons for you, Bunty; you're going to need it," she admonished.

I obediently put my arms through the armholes of the apron, which engulfed me completely from head to toe. I tied its strings around what should have been my waist, while Mom Greene poured us both a cup of coffee. She looked at the two rows of empty jars on the picnic table. "I'm hoping we'll be able to fill all those jars by this afternoon." She added: "When we get through, you won't recognize this place!"

As I put a slice of bread in the toaster, I wondered glumly what she meant, mentally visualizing a scene of carnage. I didn't want to ask, so I observed: "Well, at least we have a lovey sunny day outside." I stopped short of adding: "and I'm already wishing I were out there instead of in here!"

"I'm glad you're interested in learning how to can, Bunty. There's really nothing to it, just time and a little elbow grease. When I was a girl growing up in Shenandoah, we used to help Grandmom Millard when she did the canning. Money was scarce, so we canned all the vegetables and fruit the family would need for the winter. I still remember those rows and rows of jars on shelves in our cellar."

I looked again at the baskets of peaches. They seemed to be larger and fuller than when I saw them at the farm market. I thought morbidly: "To me it looks like at least a week's work to peel and slice all those; I wonder how you get that fuzzy skin off the wretched things? Bet I'll end up slicing my fingers instead of the fruit. How stupid I was to buy that whole basketful for Al and me."

The next few hours alternately flew and dragged. Mom Greene worked competently with confidence born of many hours of practice. My own jobs varied between monotonous and exciting. First, the peaches were plunged into the simmering pot full of hot water on the stove top, then fished out and dunked in a pot of cold water in the kitchen sink to loosen their skins. Next, they were peeled and cut in half to remove their pits. By this time, my water-soaked fingers felt and looked like permanently crinkled prunes, and I wondered if they would ever be normal again. After being cut into the exact thickness dictated by Mom Greene, the sliced peaches were packed tightly into the waiting jars. The jars were then filled with warm syrup from the pot on the stove, and each was topped with its lid assembly.

I eyed the monstrous blue-coated "canner" on the stove. It was half full of water, and I wondered how any woman short of an amazon could possibly have carried it from the sink to the stove.

"Mom, how did you ever carry that canner from the sink with all that water in it? It must have weighed a ton!"

Mom Greene chuckled: "You'll never guess! I put the lid on the washing machine and rolled it over to the sink with the canner on top of it, then I hooked up the washer's little hose to the cold water and ran the water into the canner. Then I rolled the washing machine back to the stove with the canner filled with water, and it's just the right height to slide the canner off onto the stove top!

Still chuckling, she effortlessly picked up the cage-like contraption from the floor as if it were light as a feather, lowered it into the water in the canner, placed a peach-filled jar into each of its compartments and put the lid on the canner.

She poured us both another cup of coffee. "There, Bunty! We'll take a break while that canner does its job. Takes awhile for the water to come to a boil; the jars of peaches need to be boiled for half an hour to be sterilized."

And so the day went on, while the kitchen grew hotter and hotter. I longed to go upstairs and change into my bathing suit, but I was covered with splashes of sticky syrup and drenched with perspiration so I decided to stay buried in the folds of my hot, sticky, smelly apron and grin and bear it. Our lunch was accompanied by some wonderful iced tea; I couldn't remember ever having drunk so much liquid at one time in my entire life!

By the end of the afternoon the canner had had several re-loads, and two rows of canned peaches stood on the picnic table. The kitchen looked like a war zone, but after another orgy of iced-tea drinking the two of us were sufficiently revived to clean things up in time to make dinner.

Canning peaches was an art that I never tried again; definitely not my idea of how to spend a hot August afternoon--or any afternoon, for that matter! The amount of equipment required boggled the mind, and I had almost died of suffocation from the heat of the canner bubbling away as it sterilized each cargo of peach-filled jars. Exhausted and still imprisoned in the hot, sticky apron, I sank wearily onto a chair and said to myself: "Never again! After this, a can of peaches from the store and a can-opener is definitely the way to go."

Bunty: "MONDAY, AUGUST 12: THIS EVENING WE WENT TO A BEACH PARTY WITH THE GANG. HAD A WONDERFUL TIME; THOROUGHLY ENJOYED IT."
Bill and Marjie had invited Al and me to a beach party with their friends; another experience in the continuing Americanization of Bunty. Bill had already made a trip to the Town Hall for the necessary permit to light a fire on Little Cedar River's ocean beach.

A full moon was rising. Al and I put on our bathing suits and drove over to the ocean; daylight had disappeared by the time we arrived.

Our beach picnic group had the moonlit beach to ourselves. Several young couples were already there, sitting on beach blankets, laughing and talking near a pit that had been dug in the sand. A driftwood fire had been lit in it, casting a red glow over the white sandy beach that gleamed in the light of the full moon. The tide was receding, the sound of its rhythmic swish adding to the magical spell of the warm evening. Beginning at the little waves curling at the water's edge, a dazzling white ribbon of moonlight stretched out beyond the breakers to the horizon. It was a fairytale scene of beauty so completely new to me that it took my breath away.

There were introductions and words of welcome. Shrugging off our bathrobes, Al and I ran hand in hand into the shallow, warm water. When the water was up to my thighs I began to feel strange little nips on my legs. I turned to Al.

"Is it my imagination, or do I feel something nipping at me?"

"Oh, not to worry, dear heart, it's just a few little crabs feeling you out. Maybe they fancy you as a mate; it's mating time for them, you know."

I was *not* amused! "Oh, *NO*! You go on out for your swim, and I'll go back and sit on the beach with the kids. I'd rather leave the crabs to do their courting without me!"

Several more couples arrived and unloaded paper plates, napkins, hot dogs, rolls, condiments, marshmallows. Others went along the beach, returning with more dry driftwood to add to the pile by the fire. Back from his swim, Al sat near it with a big beach towel wrapped around his shoulders to dry off and get warm. Newly-arrived couples dashed down the beach toward the waves, expert from childhood in diving through the Atlantic breakers. I was happy just to watch and revel in this new experience.

Why is it that food tastes so much better out of doors, especially on a moonlit beach on a warm night in August? I savored every bite of hot dog. After a few disastrous tries, I even learned to make a perfectly toasted marshmallow--gooey inside, crunchy outside--after quietly burying a small pile of cremated early attempts.

One of the boys had brought a guitar and another a harmonica, and after we ate we sat around the glowing embers of our fire and sang those wonderful old wartime love songs made famous by the Big Bands of the 1940s. Nobody budged until the fire's last embers had gone out, then the sand was piled back on top of the pit and everyone packed up to go home. Tomorrow would be another working day, but tonight I again felt like Alice in Wonderland.

Day by day, my American education continued. Intrigued by my accent when I shopped at the fruit store in town, the proprietor loved to make me repeat "bernaarners" several times, before I began saying "bannannas" in self defense (note, not defence.) I learned that in America "bloody" wasn't a curse word as it was in England. In my new world, "knocking up the next door neighbors" didn't mean knocking on their door for help, and "keep your pecker up" wasn't a well-meaning encouragement to be cheerful in adversity. "Aluminium" lost an "i" and was pronounced "aloominum" and "travelling" lost one of its "l"s. "Belly" was O.K. to use for humans and not just for animals, and on and on.

My sense of humor had to undergo a total makeover. In all the years since, I never have really assimilated the personal aspects of "kidding," considered in my day in England to be impolite, or sometimes insulting.

I realized how fortunate I was in having the love of a man who was not only a good husband but also my best friend, supporting me through this first difficult year with advice and caring patience. I discovered the friendliness and generosity of people who didn't even know me. My heart was swiftly being captured by this amazing and wonderful country and its people. New experiences came every day, shaping and molding my life and enriching it with memories. I felt blessed.

A Driving Disaster

Bunty: "THURSDAY, AUGUST 15: DOING REALLY WELL WITH MY DRIVING LESSONS. AL LET ME DRIVE ALL THE WAY HOME. ALMOST THERE WHEN DISASTER STRUCK!"

"Bunty, it's time you learned how to drive the car." Al brought up the subject shortly after Nathaniel became ours.

I was ecstatic: "Oh, that sounds great! I'll be able to drive over to visit Laurie, and get around to more places on my own without worrying about bus schedules or walking my feet off."

I was nervous when I began my driving lessons. Nathaniel was a large, eight-cylinder, four-door sedan with a stick shift. At his age, he wasn't equipped with an automatic gear shift, power steering or power brakes; wrenching the big steering wheel had my shoulders in a state of semi-paralysis. Learning to work the clutch and brake pedals on the floor stretched my legs to their limit; I speculated that they would be at least an inch or two longer by the time I'd learned how to drive!

Al obtained a driver's permit for me, and on those hot summer days I sat submissively in a pool of perspiration in my sleeveless blouse, shorts and new leather-soled sandals from Philadelphia, while Al did a patient and thorough job of teaching. My driving lessons took place in a deserted area just south of Little Cedar River, where several paved streets were the only remains of a building site laid out before the war as a resort. The builder went bankrupt before construction could begin, then abandoned it. The roads he left behind were ideal for learning how to drive. I'd had lesson after lesson before Al was satisfied.

One day when we arrived for my lesson, he said: "O.K., 'Junior,' move over. Take the wheel. One last trip around the course; today's the day you graduate. You can drive Nathaniel all the way home." He adjusted the rear-view mirror and moved the big bench seat of the car forward, then slipped a fat pillow under me. Even so, the discrepancy between his almost six feet and my five feet two made it difficult for me to see the road without craning my neck, and my legs ached from reaching for the pedals.

"I'm glad you can't hear my nerves jangling," I quavered.

"Nothing to it, dear heart, just do what you've been practicing; I'll be right here next to you all the time. First we'll stop in at the Nash agency. I have to see Ernie Brown about that rear tire."

"You mean I have to drive right into town?"

"Yes, love, you can do it!"

I drove slowly back to Little Cedar River, my confidence growing as I did all the things Al had explained were necessary to avoid a disastrous accident. Before we reached the agency showroom's driveway, I proudly waved my arm out the window to indicate a turn (turning-light indicators were still in the future), negotiating the entrance perfectly. However, a few feet beyond, my leather-soled sandal suddenly slipped off the brake pedal and onto the accelerator. By the time I found the brake pedal again, Nathaniel was perilously close to the floor-to-ceiling showroom window. The car came to a stop with a sickening thud against the glass. In those days before seatbelts, I jolted forward, bumping my forehead on the windshield. As I watched, transfixed with horror, a huge crack ran down the length of the showroom window!

"Are you O.K., my love?" Al was bending over me in concern.

All I could do was to nod my head and bury my face in his comforting arm. By now a small crowd had gathered, headed by the co-owner of the agency and a passing policeman. Death would have been a welcome option as I burst into embarrassed tears, but luckily my criminal notoriety was limited to a small paragraph in the weekly County newspaper. The insurance company described it as "an unavoidable accident."

A new window was installed in the showroom, which removed the grisly evidence, but when people asked: "Bunty, how did you get that bump on your forehead?" I had to repeat the wretched tale until the bruise had faded away.

Our New Home

Bunty: "FRIDAY, AUGUST 16: GREAT NEWS--THE TENANTS ARE MOVING OUT OF OUR HOUSE ON AUGUST 30TH! I CAN HARDLY BELIEVE IT."

Al and I were so excited after the phone call from our tenants that we just sat and looked at each other in disbelief.

"They sure gave us a runaround, and now they're leaving it to the bitter end of the month to get their money's worth out of their rent!" Al sounded disgusted: "Oh well, they were decent enough to give us a couple of weeks' notice, at least that's something! I'll ask for a two- week vacation to begin after Labor Day. That should give us time to get the inside looking shipshape before we move in."

Bunty: "SATURDAY, AUGUST 31ST: AL AND I WENT OVER TO THE HOUSE TO SEE WHAT WE NEED TO DO. THE TENANTS HAVE LEFT IT EMPTY, AND THEY MUST HAVE VACUUMED THROUGH, BUT LOTS OF WORK TO BE DONE BEFORE WE CAN MOVE IN. WENT TO HARDWARE STORE TO ORDER WASHABLE WALL COVERINGS FOR KITCHEN AND BATHROOM, AND PAINT FOR BEDROOMS AND LIVING ROOM."

Our new house had a large living room, and a kitchen big enough to hold a breakfast table and four chairs. The bathroom was small, but saved by the fact that it had good quality, modern fixtures. The two bedrooms were large enough to accommodate our needs.

We looked through the empty rooms. Their condition was fair, but each one looked tired. The hardwood floors throughout the house needed to be refinished. The walls in all the rooms needed a facelift.

Al observed "Well, I'm sure of *my* first priority. These rooms all need a coat of paint!"

The remedy was found in the Little Cedar River hardware store. The sales clerk fussed with his order book when he saw us coming: "And what can I do for you today, Al?" he asked, with a hopeful smile, as if he had had a run of no sales.

Al explained about our new home's need of a facelift.

"Why don't you both look through these sample books and decide on wall coverings and also the shades of paint we should use?" The sales clerk was obviously sure of that order.

One of Al's passions was to have a paintbrush in his hand. He almost seemed to think painting had therapeutic value, having already painted all four bedrooms in Mom Greene's house after he came out of the Army, and the backyard shed before my arrival.

We agreed on traditional white ceilings, and decided it would be less wasteful of paint if he made the living room and bedroom walls all the same color. We chose and ordered washable wall coverings for the kitchen and bathroom, then turned our attention to the pots of paint lining the store shelves.

The elderly sales clerk had been Al's scoutmaster when he was in the local Boy Scout troop. He said, chattily: "It's good to have you home, Al, and I'm happy to meet your missus. You know, Al, when they paint, most of our homebuilders use a neutral color; I suggest you use 'Navajo White.'" He pointed to a paint chip on the chart: a warm, ivory color. "We have plenty of it in the store," he continued, "so you could have it without waiting for an order to arrive. You'll save money by not having to waste unused paint left over from one room to another if you had chosen a variety of colors, to say nothing of having to buy new paintbrushes and rollers for each one."

Those were enough good reasons for Al. We left the store with as much "Navajo White" as we could carry. I wondered: "Now what on earth could a paint color have to do with the Navajo Indians? Even a new immigrant like me knows they didn't use it to paint their wigwams!"

(Much later, research told me that it has that name because it resembles the background color of the flag of the Navajo Nation. Whoever would have guessed it?)

Al loved to paint. He worked tirelessly for the next two weeks, sweating over his paintbrushes and rollers in the summer heat, but he was truly happy. Painting wasn't my "thing," but out of wifely loyalty at the outset I began helping him to paint a baseboard, only to be told politely to put down the paintbrush. Perfectionist that he was, my painting wasn't up to Al's standards, so after that my only contribution was to keep him supplied with something to eat and drink, and to compliment him on the finished product.

Family Picnic

Nathaniel and Al

AUTUMN 1946

— ✄ —

The Family and Me

Bunty: "MONDAY, SEPTEMBER 2: LABOR DAY, TIME FOR THE ANNUAL FAMILY REUNION. ATE AND WENT SWIMMING ALTERNATELY ALL DAY. WHAT A DAY IT WAS! UNCLE CLEM NEARLY LOST HIS PANTS IN THE RIVER!"

LABOR DAY WAS the next American holiday I experienced, that first year in my new country. Al's family celebrated it every year with a reunion picnic. Family members flocked to the occasion from all over Pennsylvania and New Jersey. I looked forward to seeing again those heartwarming people who had made my entry into the family such a welcome one. I had heard Mom Greene telling Bill to book three picnic tables at Metedeconk, but had no idea where it was, or how we would get there.

The old house was a beehive of activity on that warm September morning. The sun had barely risen; the cloudless, pale blue sky promised another hot, steamy summer's day. The kitchen bustled with activity; everyone seemed to have a job to do. When I came downstairs, Bill looked up from the preparations long enough to ask: "What's cookin', good lookin?'" by way of greeting, then went back to his packing. After a hasty breakfast, Al and I trekked back and forth to the driveway where two cars stood with trunks open (the Brits would say "boots"), helping to stow away picnic baskets filled with jars of pickled eggs and beets, along with lidded containers of coleslaw, potato salad and home-made baked beans, all of which had been prepared the day before and packed into the groaning refrigerator. A huge ham was cooked and ready to carve. Marjie and Amy carried out thermos jugs of iced tea after Al gave an extra twist to their lids to prevent spills.

Beach towels, suntan lotion and sunglasses were piled on the kitchen table, along with a set of horseshoes and two spiked wooden posts to complete the game. All of us, except Mom Greene, wore swimming gear under our tee shirts and shorts.

Mom Greene presided over the preparations like a drill sergeant: "Be careful, now don't drop anything, Bill. Put the ham in back of the salads. Amy, put that iced tea in the other car. Al, come here and carry this picnic basket. Bunty and Marjie, here's one for each of you, too."

By seven-thirty it was time to leave; the cars began to hum and we scrambled aboard for the drive through the back roads to the state park which was to be our destination.

Located several miles north of our town, the Metedeconk River was a wide stream of fresh water, faintly brackish from the swamp cedar roots in its banks, as it flowed toward the ocean. Today, the river was flowing more quickly from a recent rainstorm, but close to its banks it was tranquil--my kind of water. We stopped at a grove of scrub pine and pin oak trees shading a cluster of picnic tables, from which the river bank sloped down to a small strip of sandy beach.

We were first to arrive; no other picnickers had commandeered tables yet. Al and Bill took three picnic tables and lined them up end to end; tablecloths were spread over them, making one continuous table. An hour later the sun had risen in the sky, and we began to feel the full heat of the day. Paper plates, napkins and plastic cutlery were unloaded. Al and Bill unloaded bags of charcoal and piled it into two outdoor grills standing nearby, ready to be lit. The food would wait until everyone had arrived before being set out on the tables.

Unloading had been hot work. Marjie and Bill were the first to shed tee shirts and shorts, and run down the bank to the waiting water in their bathing suits. Marjie's voice floated up the bank: "Come on in, kids, it's not too cold, just refreshing!"

"I don't need a second invitation," yelled Al, and he barreled down into the water with a big splash.

Wading in, I thought: "I could get used to this; the water's smooth enough for me to swim a few strokes without worrying about being swept out to sea as I did over at the ocean, with those 'mile-high' breakers and that scary undertow!"

The cedar water was pleasantly cool and seductive, and I swam with increasing confidence, but being careful not to go too far out where the current was moving swiftly toward the river's estuary. I remembered the breast and side strokes I had learned as a child, then I turned on my back and floated contentedly near the river's edge. Above me the sunshine twinkled through the bordering trees, and somewhere I could hear birds singing; it was heavenly.

Bill had brought a beach ball, and the four of us played together, laughing and splashing like the kids we were then. We were still cavorting in the river when two cars appeared with Pennsylvania license plates. Quickly toweling ourselves dry, we went to meet them. Out spilled Uncle Bill Millard and his family from Harrisburg, then Aunt Mary and Tom. Another car soon arrived with Uncle Clem, Aunt Ethel and Grandmom Millard. Soon afterwards came the contingent from Camden, New Jersey. Aunts, uncles and cousins were everywhere. Aunt Kate, Grandmom's sister, struggled out of the car. As her feet emerged I noticed she was wearing a pair of red, white and blue striped ankle socks. Al explained: "That's her trademark, Bunty, she wears 'em for every national holiday!"

The two elderly family matriarchs were fussed over and made comfortable in the shade on beach chairs. Hugs, kisses and family news were exchanged and the reunion was soon in full swing. Al and Bill went to the two grills and lit the charcoal.

Al shouted: "Hey, folks, now's a good time for a dunk in the river while we wait for the grills to be ready. We'll all be too full after lunch to waddle down to the water! Let's go: last one in's a rotten egg!"

Uncle Clem was the first in, his rotund mid-section overflowing the waistband of his boxer-type swim trunks. He lumbered heavily into the water and waded off downstream, away from the cluster of relatives still exchanging family gossip as they dabbled their feet in the river's invitingly cool water. Refreshed from my earlier swim, I watched from the river bank as Uncle Clem lazily drifted away from us, carried by the mid-river current, his head bobbing along below the trees bordering the water. He was almost out of sight when I saw him waving something in one hand and heard him bellow: "Bill, come quick!"

Aunt Ethel screamed: "Oh, Clarence!" Always worried about his health, she was sure he was having a heart attack. She only called him "Clarence" on special occasions, this time as if his nickname wouldn't be adequate if he were to pass on suddenly.

"Bill" must have been a favorite name in the family. Al's brother, two uncles, two cousins and a friend of the family all responded to the distress call. "O.K., hang on, Uncle Clem," they shouted, then dashed simultaneously along the river bank with a large beach towel to where Uncle Clem was standing up to his waist in the water. We watched them surround him and wrap him in the towel as he waded ashore. Puzzled, I watched as they stood closely around him for a few minutes. When he emerged, smiling, they all trooped back to the picnic, where a crowd of relatives waited.

Uncle Clem bellowed: "Begorra, I've never been caught wi' me pants down afore! The damn things slipped down in that goddam current, they did. God save me, I grabbed the bastards just afore they floated away. I couldn't have come back to the picnic in me birthday suit, so I hollered for the boys to come and help me put 'em back on again!"

I giggled to myself: "Wait 'til I tell Mom and Dad this story in my next letter--they'll laugh their heads off!"

The picnic lunch was a feast to be remembered. Everyone brought a specialty, some with tastes and names foreign to me: Bavarian oyster stew; sugar-baked Virginia ham; hot dogs with sauerkraut; charcoal-broiled hamburgers; corn on the cob, spicy deviled eggs; crunchy coleslaw; colorful three-bean-salad; slow-cooked Boston baked beans; yellow and green succotash (from the Algonquin Indians' recipe); German potato salad; Polish kielbasa and Mom Greene's Pennsylvanian pickled

beets with peeled hard-boiled eggs stained a pretty pink as they floated in the beet juice. Desserts included Pennsylvania Dutch shoo-fly pie,
Grandmom Millard's Welsh cakes and a huge watermelon cut into de-
lightfully drippy slices. Where the juice dripped posed no problem; we
were still in our sun-dried swim suits, anyway!

Bunty: "MONDAY, SEPTEMBER 23: HOT, HUMID DAY. AL IS BACK
TO WORK ON THE DAY SHIFT. HAD A SURPRISE VISIT FROM IN-
LAWS. CAUGHT ME AT MY WORST! MUST HAVE MADE A TERRIBLE
IMPRESSION. WHAT AN EMBARRASSING DAY!"
Our house was painted, floors refinished, furniture arranged. We had
moved in. Outside and inside it was hot and humid. Al was at work; I was
alone in the house, rearranging the kitchen cabinet drawers. With nobody around to see me, I was standing with bare feet on the cool kitchen
floor, dressed in old shorts and halter top, my hair limp and damp, and
with no makeup.

As I looked out of the kitchen window, a carload of people went slowly by. I paid no attention; cars went in and out of our cul-de-sac all day. I
stiffened with a start when the doorbell rang. Looking through the screen
door I froze in horror. There stood Aunt Mary; behind her were Aunt
Ethel, Uncle Clem and Grandmom! Aunt Mary stepped inside, announcing brightly: "We thought we'd take a ride over to Ida's today while the
summer weather's still here. She said you were in your new home, Bunty,
so we came over to say 'hello.'" The others followed her in. I wanted to
sink through the floor! Why hadn't they picked up the phone to warn me?
To drop in without any warning in England was unthinkable!

Apologizing for my appearance, I snatched up the curtains I had been
hemming off the couch, and said: "How nice to see you! Sit down and
make yourselves at home." Panic-stricken, I thought: "I haven't a thing in
the house to offer them; shopping day isn't until tomorrow!" But in my
best English manner, I said: "May I offer you some tea?"

Grandmom Millard stopped fanning herself long enough to smile and
say: "Oh, if it's *iced tea*, we'd love some."

I went into the kitchen, took down my Acme Cookbook from the shelf, and looked up iced tea. I was instructed to "boil the kettle and make a pot of tea." "So far, so good," I thought, and put the kettle on. The instructions continued: "Cool tea, Pour into a pitcher. Add ice cubes, and sugar to taste. Serve with lemon slices."

I darted back into the living room. The family were all now fanning themselves at quadruple speed. Assuring them that iced tea was coming momentarily, I rushed back into the kitchen. The tea wasn't cooling; it was still almost at boiling point! Desperately, I emptied my only tray of ice cubes into the pitcher. They all promptly disappeared, leaving the tea still warm.

So there I was, with a pitcher full of warm tea and no way to cool it (back in 1946 ice cubes would take hours to make and there were no automatic ice-makers in refrigerators); no lemon in the house, no cookies, only some wilted crackers. I gave up, shrugged and said to myself: "What the heck!" I then dumped sugar into the tea, poured it into glasses and served it, explaining that I was sorry for the delay, but this was the best I could do.

It was! The visit was brief; the relatives drank the lukewarm tea minus lemon, and left soon after--probably stopping for iced tea on their way back to Pennsylvania.

A Little Stranger

Bunty: "TUESDAY, SEPTEMBER 24: OUR FIRST ANNIVERSARY. COULD IT ONLY HAVE BEEN THAT LONG? I'VE LIVED A LIFETIME'S WORTH OF EXPERIENCES SINCE I SAID 'I DO.'"

There was no mention of a celebration in either my diary or Al's, but I had kept our romantic first anniversary cards to each other in that white battered box, and I remember Al's gift to me: the fancy teapot I had been drooling over in the window of one of the local stores, which suddenly appeared in all its glory on the kitchen table that morning. I can only presume that today had been another working day for Al, and that we celebrated by going out to dinner when his shift work permitted.

I must also have been remembering the day at Rainbow Corner when Al had surprised me by asking me to marry him on the eve of his transfer to Germany, and the shock it was for Mom and Dad. I probably recalled our wartime wedding and short honeymoon, the battle with red tape to become a G.I. Bride, the wrench of parting from my beloved parents and homeland, and all the adjustments required for leading a new life in a new country.

Homesickness and loneliness for all that was familiar often overtook me and I had a "good cry", after which I always felt better! This first year of our marriage had begun with life-changing experiences for both of us, "one for the books," as Dad would have said! And it was!

Bunty: "TUESDAY, OCTOBER 1: SURPRISE! A LITTLE STRANGER!"
Al was on the evening shift. We were having lunch when the doorbell rang. There on the front walk stood Ellie Gleason, our real estate lady, cradling in her arms a tiny black terrier puppy. She greeted us with: "I have a housewarming gift for you two. Remember when we were looking at houses one day and you talked about getting a dog as soon as you had a home of your own? Well, how will this one do?"

Al and I both had fond memories of growing up in the company of a dog. When I was nine years old, I saved up my pocket money and picked "Prince," a fox terrier-mix puppy, from a basket of squirming pups in a wicker basket at an outdoor market. Al's "Bobbie" had been his faithful companion throughout his teenage years. He fondled the puppy's tiny, silky head. I put my face down near the little, wet nose and felt a small, pink tongue lick my cheek. I melted completely. Our new home had a dog!

It took a few days for us to find a name for her. Skidding along on the new kitchen linoleum, her paws made a pattering sound. We parodied the name of a queen: "Cleo the Patterer." Cleo became the undisputed ruler of the household. She was very intelligent, and with time on my hands I wondered if I could train her to do a few tricks as I had done so many years ago with Prince. A surprisingly quick learner, she turned out to be a real "ham." She *loved* to perform, then to be rewarded with a dog treat and an affectionate rub on the ears. "Give me your paw" (she lifted one paw for me to shake); "sit" (she sat); "beg" (she sat up, with front paws waving in the air); "dead dog" (she lay motionless until I said "good girl" then sprang to her feet for her treat); "roll over" (she often did several rolls for good measure); "speak" (bark); "talk" (growl); "let's go for a walk" (mad dash to the door); "go get your leash" (a jump up on the wall where her leash was anchored to a nail)--these were all mastered by the time she was a year old.

Cleo didn't seem to know she was a dog. Being spayed didn't faze her; she basked happily in our tender loving care when she came home from the vet. However, changes in the house made her nervous. Even a chair moved out of place would make her sniff around suspiciously, to compare where it had been with where it was now.

She had been with us for almost a year when the punishing heat and humidity of summer struck again. Disposable products were coming on the market to replace old-fashioned, labor-intensive ones: paper kitchen towels; expensive disposable diapers; even a disposable paper wedding dress that looked like white fabric! I was impressed by attractive disposable printed paper draperies; a welcome solution for me in pre-air-conditioned coastal New Jersey, where the summer humidity made my cloth drapes smell of mildew for the rest of the year.

I bought some flower-patterned paper drapes and hung them in the living room for the summer. Cleo was outside, taking a nap in the shade of a bush in the front yard. Nap over, she scratched on the front door to come in. Rounding the corner into the living room, she caught sight of the new drapes. She skidded to a halt, stiff-legged and with tail drooping. The hair rose in a stiff ridge down her spine. As if she had figured out how to handle this new intrusion upon her world, she looked fixedly at the drapes and began to bark at them. She was probably disappointed that she didn't scare them away! If only I'd had a camcorder--but they hadn't been invented yet!

Al: "SUNDAY, OCTOBER 6: HAD A SWELL BIRTHDAY PARTY TODAY. ALL FAMILY THERE, ALSO THE FOLKS CAME FROM CAMDEN TO SURPRISE ME. BUNTY GAVE ME A HAND-KNITTED GRAY SWEATER. BEAUTIFUL" This was Al's first birthday in America after being away for two years overseas. He was thrilled that his aunt, uncle and two cousins came from Camden to join us for Mom Greene's signature turkey dinner, crowned with his favorite apple pie. My weekly housekeeping allowance didn't stretch to buying him a gift, so I was glad I had brought enough woolen yarn, a pattern and a few sets of knitting needles in my trunk when I came to the U.S., to make him a sweater.

Great Expectations

Al: "MONDAY, OCTOBER 14: SENT A REGISTERED LETTER TO NEW YORK ASKING FOR BUNTY'S FUR COAT TO BE TAKEN OUT OF STORAGE AND SENT TO US. IT'S GETTING QUITE NIPPY OUTDOORS. SHE'LL NEED IT."
The clerk at the showroom in New York had suggested that we have my fur coat professionally stored for the summer. Not wanting to have it on my hands at Mom Greene's, where I visualized several generations of moths having an orgy in it, we decided not to mention it, nor to tell my Mom that I would soon be wearing her generous gift, until it arrived. I'm glad we didn't!

Bunty: "TUESDAY, OCTOBER 22: FALL COLORS ARE ON THE TREES. GORGEOUS! JOAN AND BUD ARRIVED THIS AFTERNOON. JOAN WILL STAY WITH US UNTIL HER BABY IS BORN."
After Labor Day, the sweaty, semitropical days of summer meandered gently into the crisp mornings of fall, with a hint of frost in the air. I had

begun to wonder if I would ever stop perspiring; the change of season came as a welcome reprieve.

Memory told me that in autumn in the south of England, most of the deciduous trees' green leaves shriveled into nondescript brown-colored attachments, then fell off. There were very few patches of evergreen forest, so the landscape remained filled with tree skeletons that were stark and naked until spring awakened them again.

The trees in New Jersey had names strange to my English ears: maple, sassafras, pin oak, sumac, hickory, catalpa. As the autumn days went by, their green leaves were transfigured before my eyes, gradually becoming bright colors: orange and scarlet for the maples and sumac, deep red for a variety of oak and the sassafras, daffodil yellow for the hickory. The glorious riot of color delighted and surprised me; I had never imagined anything like it. My effervescent enthusiasm spilled over: "Oh, Al darling," I bubbled, "I just can't believe all this gorgeous autumn color on the trees! You know, there were pictures of North American foliage in one of my encyclopedias back in England, but I didn't think the photos were real. I thought the pictures had been touched up; leaves on trees could never be that bright. But they are!"

In my letters, I told Mom and Dad to look at the pictures in my encyclopedia to see what the fall foliage really does look like here. In the years that followed, when English friends and relatives came to see us, I always steered them toward October for their visits!

Near the beginning of her pregnancy, it was with obvious eagerness that Joan had taken us up on our offer to have her stay with us when the baby was due. Now, months later, that day had come. Everyone was happy: we were happy to be in our own home; Bud was happy that Joan would be staying with us; his mother was happy that she could welcome her first grandchild at a local hospital.

Al was working the day shift. After lunch time, Bud pulled into our driveway. Cleo and I went out to meet the car, while a very pregnant Joan struggled to heave herself out of the front seat. I held the car door open for her while Bud unloaded her suitcase and clothes from the back seat.

Joan managed a faded smile: "Oh, hello, Bunty. Gosh, that was a bumpy ride from north Jersey," she said. "Once or twice we bumped so hard I thought I'd have the baby in the car!"

Bud remonstrated, but with a tolerant grin: "Aw, come on, Joan, my driving isn't *that* bad; it's your condition, you know."

"Oh, I'm so sick and tired of being told it's my 'condition'; I'll be glad when it's all over." Joan walked ponderously to the house, preceded by Bud with her suitcase and a handful of clothes hangers laden with an assortment of clothes. They both looked exhausted. Bud continued wearily toward the front door, where Cleo welcomed them with tail wagging and little leaps in the air.

Bud huffed a little from the exertion: "Well, at least there are no stairs here for you to climb like there were in our apartment, Joan. Hello, Cleo. Stay out of her way now, we don't want Joan tripping over you. Here, come here, good dog."

Joan snapped: "Oh, don't fuss so, Bud. All I want is to lie down for awhile."

I realized they were both tired from the trip down to Little Cedar River, so I offered brightly: "Joan, go on into the bedroom and get yourself settled. The hideaway bed is pulled out and it's made up all ready for you to rest. The closet's empty, Bud, for hanging Joan's things, and there are plenty of empty drawers in the chest of drawers when you're ready to unpack. I'll put the kettle on. We all need a nice cup of tea."

It's amazing what restorative powers there are in a cup of tea! By the time Al arrived home from work, everyone was on an even keel again and a dinner casserole was baking in the oven.

Al: "TUESDAY, OCTOBER 29: JOAN HAS BEEN HERE NOW FOR ONE WEEK. NO BABY YET. DOCTOR SAYS BABY DUE IN ABOUT ANOTHER WEEK'S TIME. WEATHER BEGINNING TO GET QUITE CHILLY. TRIED OUT THE SPACE HEATER."

By this time I had given up writing anything at all in my diary, but Al persevered through several more sporadic entries in his. He must have thought that Joan's arrival would produce immediate results. The baby's non-arrival was certainly important enough to him for it to be recorded!

Joan was good company for me, and she enjoyed whatever privacy she needed with a room of her own, but the little house was confining for both of us, so we took Cleo for short walks and did the shopping together, walking the few blocks into town and feeling better for the exercise.

My driving had improved with practice, I now had enough confidence to make the trip to visit Laurie, when Al's shifts left the car available. Laurie had also mastered driving by this time, and she came to visit us in Little Cedar River. The three of us shared many afternoons of English "chin-wagging" over the inevitable cups of tea and biscuits (cookies.)

The autumn days were cool and comfortable enough, but we began to need some heat on during the evenings, provided by a kerosene-fed space heater standing in one corner of the living room; it had come with the house. Al's attempt to regulate it on the first nippy evening succeeded in taking the chill off the house, but the mounting heat and kerosene fumes made me rush to the windows and open them, plunging the house back into the same chill as before. After a few more tries, Al became quite expert at regulating both heat and fumes, but in the meantime Joan and I each routinely put on an extra sweater and retreated into our bedrooms, closing their doors behind us.

Al: "SATURDAY, NOVEMBER 9: JOAN'S BABY'S DUE DATE. NO SIGN OF THE BABY OR BUNTY'S FUR COAT! SENT ANOTHER REGISTERED LETTER TO NEW YORK ABOUT COAT; CAN'T DO MUCH ABOUT THE BABY!"

In those days we still relied on the power of the printed word, rather than that of cellphones or e-mail, neither of which had yet been invented. I thought the non-arrival of my fur coat in almost a month was enough of an emergency for a phone call, but had left Al to handle it, as Mom would have done with Dad. Another registered letter was evidently what Al thought would be best to follow up on his original request for shipment, more than three weeks ago. The coat had been paid for, but where was it?

At Little Cedar River, telephone rates in general, especially long-distance ones, were considered quite costly by the average family. To reduce costs, "party lines" were common, where several customers shared the same telephone line. In our new home we were the third party on a "three-party-line." The telephone rang once for the first party, twice for the second and three times for the third. I was used to answering the phone on the first ring, in England, so the day ours was connected I automatically picked up the phone when it rang.

A squeaky young male voice inquired: "Hi, Poopsie, how's about a date tonight?"

Shocked, I asked: "Who is this? I don't receive obscene phone calls," and promptly replaced the receiver. Later, I was working in my little flower garden when one of the neighbors walking by stopped to talk. "Hello, Bunty," she said, "how are you settling in?" We chatted, and I complemented her on her cute teenaged daughter who adored Cleo and liked to stop and play with her.

"Oh, yes," she responded, "but Connie's having trouble with her current boyfriend; he says she hung up on him the other day."

I quickly changed the subject!

Al: "MONDAY, NOVEMBER 10: BUD HERE FOR THE WEEKEND, HE AND JOAN SPENT IT WITH HIS FOLKS. STILL NO SIGN OF BABY."
Bud's weekend visits made our little house even more crowded, so he and Joan spent them with his folks. Weekends were a lifesaver for Al and me, as I'm sure they were for Joan and Bud. Yes, boredom and too much togetherness put a strain on our friendship, but Joan and I were fine again after a weekend with our husbands. The company of Laurie and Amy made welcome breaks for us, too. Joan often came with Amy and me to the movies. Comments in my diary ranged from "MARVELLOUS" (English spelling,) to "I SHOULD HAVE SAVED MY SIXTY CENTS!"

A movie for sixty cents? Ah, those were the days!

On Mondays, Joan and I took the wash over to Mom Greene's house because Al and I didn't yet have a washing machine of our own. Then we usually walked into town and shopped, while the clothes dried on the clothesline. Now that I had my own iron, we didn't need to stay at Mom Greene's to do the ironing.

The days grew colder and went by more slowly for poor Joan than for anyone else, she was so uncomfortable with all the extra weight she carried around. At the beginning of another week of waiting, she felt particularly downhearted: "Oh, Bunty, I feel so top-heavy, and I'm being such a drag on everyone. I wish it were all over!"

I tried to comfort her as best I could: "Joan, you're not being a drag. You've been helping me as much as you can with the cooking, and I appreciate that so much. And you keep your bedroom in perfect condition, and I appreciate that, too. Don't worry, it won't be long now until the baby is here, and then you'll be back in your own home again. These last few weeks couldn't have been a picnic for you, I'm sure. Chin up, old girl!"

The following Monday brought us the event we had waited for.

Al: "MONDAY, NOVEMBER 18: JOAN'S BABY FINALLY DECIDED TO COME: A BABY BOY! BOTH ARE DOING WELL--CAN'T TELL ABOUT BUD--A BIT DAZED, BUT HE SEEMS O.K."

Al must have made a heroic effort to record this important diary entry, but there was no mention of when Joan had gone into labor, or how she got to the nearest hospital in Pinewood ten miles away, where the baby was apparently delivered without undue difficulty. In all probability, we had called Bud in plenty of time when her labor began and he took her to the hospital himself.

I remember calling Laurie to let her know the news. She asked: "Will Joan and the baby be coming back to stay with you when they come out of the hospital, dear; or will she be going to stay with Bud's folks?"

Laurie sounded anxious. I reassured her: "Neither, Laurie. Bud says Joan and the baby will be staying in the hospital until the doctor tells her it's O.K. for them to travel, then he will take them directly home to north Jersey. Good thinking, eh? Everything couldn't be better: the baby's arrived safely; his new grandmother saw him from his first day; Joan, Bud, Al and I are still on speaking terms; and when Joan and the baby go back to north Jersey they will have bypassed any further in-law conflict. Whew!"

Bud's mother's "heart condition" survived the thwarting of her plans for Joan's pre-delivery care and subsequent stay with her after the baby's arrival. She outlived Bud's father.

Where's That Muskrat?

Al: "THURSDAY, NOVEMBER 21: STILL NO FUR COAT! WROTE A THIRD REGISTERD LETTER TO NEW YORK. IF NO RESULT WILL HAVE TO SEE A LAWYER. BUNTY'S GETTING TO BE A SOCIAL BUTTERFLY--STATIC CLUB, MARJIE'S SEWING CLUB, WHAT NEXT?"

In Al's diary entry was a cry of despair. I still didn't understand why there was no telephone contact about my fur coat, but I suppose Al felt that a tangible receipt to show he had sent a third letter would be more effective if we had to go to court. We decided to give the matter a few more working days.

My future sister-in-law Marjie was an accomplished seamstress. She had taken lessons in sewing in high school--something that no British prep school in those days would have offered, considering it "non-academic," and to be pursued as a hobby to be picked up from one's female relatives. There were tailors like our Mr. Anderson to do the professional stuff.

Having heard that I did knitting and embroidery as a hobby, Marjie invited me to join her sewing club. Its attendance varied between six and a dozen girls who brought sewing projects to the meetings, but not much sewing was done. The main focus seemed to be on local gossip, and I learned to act like the proverbial mouse in the corner and listen without comment. I was fascinated to learn that there were four or five prominent families in Little Cedar River, all interrelated, so I made a mental note to be careful to speak only good things about everyone; they might be someone's second cousin once removed!

Marjie was talented and creative, able to visualize how a fabric would be suited to a pattern even before she bought the yardage in the "dry goods store". She produced beautiful clothes on her sewing machine, including tailored shirts for Bill. On our way home, she counseled: "Bunty, you really should get a sewing machine; I can show you how to save a lot of money sewing your own clothes, and we could make slip covers for that nice furniture of yours." With a sudden flash of inspiration she added: "Jeepers creepers, hon, how's about asking Santa Claus for a sewing machine this Christmas?"

Social Life Galore!

Al: "MONDAY, NOVEMBER 25: BUNTY AND I WENT TO A DINNER DANCE SPONSORED BY DOVER TOWNSHIP FOR THE WORLD WAR TWO VETERANS IN OCEAN COUNTY. LAURIE AND BUNTY ARE ORGANIZING A CLUB FOR THE ENGLISH GIRLS."

The dinner dance for the county's war veterans and their ladies was a gala affair, sponsored by citizens of the township of Dover, centered at Little Cedar River, the county seat. It was held in the opulent *Laurel in the Pines* hotel in Pinewood. I still have the official invitation and program for the evening, yellowed with age, which lists the names of all the servicemen and women from the county who served in World War Two.

As we entered the gilded foyer, each of the ladies was presented with a pretty flower corsage supplied by the local florist. I remember meeting Laurie and her husband in the main banquet room and sitting with them at one of the tables for eight.

I dimly recall listening to a series of dreary speeches from local politicians. Following them were American Red Cross representatives who narrated the saga of the G.I. Bride invasion of America earlier in the year, emphasizing the part the American Red Cross had played in helping to ease the problems of this flood of women and children, before, during and after they crossed the Atlantic Ocean.

While their husbands exchanged war stories, the G.I. Brides chatted excitedly: "Where do you come from in England? When were you married? When did you come to America? On which ship? Where do you live now?"

Two excellent dance bands had been hired for the occasion. After the speeches were over they played alternately; the dance floor was soon filled with whirling couples. As we paused for breath at our table between dances, I saw Laurie's eyes light up; I could tell something was brewing in that fertile brain of hers. She leaned over toward me and whispered: "Bunty, this is the perfect opportunity to begin thinking about organizing a club for G.I. Brides from all over Ocean County! We can start with those within a small radius of Little Cedar River and work our way further out when we get established. I'm sure it would help them all to have a breath of home to share with each other."

"Oh, Laurie, what a lot of work that will be. I'll have to think it over, but it certainly sounds good in theory!"

"We can do it, Bunty; think what a godsend it will be for those girls who are terribly homesick."

That ended the conversation for the time being, and we went to explore the magnificent buffet supper, returning to our table with laden plates, to be entertained in turn by nine different performers on the stage, while we ate.

The G.I. Brides' club eventually became a reality. It continued for several years, but interest waned as the girls became more settled and integrated. When they began to have their families, they found it more difficult than ever to travel from their scattered little towns to meetings. The club gradually died a quiet death, but not before it had served its purpose.

By now, I had stopped chronicling my life in a diary. Our history was recorded in my weekly letters home to Mom and Dad, which somehow disappeared over the years. The only other record was in a series of black and white--later followed by color--photographs, all methodically stored (without dates or narrative) in albums.

Al's diary entries had faltered, but he rallied enough to record one more.

Surprises and Reflections

Giving Thanks

"THURSDAY, NOVEMBER 28: THANKSGIVING DAY."

NEITHER AL'S NOR my diaries recorded my first Thanksgiving Day, another traditional American holiday new to me. I remember Al had to work that day, so Mom Greene postponed dinner until he returned from the radio station in the late afternoon. Amy and I helped her with the preparations.

Bill had been invited to the McCaffertys' for Thanksgiving. Mom Greene had bristled, but was having to accommodate herself to the fact that he was now torn between two families, which she knew she would have to accept. He had hugged her and said: "Mom, by that time we'll be 'fit to bust' after one turkey dinner, but Marjie and I will be over to join the family for our Thanksgiving after Al gets home, not to worry."

As usual, Mom Greene said grace before dinner. After giving thanks for the food, she added: "And thank you, Lord, for bringing my two boys safely back from the war, and for my new little daughter Ida."

Mom Greene's first child had died in the 1918 influenza epidemic; a two-year-old girl they had named Ida. After she recovered from the shock of Al's engagement, Mom Greene had written in a letter to me: "I never dreamed, when I lost one daughter Ida, that God would give me another daughter Ida." Her simple words at the Thanksgiving table left us all with tears; tears of thanksgiving.

Behold! Bunty's Muskrat

Mom and Dad

At Last, the Muskrat!

Al: "TUESDAY, DECEMBER 3: BUNTY'S NORTHERN BACK MUSKRAT FUR COAT FINALLY ARRIVED BY REGISTERED MAIL, IT'S VERY BEAUTIFUL, VALUED ON THE SHIPPING DOCUMENT AT $350. WROTE TO NEW YORK AND CONFIRMED RECEIPT OF THE COAT."

The custodians of my fur coat must have had extrasensory perception! We were going to make an appointment with the lawyer today! The post office delivery van pulled up outside our house, and I signed the receipt which valued the fur coat at about seventy-five dollars more than it had cost us at a discount price--in those days, a fortune. No wonder Al recorded it in his diary!

I remember enthusing: "Thank goodness that's over! It's even more gorgeous than when I saw it in the store! You know, dear, even though it took forever, it was worth waiting for! But I'm not going to tell Mom and Dad how long we've waited for it to be delivered; that would spoil their pleasure in knowing that now, thanks to them, I'm well insulated for the winter!"

Behold, the Holidays

"SATURDAY, DECEMBER 21: 'O CHRISTMAS TREE.'"

The Saturday before Christmas was the day the family traditionally put up their Christmas tree. With the separation pay Bill had received after his service in the Navy, he had bought a small tract of land on the outskirts of Little Cedar River covered with swamp cedars, where he intended some-day to build a restaurant. Al and I dressed warmly, and piled into Bill's car with Amy and Marjie to drive out of town and park at the edge of the land. Ropes, saws and axes were unloaded, and a young cedar tree with a full, bushy top was chosen for the supreme sacrifice. The men did the chopping, and yelled "TIMBER" just before the tree fell with a "whomp" to the ground. Next, they measured down five feet from the top, and sawed the trunk through at that spot, resulting in a beautiful, fully-leafed Christmas tree. We all helped drag it to the car. Securely roped to the roof, the tree made the journey to Mom Greene's. In the living room, it was wedged with several bricks into an upright position in a bucket. Water was then poured into the bucket to keep the tree green throughout the Christmas season. A wrapping of bright red crepe paper to conceal the bucket added the finishing touch.

As I helped hang the dancing, multicolored glass balls, I pictured Mom and Dad bringing down our little artificial Christmas tree from the attic along with its boxes of glass decorations, and a familiar lump of homesickness came into my throat.

"TUESDAY, DECEMBER 24: CHRISTMAS EVE."
Our diaries both contained blank pages again, but I remember with plea-sure the excitement of Al's family tradition of exchanging Christmas pres-ents around the tree on Christmas Eve, opening up our gifts as the lights twinkled on its branches. After a festive buffet supper, we bundled up and went to the midnight Christmas Eve candlelight church service, which I found meaningful and full of wonder.

With Christmas, my first year in America was drawing to a close. Santa really did bring me a sewing machine; along with my fur coat it made the most luxurious Christmas in my life.

"TUESDAY, DECEMBER 31: NEW YEAR'S EVE."
Al had to work the night shift on our first New Year's Eve, so when he left the house before midnight for his commute, I didn't see him again until 9 a.m. on New Year's Day. Bill was at the McCaffertys'. Mom Greene and Amy were at the American Legion Hall. I felt lonely, but I chose not to join them, with no desire to spend New Year's Eve there without Al.

As midnight approached, I turned on the radio to a New York sta-tion. Guy Lombardo and his orchestra were playing at one of the big city hotels in a ballroom crowded with New Year's Eve revelers. Just before midnight, the broadcast switched to the tightly-packed masses in Times Square as they roared the countdown to midnight. A hysterical cacoph-ony of sound broke out at the stroke of twelve: horns hooting, tooters tooting, people screaming, cheering and singing, to welcome in the New Year.

In my mind's eye, I could see Mom and Dad sharing a glass of wine with the neighbors. The memory of past New Year's Eves at the Ditchfields flooded back: Uncle Hal McKenzie shaking the snow off his boots on the front doorstep, then leading the men into the house as Gram's First Foot, to enjoy the Christmas buffet with the family. Tonight it would be peacetime in Sunderland. I could almost hear the church bells joyfully pealing all over town to welcome in the New Year, now free from their wartime silence, when they were to ring only to announce a Nazi invasion. By the grace of God we were spared this horror, and the bells had broken their silence to ring out with joy on V-E Day.

The memories were poignant, but I shook off the wave of nostalgia and began to count my blessings. I was thankful for the adventurous spirit that Mom and Dad had passed on to me. It had helped me to weather what, in some respects, had probably been the most difficult and challenging year I had ever known. But Al had been with me through the ups and downs, helping me to bear the pain of homesickness, and, with loving care and patience, steering me to becoming assimilated into my new country. Now, in our own home, we had the freedom to build our marriage, and with plenty of mistakes I could learn to adapt to my new world.

So here we were, on the threshold of the New Year, with the promise of more adventures when Mom and Dad's letter arrived to say that they would be booking passage on the newly refurbished *Queen Elizabeth* for a visit next May! My happiness was complete.

Epilogue

You have finished reading my story, and have traveled with me into Bunty's New World. By the end of that first year, driving, cooking and housekeeping had become became less daunting for me; lessons learned mostly through trial and error! Soon, I would learn to use my sewing machine and make thrifty items with the help of Marjie, my new sister-in-law and ally.

Monthly Static Club meetings broadened my knowledge of life in other parts of America, as each member described her background in her native state. The coming year held the promise of a different kind of club; a group of British fellow-newcomers who could strengthen each other's confidence in this new world.

"American English" spelling, as well as vocabulary, was gradually being assimilated after many unwitting "foot-in-the-mouth" remarks--some hilarious, some embarrassing--especially when identical American words and phrases often had extremely different meanings from English ones.

Knowledge of an entire year's worth of American holiday customs could now be stowed away for future use, each one another milestone in my new world.

In the months to come, my new husband would open up for me a wonderland of knowledge as I learned about the history of this new world. I would learn about the first settlers in my new home state, New Jersey--the Leni-Lenape Indians. The painting of George Washington crossing the Delaware that I had seen in his ancestral home in England came to life for me when we visited the exact spot where it took place.

Al took me on one of his "four-day weekends" to Washington, D.C., gleaming with its white marble buildings, where I was thrilled to see the

Declaration of Independence and sat in the public gallery in the halls of Congress to witness a vote on a new piece of legislation. Already familiar with his smaller image in Parliament Square in London, I looked with awe upon the enormous statue of Abraham Lincoln enshrined in the white marble of the spectacular Lincoln Memorial. In one museum I paid tribute to the wonderful exhibit showing the reverence for their land by the first native Americans. In another, I gazed at the "Spirit of St. Louis" as it hung from the ceiling. I saw for myself that the White House was really painted white.

Despite the fact that I was married to an American citizen, U.S. immigration laws dictated that I would have to wait two more years before I could apply for citizenship. Having to report regularly to Little Cedar River's Town Clerk as an "alien" made me cringe. Looking forward impatiently to studying the requirements needed in order to adopt my new country, I wanted to belong; after all, I didn't want to be an "alien" forever--that made me sound like someone from outer space! When I eventually did became a U.S. citizen, having to renounce allegiance to the Queen caused me to suppress a tear or two, yet when I received my citizenship papers I knew my new world wasn't so new to me any more, and that at last I had a real home of my own.

I've traveled a long journey to find my way home. Along the way I often wondered: "Where is home, anyway? First there was one in central Africa, two in northern England, then three in southern England. World War Two brought me eleven different homes, and in America there have been seven more before my final home in retirement!

My wartime diary reminded me that when I came home to Upper Woodside from work in London that day during the V-1 and V-2 rocket air raids, hardly daring to look down Bishop's Hill in fear that I would see our home reduced to rubble along with all our possessions, I suddenly remembered the old saying: "Home is where the heart is." Home had been wherever I was with the people I loved, and it helped me to realize, even then, that home is not just a building where material "things" are stored.

With this book, you joined me, so many years later, as I had just moved into our retirement home in Connecticut. I was sitting on the porch floor, surrounded by unpacked moving cartons full of extra "stuff". I knew I would have to "downsize" again--ugh! But that reminder in my wartime diary put into perspective the reality that discarding excess "things" was really not the painful process I had dreaded.

Even so, let's hope I've done my final "downsizing!"

References

Croydon, Old and New (1975): Local publication, Croydon, Surrey, England

Eden Camp Museum, Malton, North Yorkshire, England (exhibit information)

Mantale, Ivor: *World War II* (1987): Military Press

Mason, David: *Churchill* (1972) Ballantine Books

Reader's Digest article (1945): *Brides from Overseas*

Virden, Jenel: *Goodbye Piccadilly: British War Brides in America (1996)*: University of Illinois Press

Video Series: *Winston Churchill, PBS*

World Book Encyclopedia: Field Enterprises Educational Corporation (1965)

In addition: careful verification, where necessary, of information and historical data via countless articles and links on the Internet.

Made in the USA
Middletown, DE
13 June 2017